Writing Skills for LAW ENFORCEMENT

SENTENCES, ESSAYS, AND PRESENTATIONS

H. Carol Doughty
Durham College

Australia Canada Mexico Singapore Spain United Kingdom United States

This book is dedicated to Lauren Megan, my first grandchild,
born June 20, 2003, to Colin and Darcie.
Lauren, you are one of the rays of sunshine in my life.

Writing Skills for Law Enforcement: Sentences, Essays, and Presentations

by H. Carol Doughty

Associate Vice-President, Editorial Director:
Evelyn Veitch

Executive Acquisitions Editor:
Anne Williams

Acquisitions Editor:
Rod Banister

Marketing Manager:
Lisa Rahn

Publisher's Representative:
Bill More

Senior Developmental Editor:
Mike Thompson

Permissions Coordinator:
Nicola Winstanley

Production Editor:
Tammy Scherer

Copy Editor:
Tara Tovell

Proofreader:
Laurel Sparrow

Indexer:
Elizabeth Bell

Production Coordinator:
Ferial Suleman

Creative Director:
Angela Cluer

Interior Design Modifications:
Katherine Strain

Cover Design:
Roxanna Bennett

Compositor:
Starlight Design

Printer:
Webcom

Printed and bound in Canada
1 2 3 4 07 06 05 04

For more information contact Nelson, 1120 Birchmount Road, Toronto, Ontario, M1K 5G4. Or you can visit our Internet site at http://www.nelson.com

Library and Archives Canada Cataloguing in Publication

Doughty, H. Carol (Helen Doughty), 1945-

Writing skills for law enforcement : sentences, essays and presentations / H. Carol Doughty.

Includes index.

ISBN 0-17-641487-8

1. Police reports. 2. Report writing. 3. English language–Rhetoric. I. Title.

HV7936.R53D69 2004
808'.066363 C2004-905227-6

Brief Contents

Contents

Preface

Welcome to the Law and Security or the Police Foundations program at the college you have chosen. You have made an important career decision and are about to start a very exciting two years of your life.

When you looked over the college calendar, you were probably surprised to find that you would have to take courses with names like "Communications" as part of your program. You likely wondered just what communications was all about. Simply put, "communications" is the term used to refer to courses dealing with written language, oral presentations, and interpersonal communication. In policing, all of these communication skills are used daily, in both obvious and subtle ways.

In fact, communication skills are so important in policing that most services use some form of communications test as part of the hiring process. Some services will have a spelling test; others will ask you to write an essay in a test situation; and others will ask you to write and pass the Written Communications Test.

The ability to communicate correctly, concisely, and clearly is key when writing police reports and when speaking to groups of people or one-on-one as an officer. You will need to communicate well with both your colleagues and the public, often under difficult circumstances.

Officers do not just write reports, fill out forms, and keep their notebooks up to date. They may be required to write an article for a newspaper or a magazine; write an essay as part of the promotion process; or write memos, letters, and reports for different situations.

Officers also may be asked to speak to a classroom of elementary students about bicycle safety; to a community group about Neighbourhood Watch; or to a school board about security issues. Therefore, as you can see, writing and speaking are integral parts of an officer's day.

It should now be clear to you why written, verbal, and interpersonal communications courses are included in your course of study during your two-year program. Excelling in these skills will go a long way towards helping you excel overall in your career.

You have come to college with a number of years of writing and presenting skills behind you. You will have many strengths in these areas, as well as some weaknesses. We all have at least one area in which we need to improve. Through this course, it is hoped that you will be able to build on your strengths, fine-tune your writing and presenting skills, and improve your weaknesses. Your goal should be to submit error-free written assignments and clear, organized, attention-keeping presentations.

All the best to you as you strive to be the best communicator you can be so that all of your messages are clear, concise, and correct.

About This Book

This Canadian textbook about writing and presenting in law enforcement guides students through a step-by-step process, moving from basic writing skills to the writing of a research essay, and then on to giving a presentation.

This text can be used for any law enforcement training program. It is particularly suitable for the Police Foundations course because it fulfills the learning outcomes for the communications courses requiring students to write essays and give presentations.

The book starts off with spelling, grammar, and punctuation rules and their applications (Chapter 1) and then discusses the sentence and its varied forms (Chapter 2).

Next is an explanation of the paragraph (Chapter 3), followed by the five-paragraph essay style (Chapters 4–5), which is the cornerstone of essay writing. Students are then shown how to use this style to write a five-paragraph essay (Chapter 5), a process essay (Chapter 6), a research essay (Chapters 7–9), and a comparison/contrast essay (Chapter 10). The book ends with a chapter on how to give an oral presentation (Chapter 11).

The appendices contain resource pages for students to use in the research essay process (Appendix A); information on the MLA style of essay documentation (Appendix B); samples of a memo, a police report, and a business letter (Appendix C); a personal spelling list for students to maintain and refer to when they do any written assignment (Appendix D); sample research essays (Appendix E); and an answer key (Appendix F).

WHAT IS UNIQUE ABOUT THIS BOOK?

This book contains many examples and references related to a career in law enforcement. While the references and examples are not restricted to that career, all the exercises are career related or have a law-enforcement theme. Many of the examples of good writing are by actual police officers and are excerpted from the Canadian policing magazine Blue Line. The majority of the essays and magazine excerpts in this book are directly related to law enforcement, although general interest pieces are included as well, in order to provide variety, depth, and a wider perspective to the learner. Most of the essays were written by Ontario college students enrolled in a communications course in a Police Foundations or Law and Security program. All the examples in the book can act as excellent examples when students do their assignments. (Note that all essays in this textbook have been used with permission from the authors.)

Another unique aspect of the book is the chapter that deals with note taking (Chapter 8), which presents an easy-to-use process for summarizing and note taking. This chapter also shows students how to take notes from a video newscast or documentary. This last process should be especially helpful to students who are visual learners and enjoy using documentaries as a source of information.

This text is also a workbook that contains exercises to complete within each chapter. Lines are provided and the perforated pages make it easy to tear out the work to submit for marking if the teacher requests this.

Furthermore, this text can be used as a reference in other and future classes in which the students are required to write an essay or give a presentation.

The goal of the text is also to help the students to identify their structural errors and to work to improve them. The personal spelling list (Appendix D) is a place for students to write the correct spellings of words they misspell, which they can then use as a study tool. It is hoped that the students will learn the correct spellings and eliminate these errors in their work.

Also included in this book are sample business documents, such as memos and letters, plus a police supplementary report (Appendix C). These have been added because some instructors like to incorporate the coverage of writing these business documents and police reports into their writing courses at various levels.

(Please note that sample documents in this book are not sized to scale. Students should consult the MLA documentation guidelines in Appendix B for accuracy when preparing material.)

TEST BANK/INSTRUCTOR'S MANUAL

A separate test bank/instructor's manual to accompany this book is also available to instructors. Please contact your Thomson Nelson sales representative to order one.

ABOUT THE AUTHOR

Carol currently teaches Communications I, Communications II, Interpersonal Communications, and Psychology to Police Foundations and Law and Security students at Durham College in Oshawa, Ontario. She has been at Durham for over twenty years, teaching in every division and a variety of programs, but has spent most of the past eight years in the School of Justice at Durham.

In addition to writing this and one other book for law enforcement courses, Carol has also written a number of skits and one-act plays.

Carol holds Specialist's credentials in Physical Education and Health, Elementary Mathematics, and Special Education–Learning Disabilities. In her spare time, Carol can be found working with the Carruthers' Creek Performing Arts Company, where she is the director and a performer, or with community theatres in Durham. She continues to work at perfecting that golf swing, and enjoys spending fun times with her family and loving her first granddaughter to pieces.

ACKNOWLEDGMENTS

Thank you to my family for all their support once again. In particular, to Bruce for contributing just the right advice at the right time, and to Nancy for making all those meals while I was writing this book.

In addition, I would like to thank Bert Dejeet, Dean of the School of Justice, who encouraged me and inquired about my progress regularly; the students at Durham College who contributed to this book; all my students who critiqued the work-in-progress; the staff at the Police Learning Centre at Durham College for answering all my questions; the staff at Blue Line for allowing the use of their material; and Constable Brendan Kennaley, for the use of his article. I would also like to extend my thanks to the staff at Thomson Nelson: to sales representative Bill More, for initiating this process; to executive acquisitions editor Anne Williams, for accepting my proposal for this book and seeing it through; to production editor Tammy Scherer, for keeping things on track; to copyeditor Tara Tovell and proofreader Laurel Sparrow, for their expertise; to editorial assistant Erica Smith, for her contribution to this project; and especially to developmental editor Mike Thompson, for being so patient with me as he expertly guided me through the writing process in such a timely manner.

The author and editors wish to thank the following reviewers for contributing their suggestions and insights during the development of this book: Gina Antonacci, Humber College; Stephen Boaro, Northern College; Dilys Denning, Lambton College; Dianna McAleer, Algonquin College; Jane Anne McLachlan, Conestoga College; Kevin Pickell, Algonquin College; and Andrew Stracuzzi, Fanshawe College.

Spelling, Grammar, and Punctuation

Learning Objectives

After students have learned the content of this chapter, they should be able to do the following:

- Identify the correct spellings of some of the most frequently misspelled words and use them correctly in their writing.
- Know the correct usage and spellings of some of the most frequently misused and misspelled words and use them correctly in their writing.
- Know some of the most common grammar errors and how to correct them in their writing.
- Correct some of the most common punctuation errors, and apply these punctuation rules to their writing.

Learning Benefits

You must be able to write correctly for every career. People have to be able to understand what you are trying to say. Don't force your readers to work hard to figure out what you are saying by rereading your words two to three times before they understand what you've written. Sometimes, leaving out one little comma can cause a major misunderstanding.

In policing, the ability to write correctly and clearly is of utmost importance. Notebooks and reports that are written correctly speed up the judicial system. Furthermore, an officer's ability to write well is a major consideration for promotion.

SPELLING

Being able to spell correctly is a very important skill. Spelling English words correctly is difficult because we use phonetics and memorization to help us use the correct words at the right times, and in English, there are often exceptions to rules. Also, many people depend upon a variety of spell checkers on their word processors to correct the spelling for them. Unfortunately, these spell checkers do not pick out some of the spelling errors. For example, look at the following sentence. *The constable went fro his gun.* The word "fro" is incorrect in this sentence. "Fro" is a word, and it means to go back and forwards. The spell checker would not point out this word as an error because "fro" is a word. Therefore, you must learn how to spell words correctly and use them correctly. Developing and using your proofreading skills also enhances your spelling a great deal. So, to help you with your spelling of some commonly misspelled and/or misused English words, this section of the chapter is divided up into three parts, covering commonly misspelled words, misused words that are considered to be either spelling or grammatical errors, and a spelling reference list of words frequently used in law enforcement.

Commonly Misspelled Words

There are many words that get misspelled by a variety of students, but there are a few that seem to be misspelled more than others. This section, and much of this chapter, will concentrate on helping you correct these. A list of these words appears in Table 1.1.

Table 1.1: Commonly Misspelled Words and Their Corrected Spellings

Wrong Spelling	Corrected Spelling
admissable	admissible
cheif	chief
commited	committed
definately	definitely
do n't or don't'	don't
Febuary	February
Firday	Friday
i	I (the pronoun "I" is never in lower case)
knifes	knives
layed	laid
leutenant	lieutenant
occurence	occurrence
patroled	patrolled
recieve	receive

(continued)

Table 1.1: Commonly Misspelled Words and Their Corrected Spellings *(continued)*

Wrong Spelling	Corrected Spelling
sargeant	sergeant
tommorrow	tomorrow or to-morrow (This spelling is outdated, but it is still used.)
Teusday	Tuesday
Wendsday	Wednesday
wifes	wives
wuz	was

As you can see, the list in Table 1.1 includes only some of the most commonly misspelled words. If you always spell all these words correctly, then congratulations! However, if your teacher points out to you in your written work that you are spelling any of these wrong, write them in the Student's Personal Spelling List (see Appendix D) and make an effort to correct them in your writing.

Exercise 1.1 Spelling Exercise

Without looking at Table 1.1, circle the correct spelling of the word in parentheses.

1. The tape recording of the phone message was (admissable / admissible) in court.
2. (Cheif / Chief) Pagani started his term on (February / Febuary) 24th.
3. The (leutenant / lieutenant) told me that (I / i) needed to report to my (sergeant / sargeant) by (tommorrow / tomorrow) morning at 09:10.
4. (I / i) (was / wuz) relieved of my duty on (Wednesday / Wendsday).
5. Officer Ing (received / recieved) an order to patrol Queen Street.

Exercise 1.2 Writing Exercise

1. Choose any ten of the words listed in Table 1.1. In particular, choose the words that you know you tend to spell incorrectly.
2. Write sentences using those words on the lines below. You can also try using more than one of the words in the same sentence if you wish.
3. Underline the words so that they stand out.
4. After your teacher has marked your work, record **any** word that you misspelled in your personal spelling list at the back of this textbook.

   1. ______________________________

   ____

2. ____

____

3. ____

____

4. ____

____

5. ____

____

6. ____

____

7. ____

____

8. ____

____

9. ____

____

10. ____

____

E-mail and chat line spellings

While chatting with people through e-mail messages and chat lines, you may have used abbreviated forms for words, such as "u" for "you," "4" for "for," "r" for "are," and so on. Other common e-mail spellings are "c u " for "see you" and "ttul" for "talk to you later." There are hundreds more.

Although these spellings are acceptable when writing to your friends via e-mail or chat lines, they are **not** acceptable in an essay unless you are quoting someone who is using them. Have fun on e-mail and chat lines with creative spellings, but use the appropriate ones for all your written work in school and in your career.

Commonly Misused Words

There are many words that are often misused, resulting in spelling or grammatical errors. The words listed below cause a lot of problems for many students. Some of these words are homonyms—that is, words that sound the same but are spelled differently, such as "bear" and "bare." The first spelling, "bear," is used for the animal, and the second spelling, "bare," refers to being naked. It is important to know which one to use in the context of your sentences. In many cases, it is just a matter of memorizing which word is the correct word to use in your sentence. Table 1.2, below, provides some hints and examples to help you learn the correct usage of these words.

Table 1.2: Commonly Misused/Misspelled Words

affect, affected - verbs *The noise from the boom box affected the teen's hearing.*	**effect** - a noun *What were the effects of September 11?* Hint: "Effect" usually has "the" or "an" in front of it.
bear - an animal *The officer investigated the incident involving the bear attacking the tourist.*	**bare** - having nothing on, naked *The young man was bare-chested when his body was found by the river bank.*
choose - present tense of the verb *to choose* *Lieutenant Pawlak will choose his team.* Hint: Listen for the "oooo" sound, like in "moose."	**chose** - past tense of the verb *to choose* *Lieutenant Pawlak chose his team yesterday.* Hint: Listen for the letter "o" sound, like in "toes."
compliment - to say something nice to or about someone *Chief Gomez complimented his officers after the suspect was arrested.* Hint: Look for the "i" in the word: "I like to get compliments."	**complement** - to match, to go along with *The gold trim on the hat complemented the dark blue uniform.*
could of - This combination does not exist in the English language. Replace it with the choices in the right column.	**could have/could've** *The officer could have done another shift.* *The officer could've done another shift.*
desert - a dry barren land *The military police patrolled a four kilometre square section of the desert during Desert Storm.*	**dessert** - the part of the meal that usually comes after the main course. e.g., pie, cake, fruit *The new recruits received cherry cheesecake as the dessert at their banquet.* Hint: To help you remember that "dessert" has a double "s", think of this: *I would rather have two desserts than cross a desert twice.*
it's - the contraction for the two words "it" and "is." The apostrophe (') replaces the letter "i" in "is." *The judge told the jury, "It's time to make your decision. Please leave the court room and report back when you have made your decision."* Hint: You would never use "it's" in a formal essay. Always write "it is" and you will get it correct.	***its*** *- the possessive form; a sense of belonging to someone/something* *The officer pulled her gun out of its holster.* The "its" in this sentence refers to the "gun," and the holster, in this sentence, belongs to the gun.

(continued)

Table 1.2: Commonly Misused/Misspelled Words *(continued)*

quite - an adverb showing comparison; can usually be replaced by "very" *The officer's writing in his notebook was quite small; therefore, his supervisor had trouble reading the notes.*	**quiet** - (qui- et) a two syllable word; state of no noise *The suspect remained quiet on the stand; he refused to answer any questions or say anything.*
should of - This combination does not exist in the English language. Replace it with the choices in the right column.	**should have, should've** *The officer should have written more detailed notes because when he went to write his report, he could not remember many of the details.*
suppose to - This combination does not exist in the English language. Replace it with the correct spelling in the right column.	**supposed to** - Note the "d" at the end of "suppose." This is the correct spelling. *The recruits were supposed to polish their boots every day.*
than - a comparison: greater than, rather than, bigger than, etc. *The drill sergeant was taller than the corporal.* Hint: Pronounce these words correctly and you should get them correct. *Stress the "an" in "than."*	**then** - next in line, next in time sequence *The officer yelled, "Stop! Police!" Then he yelled, "Drop your gun!"* *Stress the "en" in "then."*
their - possessive plural form *The police bagpipe band looked great in their kilts.*	**there** - a place, a position *The organizer of the recruit graduation ceremony told the bagpipe band to assemble over there.* Hint: The word "there" contains the word "here." They both refer to placements. If you can substitute "here" for "there," then use "there," not "their."
to - motion, usually goes after a verb to indicate movement or action or goes in front of a verb in the infinitive form. *The recruit went to the provincial police training centre to take his six month training course.*	**too** - also/very *Officer Anderson went to the provincial training centre too.* *Officer Hazell thought that the accommodations at the training centre were too dark and small.* Hint: For "too," stress the "oo" sound when you say it and think of *excess* or *too much* when you write it to help you put in the extra "o."
use to - This combination does not exist in the English language. Replace it with the correct spelling in the right column.	**used to** - Note the "d" on "used." *In Ontario, the police uniforms used to be blue; now they are black.*

(continued)

Table 1.2: Commonly Misused/Misspelled Words *(continued)*

you're - contraction for "you are" The apostrophe replaces the letter "a" in "are." *The instructor said to the recruit, "You're going to be a great officer because you have such good common sense!"* Hint: You would never use "you're" in a formal essay unless you are quoting someone. "You" is a second person pronoun, and you should use only third person pronouns in formal essays.	**your** - belonging to someone *"That is your uniform," said the training officer to the recruit.* Hint: "Your" is only one word. If you need to use the two words, "you" and "are," where you have written "your," then replace "your" with " you're" or " you are," as described in the left column.

Once again, Table 1.2 contains only some of the most commonly misspelled and misused words. If you get any of these wrong in your writing, put them in your personal spelling list in this textbook. Try very hard to correct your errors. Not only will you save some potentially lost marks on your essays, but you will also write correctly in the workforce.

Exercise 1.3 Word Choice

Circle the correct word.

1. Whatever you (chose / choose) to do as an officer in any situation, it will (effect / affect) you in some way or other.

2. The sergeant told the officers to buy a workbook for the course because the workbook would (complement / compliment) the textbook, and they would find this workbook (quiet / quite) useful.

3. The recruits were just getting (used to / use to) (their / there) instructor for one course when that instructor took sick and was replaced by another instructor.

4. "(Your / You're) going to get (used to / use to) the feel of the gun," said the instructor. "(Its / It's) the weight of the gun that bothers people!"

5. "Did you participate in (Dessert / Desert) Storm?" the announcer asked the Canadian soldier.

Exercise 1.4 Writing Exercise

1. Choose any ten of the words listed in Table 1.2. In particular, choose the words that you know you don't spell correctly.

2. Write sentences using those words on the lines below. If you use more than one of the words in a sentence, then that is fine.

3. Underline the words so that they stand out.

4. After your teacher has marked your work, record **any** word that you misspelled in your personal spelling list.

1. ______________________________
____
2. ______________________________
____
3. ______________________________
____
4. ______________________________
____
5. ______________________________
____
6. ______________________________
____
7. ______________________________
____
8. ______________________________
____
9. ______________________________
____
10. ______________________________
____

Spelling Reference List

The following list contains many of the words used frequently in law enforcement. Use this list as a reference or as a spelling practice list. Knowing how to spell these words correctly will help you communicate clearly and correctly. This list should act as a complement to your dictionary.

A	administration	admit	admittance	admitting	argument
	assault	authority	authorize	automatic	
B	bail	ballistics	barricade	behaviour	blond (male)
	blonde (female)	boundary	border	brakes	bruise
	brunette	bulletin	bureau	burglary	
C	calibre	captain	cartridge	caution	chased
	chief	cigarette	circumstantial	citation	clemency
	coercion	committed	complainant	condemn	confiscate
	conjecture	counterfeit	credible	criminal	custody
D	deceased	deduction	defendant	defence	deferred
	definitely	defraud	delinquent	denial	denied
	description	detective	detention	disappear	disciplinary
	discrepancy	disguise	drunkenness	dying	
E	ejected	eligible	embedded	emergency	employee
	encounter	endorsement	enforcement	environment	equipped
	establish	ethical	evidence	exemption	existence
	exonerate	expedite			
F	facility	falsified	familiarize	fatality	fault
	faulty	feasible	felony	foreign	forfeit
	formally	forty	fraudulent	frequency	
G	gasoline	gauge	government	grievance	guard
H	hearing	height	heroin	homicide	
I	identical	identify	immaterial	immediately	impersonate
	implicate	incarceration	incident	incompatible	independent
	indication	indict	informant	initiate	innocence
	inquired	inspector	instrument	insufficient	intelligence
	intention	interrogate	intersection	interview	intoxication
	investigation	irrelevant			
J	jewel	jewellery (or jewelry)		judgment (or judgement)	
	judicial	jurisdiction	jury	justice	justified
K	kidnap	kidnapped	knowledge		
L	laboratory	larynx	law	league	legitimate
	length	liability	liable	libel	licence–noun
	license–verb	lieutenant	logical	lying	
M	magistrate	malfeasance	manual	marijuana	marital
	mayor	measure	minimum	minor	morale
	motive	multiple	murder		

N	narcotic	necessary	negligence	negligible	neighbour
	noticeable				
O	obstruction	occasion	occurred	offence	officer
	omitted				
P	paid	pale	paraphernalia	parole	patrol
	patrolled	penalty	penitentiary	perjury	perpetrate
	plausible	plea	poison	possess	possession
	preceding	premise	prisoner	procedure	prosecutor
	puncture	pursue			
Q	qualify	quality	quantify	quantity	quarrel
	quarry	queen	query	queue	quiet
	quit	quite	quorum		
R	receipt	receive	recommend	reference	regulation
	rehabilitate	relevant	removable	repossess	reprimand
	resolution	restitution	rhythm		
S	sabotage	scene	scheme	secrecy	seized
	separate	September	sergeant	serial	similar
	siren	situation	slander	slippery	solemn
	soliciting	solution	specimen	statutory	stereotype
	stripped	substitute	suicide	superintendent	superior
	suspicion				
T	tactics	tattoo	technical	testified	through
	tobacco	transient	trespass	twelfth	
U	umbrella	use	used	using	
V	vault	vegetable	vehicle	velocity	verify
	veteran	violate		visual	
W	waist	warrant	weather	weight	wrecked
X	x-ray				
Y	yesterday	yield			
Z	zinc				

GRAMMAR

Not only is it important to spell correctly, but it is also important to use the correct words at the correct times when you speak and write. Some of the most commonly misused homonyms were discussed in the Spelling section, but there are also many adjectives, adverbs, pronouns, and verbs that are commonly misused in English. Below are some of these words and how to use them correctly. Using these words correctly will ensure that your message is being communicated accurately and with correct grammar.

Common Grammatical Errors

Listed below are some of the most common grammatical errors.

well / good

well = an adverb; refers to a verb
good = an adjective; describes a noun

Correct: *The recruit did well on his exams.*

did = verb
well = adverb

Correct: *The officer wrote good notes in his notebook.*

good = adjective
notes = noun

Incorrect: *The recruit did good on his exams.*

Starting an assertive sentence with *which*

Correct: *The officer chased down a 24-year old male.*
Incorrect: *The officer chased down a suspect. Which was a 24-year old male.*

Misuse of the verb *to go*

Correct: Present tense: Use "go" or "goes."

*The officer **goes** to work four days out of seven.*

Past tense: Use "went."

*The officer **went** to work four days last week.*

Past participle (helper verb): Use **"has," "have," "was,"** or **"were"** with **"gone."**

*The officer **has gone** to work every day this week.*

Incorrect: *The officer has went to work every day this week.*

Misuse of the verb *to see*

Correct: Present tense: Use "see" or "sees."

*"I can **see** the suspect very clearly now," reported the officer doing the surveillance.*

Past tense: Use "**saw.**"

*"I **saw** Mrs. Barber swaying from side to side, putting her arms out to her sides, and holding onto her car while she tried to walk along the yellow curb line along highway 41," reported Constable Raz.*

Past participle: Use "**seen**" with "**has," "have," "was,"** or **"were."**

*"The four suspects **were seen** running from the Macs store at approximately 04:15," reported Constable Blythe.*

Incorrect: *"I seen two suspects running north on Centre Street," reported Constable Cox.*

"**Seen**" must be used with a helping verb, such as "**has," "have," "was,"** and **"were."**

Misuse of the verb *to drive*

Correct: Present tense: Use "drive" or "drives."

During Call-To-Duty, Sergeant England told Constable French that he could ***drive*** *patrol car #987.*

Past tense: Use "**drove.**"

"The 84-year old woman ***drove*** *her car at the exact speed limit of 50 km per hour," stated her lawyer.*

Past participle: Use "**driven**" with "**has,**" "**have,**" "**was,**" or "**were.**"

"Mrs. Gale ***has driven*** *for 58 years," stated her lawyer.*

Incorrect: *"Mrs. Gale droved for 58 years," stated her lawyer.*

"Mrs. Gale has droved for 58 years," stated her lawyer.

Misuse of the pronouns *I* and *me*

I = first person singular, subjective

Correct: *I am an RCMP officer.*

My friend and I want to be police officers.

(You always state yourself last when naming yourself with others.)

Incorrect: *Me and* **my friend want to be police officers.**

Me = first person singular, objective

Correct: *The suspect* ***came*** *with me down to headquarters.*

("Me" answers the question, "With whom?" after the verb, "came.")

"Look over your notebooks before you hand them to ***me,*** *" stated the Staff Sergeant.*

Incorrect: *"Me and my partner are coming in," said Constable Hyde.*

Agreement rules for *each, everyone, someone, either, neither,* and *one*

All these words are **singular** and, therefore, take a singular adjective.
Correct: If all the students are male:

Each *student must buy all* ***the*** *textbooks on* ***his*** *book list.*

If all the students are female:

Each *student must buy all* ***the*** *textbooks on* ***her*** *book list.*

If the students are co-ed, male and female:

Each *student must buy all* ***the*** *textbooks on* ***the*** *book list.*

Or:
Change the singular "each" to the plural "all" and make everything plural:

All *student****s*** *must buy* ***all the*** *textbook****s*** *on* ***their*** *book* ***lists.***

Incorrect: *Each student must buy all the textbooks on their book list.*

The same rules apply to all the words in the list above: *everyone, someone, either, neither,* and *one.*

Exercise 1.5 Using Correct Grammar

Circle the correct answer.

1. The officer did (well / good) on his fitness test because he used his time (well / good) during the practice sessions, which were taught (well / good).
2. Our neighbour's son (has went / went) to Alberta to train for the RCMP.
3. The instructors (seen / saw) a big difference in the new recruits' driving skills.
4. At the beginning of the course, each recruit (drived / droved / drove) the patrol car too fast and ended up failing (the / their) (tests / test).

Exercise 1.6 Writing Exercise

1. Choose any five of the words listed in the Grammar section above. In particular, choose the words that you know you have trouble using.
2. Write sentences using these words on the lines below. If you like, try to use more than one of the words in a sentence.
3. Underline the words so that they stand out.
4. After your teacher has marked your work, record **any** word that you misspelled in your personal spelling list.

1. ____

____

2. ____

____

3. ____

____

4. ____

____

5. ____

____

Parallelism

When you are listing one or more things or items in a series, each item in the series must be parallel to the other items in the series. "Parallel" means two or more listed items having a similar grammatical construction, the same order of the parts of speech, and, usually, about the same number of words as the others in the items listed in the series.

Correct: *I like apples and peaches.*

The two items in the series, "apples" and "peaches," are both one word in length; they are both nouns, and importantly, they are both plurals, which keeps them consistent with one another. Therefore, this sentence contains parallelism and is correct.

I like apples, peaches, pears, and plums.

The items listed are each one word long, plural, and they are all nouns. Therefore, the sentence contains parallelism and is correct.

I like Macintosh apples, Bartlett pears, and Niagara plums.

This time, the items in the series contain two words, and the first word is an adjective describing the other word, which is a noun.

Incorrect: *I like Macintosh apples, pears, and Niagara plums.*

"Pears" should have an adjective to make it parallel to the other two items in the series.

Also, you wouldn't say *I like Macintosh apples, a pear, and Niagara plums.* Speaking generally about two items and specifically about one ("a pear") would make this non-parallel, and therefore incorrect.

Exercise 1.7 Creating Parallel Sentences

Correct the lack of parallelism in these sentences by adding or deleting words where necessary.

1. Officer Kim removed his gun, holster, and his badge.
2. The menu for the recruits' banquet consisted of salad, roasted potatoes, Yorkshire pudding, roast beef, and cake.
3. The instructor told the officers to bend and shoot low.
4. Black pants, shirt, black socks, and black shoes was the dress code for those Police Foundations students.
5. For about an hour, the residents heard the sirens and ambulances.

Exercise 1.8 Writing Exercise

Write sentences to answer the following questions. Be sure that the responses are written in parallel form.

1. Name three vegetables that you like eating.

   ____

   ____

2. What are three reasons why you should be physically fit?

   ____

   ____

3. What three characteristics should a police officer possess?

____

____

4. Name four subjects that you are studying now in your program.

____

____

5. Name two sports that you enjoy.

____

____

PUNCTUATION

Rules to Remember

Besides learning the rules for some of the most common spelling and punctuation errors, learning how to punctuate is very important. The misuse of a question mark for a period can change the sentence from an **assertive sentence**, which states facts, to an **interrogative sentence**, which asks a question. Also, leaving out one comma in a sentence can cause a reader to misinterpret the meaning of the sentence and may also force the reader to reread the words a few times before understanding the content. There are many punctuation rules. Below are the most commonly used and often the most misused ones. Learn these and apply them to your writing so that whoever reads your writing will be able to do it with ease and clarity.

Period

1. Put a period at the **end of every sentence.**

   Mr. Smith was sentenced to fifteen years in jail.

2. Put a period **inside the end quotation marks** when writing a conversation (dialogue), if the speaker information is at the beginning of the sentence and introduces the words of the speaker.

   The judge said, "Mr. Smith, your sentence is fifteen years in jail."

3. Use period(s) in **abbreviations** (short forms).

   Mon. = Monday; Mr. = Mister; Sgt. = Sergeant; P.C. = Police Constable

Comma (,)

1. Put commas in the **date** to separate the day from the month and the date from the year.
   Day, month date, year

   Friday, August 19, 2005

2. Put a comma before the coordinating conjunction joining two independent clauses (sentences).

   Greg worked out at the gym three times a week, for he was preparing for his physical fitness test.

   Coordinating conjunctions:

   ,for ,and ,nor ,but ,or ,yet ,so

   If you put the first letter of each one of these conjunctions together, you get the word "fanboys." Use this acronym to help you remember the coordinating conjunctions and the comma needed before them when joining two independent clauses. (**Note:** For more information on independent and dependent clauses, see Chapter 2).

3. Put a comma after the transitional adverb when joining two independent clauses.

   So, the structure is as follows: independent clause; transitional adverb, independent clause.

   Here are some common transitional adverbs: *therefore, however, for example, consequently, furthermore, subsequently, otherwise,* and *then.*

   Greg trained for the physical fitness test; therefore, he was ready to take it.

4. Put a comma after a dependent clause that starts a sentence, to make a complex sentence.

   A **dependent clause** is a group of words that has a subject and a verb, but this group of words does not make sense on its own.

   Example of a dependent clause:

   When I attended a community college for Law and Security

   Subject: *I*
   Verb: *attended*

   This group of words does not make sense on its own. It needs more information to make it complete. You would add an independent clause to this group of words to make a complete sentence.

   When I attended a community college for Law and Security, I studied psychology, communications, and sociology.

   When you join a dependent clause to an independent clause, you have formed a complex sentence.

   Structure of a complex sentence: dependent clause, independent clause.

   Since Sara had her motorcycle licence before she became an officer, she started her motorcycle training before the other recruits who didn't have their motorcycle licences.

5. Put commas **around words that are extra information** in the sentence. This applies to words that don't have to be in the sentence for the sentence to make sense.

   Sara Hing, the officer who had her motorcycle licence before she joined the service, is here for her training.

6. Put a comma **after the introductory** word, phrase, or clause in a split sentence.

   Yesterday, the division received four calls about domestic disputes.

   During the blackout of 2003, Ottawa had 22 cases of looting.

When the electrical power failure occurred in August of 2003, all the traffic lights in Southern Ontario stopped functioning.

7. Put a comma after items in a **series** when there are **three or more items** being listed.

   Officer Maranofski put his gun, holster, and notebook into his locker.

   The investigating officers found bits of tissue, paper, gravel, and hair on the body.

8. Use a comma when introducing what someone is saying in a dialogue if the speaker is mentioned first.

   A person came to the front counter of Division 14 and said, "I witnessed the accident that happened last night at around 10:15."

9. Put a comma after the words of a speaker if the speaker is mentioned last and the words spoken make up an assertive sentence.

   "I witnessed the accident that happened last night around 10:15," said the person standing at the counter of Division 14.

10. Put a comma after the name of the person to whom an informal letter is written.

    Dear Dad,

Semi-colon (;)

1. Put in a semi-colon to **join two independent clauses (sentences)** in order to make a compound sentence.

   Structure: independent clause; independent clause

   The instructors taught the officers how to use the batons; this training was part of their course.

2. Put in semi-colons to **separate items in a series if each item is lengthy** or has other punctuation in it.

   The student chose to take Police Foundations at the college in his hometown because of the closeness to his home; the reputation of the college; and the quality of the teachers.

   This man, John Charles Hanslip, committed robberies on Monday, August 18, 2003; Tuesday, August 19, 2003; and Friday, August 22, 2003.

Colon (:)

1. Use a colon to introduce a list after a complete thought.

   Correct: *The following things were found at the scene: four fragments of green tinted glass; five strands of blonde hair; six white pieces of tissue; and three pages from a book.*

   Note: Never put a colon after words such as "to, is, are, and were." Colons come after complete thoughts. Groups of words ending with "to," "is," "are," or "were" are not complete thoughts.

   Incorrect: *The subjects that you will take are: psychology, communications, immigrations, and investigation.*

2. Put in a colon at the **end of a salutation** in a formal letter/ business letter.

   Dear Mr. Matthews:

3. Put in a colon to separate the hour from the minutes.

   The incident took place at 09:56.

4. Put in a colon after the words *To, From, Date,* and *Subject* in a memo.

   To:
   From:
   Date:
   Subject:

Apostrophe (')

Usage 1: Put an apostrophe in to replace letters left out in contractions.

Don't, won't, wouldn't, haven't, let's, it's, etc.

Usage 2: Put in an apostrophe to show **possession/ownership.**

Look at the spelling of the person who owns something in the sentence.

a) If the person who owns the thing ends with an "s" already, just add an apostrophe after the "s".

   The four officers' uniforms were lying on the table.

   Officers own the uniforms. The word "officers" ends with an "s"; therefore, just add the apostrophe after the "s" in "officers" to show possession.

b) If the person who owns the thing does not end with an "s" already, then add an apostrophe and an "s" to show possession.

   That officer's uniform was just cleaned.

   Who owns the uniform? The "officer" does. Only one officer owns the uniform. The word "officer" does not end in "s"; therefore, you need to add "s."

   Note: Do not put an apostrophe before or after the "s" at the end of every word that ends with an "s". There has to be a sense of ownership in the sentence to use the apostrophe. Read the sentence carefully. If the word that ends in "s" is simply a plural, then **do not** add an apostrophe.

Correct: *The duty officer put the guns in their cases.*

Incorrect: *The duty officer put the gun's in their cases'.*

Quotation marks

1. Put quotation marks (" ") around words **spoken in a dialogue**.

   "Where were you on the night of August 13th?" asked the officer.

   "I was at home," replied the suspect.

   "What were you doing at home?" asked the officer.

   "I was at home because there was a power failure, and I didn't have enough gas in my car to go anywhere!" responded the suspect.

   The officer then asked, "Who was with you at home?"

   The suspect stated, "All my buds came over for a barbecue because they had gas for their cars, but I had propane for the barbecue and beer!"

2. Put quotation marks around the titles of newspaper articles, magazine articles, chapter titles in books, and video clips.

   "Alberta introduces pepper spray guidelines for police to follow" – Article

   "The Five-Paragraph Essay Model" – Chapter title

   "Raves: Dancing the Night Away" – Video clip

Exercise 1.9 Correct Punctuation

Correct the punctuation in the following sentences.

1. The police sirens were going from 12:09 until 12:28, while the officer chased the speeding car along the 401 on Friday, August 19, 2005.

2. During the chase, all the cars going eastbound pulled over to the shoulder and stopped to give the officer free access to the road.

3. When the officer got up to the speeding car and pulled it over, the officer found the following people in the car: a teenaged boy; a middle-aged father; a middle-aged mother; and a ten-year-old girl.

4. The father was not driving the car; the son was.

5. The father's licence had been suspended and the sixteen-year-old who had his G1 was driving the car; the mother had a valid licence.

Exercise 1.10 Writing Exercise

1. Choose ten of the punctuation rules that you find the most difficult and write one sentence for each to illustrate the correct usage.

2. Write the sentences on the lines provided.

3. After your work has been marked, write all corrections of all your spelling errors in your personal spelling list.

   1. ______________________________

      ____

   2. ______________________________

      ____

   3. ______________________________

      ____

   4. ______________________________

      ____

5. ______________________________

____

6. ______________________________

____

7. ______________________________

____

8. ______________________________

____

9. ______________________________

____

10. ______________________________

____

Summary

To improve your writing skills, do the following:

- Identify all the words you are misspelling; write them in your personal spelling list; and study these words until you spell them correctly every time that you use them.
- Learn and use the correct spellings for the most commonly misspelled words.
- Learn and use the correct usage for the most commonly misused words.
- Learn how to spell all the words commonly used in law enforcement and use them correctly.
- Apply the grammar rules for common grammatical errors.
- Apply the punctuation rules for the period, comma, semi-colon, colon, apostrophe, and quotation marks.
- Work hard to be the best writer that you can be so that your writing will benefit the judicial system rather than hinder it.

Sentence Structure

Learning Objectives

After students have learned the content of this chapter, they should be able to do the following:

- Understand the definitions of the following terms: sentence, subject, predicate, independent clause, dependent clause, fragment, run-on sentence, and comma splice.
- Identify and write the four types of sentences: assertive, imperative, interrogative, and exclamatory.
- Identify and write the three sentence orders: natural, split, and inverted.
- Identify and correct fragments and run-on sentences.
- Identify and write compound sentences and complex sentences.

Learning Benefits

Being able to write in proper sentences is essential to effective communication. When you are writing in sentences, you are logically expressing complete thoughts, concepts, and information, thus allowing your reader to understand accurately what you are saying. All narrative-style law enforcement reports are written in sentences. These reports are read by officers, lawyers, and other law enforcement personnel. Clear, concise, correct sentences will help your readers understand the content of your narrative.

SUBJECTS AND PREDICATES

A sentence is one or more words that state a complete thought that makes sense on its own and contains a **subject**, the main idea of the sentence, and a **predicate**, what the subject is or is doing.

Sentences

I am a student in Law and Security.

Subject = *I*; Predicate = *am a student in Law and Security*

Drop the gun!

The subject (*You*) is understood to be there.
Subject = (*You*); Predicate = *Drop the gun*

Stop!

The subject (*You*) is understood to be there.
Subject = (*You*); Predicate = *Stop*

Why did you join that security company?

Subject = you; Predicate = did join that security company why

Simple sentences are also called **independent clauses** (IC) because they make sense on their own.

FRAGMENTS

What do you call groups of words that are **not** complete thoughts and **do not make sense** by themselves?

These are **fragments.** Fragments are groups of words that are lacking words or have too many words, so you end up with an incomplete thought. Fragments are major writing errors. These groups of words do not make sense and are not considered proper sentences.

Examples of fragments: These are **incorrect** and are major writing errors.

The officer drove cruiser at 75 km/h during the chase through the town.

Ran out of gas.

Because the officer told him to stop.

The officer killed in the accident.

Which is my gun.

Because he wrote incomplete reports.

How do you correct fragments? You add the necessary words or change words to make the thoughts complete. Here are some examples of correct versions of the sentences presented above:

The officer drove **the** *cruiser at 75 km/h during the chase through the town.*

The suspect's car *ran out of gas.*

The suspect stopped running *because the officer told him to stop.*

The officer **was** *killed in the accident.*

***That** is my gun.*

Because ***Constable Thompson*** *wrote incomplete reports, he* ***had to attend a forty-hour seminar on report writing.***

Exercise 2.1 Fragments

Write F in the column if the group of words is a fragment. Write IC if the group of words is an independent clause (sentence).

F

[illegible] 1. Police arrested that man after the police found 650 pot plants in house.

F 2. The street value of pot plants was $330,000.

IC 3. The police also confiscated $32,000 worth of hydroponics equipment.

F 4. The police investigators also found a bypass a hydro line that was being used to illegally connect electricity to the man's house.

F 5. This man is facing charges of the growing and producing marijuana, possession for the purpose of trafficking, and stealing hydro.

Exercise 2.2 Correcting Fragments

Correct the fragments in Exercise 2.1 by deleting or adding words to the groups of words above. Write out the correct sentences below.

1. ____________________

2. ____________________

3. ____________________

4. ____________________

5. ____________________

Exercise 2.3 More Fragments

Change these fragments to complete thoughts/sentences.

1. Officer James gave chase to speeding car.

____

2. Because the suspect was speeding.

____

3. Which he gave to him.

____

4. Rather than wait until they got to the station.

____

5. In that prison.

____

TYPES OF SENTENCES

In English, there are many different types of sentences, and there are different ways to write sentences. Using all these types of sentences will add variety to your writing and make your writing enjoyable to read. However, you must learn to write them correctly.

Table 2.1: Types of Sentences

Type	Definintion	Example	End Punctuation
Assertive	states information	*Students who wish to become police officers are encouraged to take Police Foundations at a college.*	Period (.)
Interrogative	asks a question	*Which colleges offer Police Foundations?*	Question mark (?)
Exclamatory	shows expression	*Two years is a long time to have go to school to become an officer!*	Exclamation mark (!)
Imperative	an order to do something	*Take Police Foundations at a college of your choice.*	Period or exclamation mark

Exercise 2.4 Writing Exercise

1. Choose a topic from law enforcement for this writing exercise and write it on the line below.
2. Write one example of each type of sentence based on that topic in the following table. Be sure to add the correct end punctuation.
3. Once you have your work marked by a teacher, be sure to write all the spelling corrections in your personal spelling list in Appendix D.

Topic: ____________________

Type	Example
Assertive	
Interrogative	
Exclamatory	
Imperative	

SENTENCE ORDER

The order within a sentence is determined by **the position of the subject.** The subject is the main focus or topic of a sentence and can appear in three different places in the sentence.

Table 2.2: Sentence Order

Sentence Order	Example	Position of Subject
Natural	*The officer put his gun into his holster before leaving the firing range.*	Beginning of sentence
Split (Note the comma after the introductory phrase)	*Before leaving the firing range, the officer put his gun into his holster.*	In the middle (approximately)
Inverted	*During the night shift, there were four arrests.*	The end

Exercise 2.5 Writing Exercise

1. Choose a topic from law enforcement for this writing exercise and write it on the line below.

2. Write one example of each type of sentence order based on your topic in the following table.

3. Once you have your work marked by a teacher, be sure to write all the spelling corrections in your personal spelling list.

Topic: ____________________

Sentence Order	Example
Natural	
Split	
Inverted	

COMPOUND SENTENCES

The above sentences are all simple sentences with one subject and one verb. It is possible to join two sentences (independent clauses) together to write compound sentences. Compound sentences have **two independent clauses** in them.

Table 2.3: Compound Sentences

Ways to Write Compound Sentences	Examples
1. Join two independent clauses with a semi-colon.	*I finished Police Foundations when I was twenty years old; I started as an officer for Milton when I was twenty-two.*
2. Join two independent clauses with a comma and a coordinating conjunction.	Coordinating conjunctions: *for, and, nor, but, or, yet, so* *I did not get a job with a police force right after graduating from Police Foundations, so I got a job with a security company.* *I enjoyed the job, but I still wanted to be on a police force.* *I always wanted to be an officer, for my grandfather was a police officer.*
3. Join two independent clauses with a semi-colon, then a transitional adverb, and finally a comma.	Transitional adverbs: *therefore, however, consequently, for example, then, subsequently, moreover, furthermore,* etc. *During the state of emergency in Ontario caused by the hydro failure in the summer of 2003, there were many vehicle accidents; therefore, all officers were on call so that the public could be served.*

Exercise 2.6 Writing Exercise

1. Choose a topic from law enforcement for this writing exercise and write it on the line below.
2. Write one example of each way to write compound sentences based on that topic in the following table.
3. Once you have your work marked by a teacher, be sure to write all the spelling corrections in your personal spelling list.

   Code for abbreviations:

   IC = independent clause

   Co = coordinating conjunction: *for, and, nor, but, or, yet, so*

   Ta = transitional adverb: *therefore, however, consequently, for example, then, subsequently, moreover, furthermore,* etc.

Topic: ______________________________

Type of Compound Sentence	Example
IC; IC	
IC, Co IC	
IC; Ta, IC	

Complex Sentences

A complex sentence is formed when you **join an independent clause to a dependent clause.** A **dependent clause** (DC) is a group of words that has a subject and a verb, but doesn't make sense on its own.

Dependent Clauses

Dependent clauses, as their name implies, are not complete "thoughts" on their own.

Examples:

When I was a recruit

Because I want to

Once you join the dependent clause to an independent clause, you have a complete thought and a sentence.

When I was a recruit, I really enjoyed the training sessions.

DC *IC*

Because I want to be a police officer, I will work hard to get very good

DC *IC*

marks in my Police Foundations courses.

Yes, you can start a sentence with the word "because." Be sure to complete the thought of the dependent clause started with the word "because" by adding an independent clause, and make sure that the sentence is not a fragment.

To write a dependent clause, start the clause with a **subordinating conjunction**, such as the following: *after, although, because, when, if, whenever, until, while,* etc.

The dependent clause can be the first or the second clause in the sentence. If the dependent clause is **first** in the sentence, you separate it from the independent clause with **a comma**.

If the dependent clause is **second** in the sentence, there is **no comma** between those two clauses. See Table 2.4 below.

Table 2.4: Ways to Write Complex Sentences

Code for abbreviations: DC = dependent clause
IC = independent clause

Ways to Write Complex Sentences	Examples
DC, IC (Note the comma after the dependent clause)	*After the officer chased the suspect for approximately one kilometre, the officer caught him and read him his rights.* *Because the suspect resembled the description of the person who robbed the jewellery store, the officer arrested him.* *Although some cases are not resolved immediately, many cases are solved within two weeks' time.*
IC plus DC There is **no comma** between the two clauses.	*The officer caught the suspect and read him his rights after the officer chased the suspect for approximately one kilometre.* *The officer arrested the suspect because he resembled the description of the person who robbed the jewellery store.* *Many cases are solved within two weeks' time although there are some cases that do not get solved immediately.*

Exercise 2.7 Writing Exercise

1. Choose a topic from law enforcement for this writing exercise and write it on the line below.

2. Write one example of each way to write complex sentences on that topic in the following table.

3. Once you have your work marked by a teacher, be sure to write all the spelling corrections in your personal spelling list.

Topic: ______________________________

Ways to Write Complex Sentences	Example
DC, IC	
IC plus DC	

RUN-ON SENTENCES

A run-on sentence (ROS) is a major error in writing. It typically consists of two sentences that are side-by-side and have no punctuation between them. These two sentences can usually be corrected by adding the proper punctuation.

The following is a run-on sentence, and it is incorrect:

The officer arrested the suspect the officer forgot to read him his rights.

There are two complete thoughts here. This example contains two independent clauses or simple sentences written as one sentence, with no punctuation between them.

The officer arrested the suspect + *the officer forgot to read him his rights.*

IC *IC*

To correct this run-on sentence, you can use any one of six methods:

1. Write that group of words as two distinct sentences or independent clauses:

   The officer arrested the suspect. The officer forgot to read him his rights.

2. Write it as a compound sentence using the IC; IC method:

   The officer arrested the suspect; the officer forgot to read him his rights.

3. Write it as a compound sentence using the IC, Co IC method:

   The officer arrested the suspect, but the officer forgot to read him his rights.

4. Write it as a compound sentence using the IC; Ta, IC method:

   The officer arrested the suspect; however, the officer forgot to read him his rights.

5. Write it as a complex sentence by changing one of the ICs to a DC by adding a subordinating conjunction in front of it and using the IC DC method:

   The officer forgot to read the suspect his rights ***when*** *the officer arrested him.*

6. Write it as a complex sentence by changing one of the ICs to a DC by adding a subordinating conjunction in front of it using the DC, IC method:

   When *the officer arrested the suspect, the officer forgot to read him his rights.*

Exercise 2.8 Run-on Sentences

Correct the run-on sentence below using each of the six methods listed above:

The officer in patrol car #24 noticed a vehicle with an expired licence he pulled the driver over to investigate.

a) two separate ICs

____

b) IC; IC

____

c) IC, Co IC

____

d) IC; Ta, IC

____

e) IC DC

____

f) DC, IC

____

COMMA SPLICES

Comma splices (CS) are another common major error in writing. Comma splices occur when you put only a comma between two independent clauses. You should never join two sentences with a comma. Commas alone never join two sentences.

The following is a comma splice, and therefore it is incorrect:

The officer arrested the suspect, the officer forgot to read him his rights.

Note the comma. This comma should not be here by itself, unaccompanied by a coordinating conjunction.

The difference between a run-on sentence and a comma splice:

ROS: Run-on sentences have no punctuation between the two sentences, but there should be some punctuation.

CS: Comma splices have a comma between the two sentences, but that punctuation alone is insufficient to join the two sentences.

To correct comma splices, use any one of the six methods outlined above for correcting run-on sentences.

CS = The officer arrested the suspect, the officer forgot to read him his rights.

1. Write the group of words as two distinct sentences or ICs:

   The officer arrested the suspect. The officer forgot to read him his rights.

2. Write it as a compound sentence using the IC; IC method:

   The officer arrested the suspect; the officer forgot to read him his rights.

3. Write it as a compound sentence using the IC, Co IC method:

   The officer arrested the suspect, but the officer forgot to read him his rights.

4. Write it as a compound sentence using the IC; Ta, IC method:

   The officer arrested the suspect; however, the officer forgot to read him his rights.

5. Write it as a complex sentence using the IC DC method after first changing one of the ICs to a DC:

   The officer forgot to read the suspect his rights when the officer arrested him.

6. Write it as a complex sentence using the DC, IC method after first changing one of the ICs to a DC:

   When the officer arrested the suspect, the officer forgot to read him his rights.

Exercise 2.9 Correcting Comma Splices

Correct this comma splice by using all six methods described above:

The officer wrote his notes in his notebook, then the officer wrote his reports.

a) two separate ICs

____

b) IC; IC

____

c) IC, Co IC

____

d) IC; Ta, IC

____

e) IC DC

____

f) DC, IC

____

Exercise 2.10 Writing Exercise

1. Choose one topic related to law enforcement, or use your teacher's topic, and write a nine- to twelve-sentence paragraph about that topic on the first set of lines provided. This will be the first draft.

2. Your paragraph should include the following:
   - at least two types of sentences: assertive, imperative, interrogative, or exclamatory;
   - at least two different sentence orders: natural, split, or inverted;
   - one IC; IC (compound sentence)
   - one IC; Ta, IC (compound sentence)
   - one IC, Co IC (compound sentence)
   - one IC DC (complex sentence)
   - one DC, IC (complex sentence)

3. Proofread the paragraph and eliminate all run-on sentences, comma splices, or fragments. Also correct any spelling, punctuation, and grammar errors.

4. Ask a classmate to proofread your first draft and point out any errors to you. Ask your classmate to sign the line at the bottom of the first draft indicating that he or she has proofread your paragraph.

5. Correct your errors.

6. Rewrite your first draft, making all corrections on the second set of lines provided, and entitle it "Second Draft."

7. Submit your paragraph to your teacher for marking.

8. Once your paragraph is returned to you, write any misspelled words in your personal spelling list and take note of all the comments and errors noted by your teacher.

Summary

Important points to remember from this chapter are as follows:

- Always write in complete, proper sentences.
- Make sure your groups of words make sense and have subjects and predicates.
- Use a variety of sentences and sentence orders: assertive, exclamatory, interrogative, imperative, natural, split, and inverted.
- Join independent clauses to make compound sentences by inserting one of the following between the clauses: a semi-colon; a comma and a coordinating conjunction; or a semi-colon followed by a transitional adverb and a comma.
- Write complex sentences by joining a dependent clause to an independent clause. The independent clause can be first or second in this combination.

First Draft

Topic: ______________________________

First draft proofread by: ______________________________

Second Draft

Topic: ____

The Paragraph

Learning Objectives

After students have learned the content of this chapter, they should be able to write a paragraph that includes the following:

- An introductory topic statement.
- Body sentences that develop the topic.
- A concluding statement that concludes and sums up the topic.
- Transitions that link all the ideas together and make the paragraph coherent.
- Information that is logical.
- Information that relates to the topic of that paragraph.

Learning Benefits

Why do you need to know how to write a paragraph? The paragraph is the framework in which you write consecutive thoughts on one topic in a logical order. You write in paragraphs in memos, letters, reports, and, of course, essays. Knowing how to write in paragraphs is an essential skill.

In law enforcement careers, you will need to write all your memos, letters, and reports in paragraph form. Point form writing is reserved for your notebooks. You will need to take those points from your notes in your notebook and write them in paragraphs in the incident reports, narrative reports, and supplementary reports, to name just a few types of reports in law enforcement. Furthermore, many police services and law enforcement agencies require applicants to provide a writing sample as part of the application process. It is understood that you will write this in paragraph form.

ELEMENTS OF THE PARAGRAPH

A paragraph is a self-contained unit of sentences about one topic, and this group of sentences meets certain criteria. A proper paragraph:

- is based on one topic;
- has a topic sentence as the first or second sentence that states the topic of the entire paragraph and gets the reader's attention;
- discusses and develops that point in a series of sentences in the body of the paragraph;
- has a concluding sentence that sums up the topic and brings the topic to a close;
- has transitions that link all the ideas together and create coherence; and
- contains information that is logical.

One helpful way of thinking about a paragraph is to imagine it as piece of plywood, or perhaps as a set of laminated sheets of wood glued together. See Figure 3.1.

Figure 3.1 The Paragraph

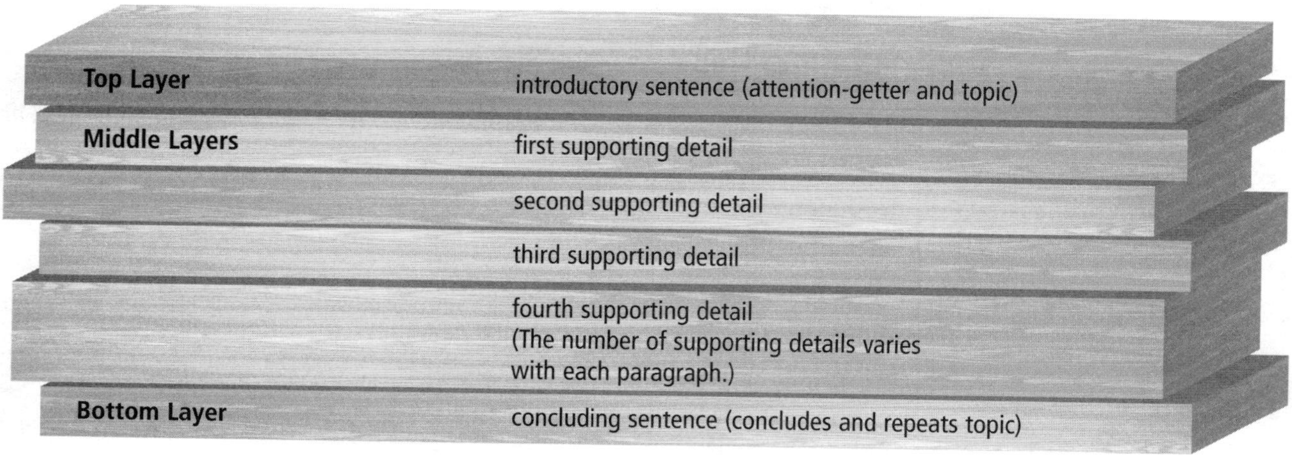

Top Layer	introductory sentence (attention-getter and topic)
Middle Layers	first supporting detail
	second supporting detail
	third supporting detail
	fourth supporting detail (The number of supporting details varies with each paragraph.)
Bottom Layer	concluding sentence (concludes and repeats topic)

You should be able to take a series of paragraphs and link them together into other forms of writing, such as essays. For examples of paragraphs flowing together in essays, see Chapters 5, 6, 7, and 10, and Appendix E.

SAMPLE PARAGRAPH

This sample paragraph has been taken from an essay in Chapter 5, but it has been changed slightly to allow it to stand alone, unlinked to other paragraphs. To see this paragraph in its original format in an essay, see the essay entitled "A Friend," in Chapter 5.

My friend, John, is one of the most encouraging people I know. He doesn't hesitate to encourage me when I have done something well. Let's look at the time when we got back our second psychology test. This was a very hard test because it was based on six chapters, and the questions were all multiple choice. John knew that I often did not do well on multiple choice tests and didn't like them, so when I got back my mark, and it was a 68, he told me that I had done well because I had improved my percentage on multiple choice questions. This made me feel good! Another time, John kept coaching me when we were preparing for the P.R.E.P. Test. I had practised that test five times, and I just couldn't consistently do it in the required time. With his coaching, I was finally able to do it in the right amount of time every time we practised and on the final test. Besides encouraging me during actual tests at school, John cheered me up when my dog died. My dog, Boots, was my companion for ten years. When he died, it was like losing a family member. John sympathized with me and encouraged me during my grieving time by listening to me reminisce about Boots. His encouragement helped me a great deal. Because of John's encouraging words in many situations, I value him as my friend.

Let's look at this paragraph to see how it fits into the structure in Figure 3.1.

Top Layer
My friend, John, is one of the most encouraging people I know. *He doesn't hesitate to encourage me when I have done something well.*

Second Layer
Let's look at the time when we got back our second psychology test. This was a very hard test because it was based on six chapters, and the questions were all multiple choice. John knew that I often did not do well on multiple choice tests and didn't like them, so when I got back my mark, and it was a 68, he told me that I had done well because I had improved my percentage on multiple choice questions. This made me feel good!

Third Layer
Another time, John kept coaching me when we were preparing for the P.R.E.P. Test. I had practised that test five times, and I just couldn't consistently do it in the required time. With his coaching, I was finally able to do it in the right amount of time every time we practised and on the final test.

Fourth Layer
Besides encouraging me during actual tests at school, John cheered me up when my dog died. My dog, Boots, was my companion for ten years. When he died, it was like losing a family member. John sympathized with me and encouraged me during my grieving time by listening to me reminisce about Boots. His encouragement helped me a great deal.

Bottom Layer
Because of John's encouraging words in many situations, I value him as my friend.

The Introductory Sentence

The introductory sentence, the top layer in the above example, should do two things:

1. Get the reader's attention; and
2. State the topic.

Example

My friend, John, is one of the most encouraging people I know.

Let's examine this introductory statement.

1. Does it have an attention-getter?
   Yes, it does because of the words, "most encouraging people I know," and the name of the person; many people would want to read the rest of the paragraph to find out why John was given such a high compliment.
2. Does it state the topic?
   Yes, it does. The words "encouraging people" and "John" state the topic. Right from the start, the reader knows that this paragraph will have examples of how John is encouraging to the author of this paragraph.

The Body Sentences

Let's examine the body sentences (the second, third, and fourth layers) in the above example. The author has organized the supporting details into three examples. The first one is as follows:

He doesn't hesitate to encourage me when I have done something well. ***Let's look at the time*** *when we got back our second psychology test.* ***This*** *was a very hard test because it was based on six chapters, and the questions were all multiple choice. John knew that I often did not do well on* ***multiple choice*** *tests and didn't like them, so when I got back my mark, and it was a 68, he told me that I had done well because I had improved my percentage on multiple choice questions.* ***This made*** *me feel good!*

The second example is as follows:

Another time, *John kept coaching me when we were preparing for the P.R.E.P. Test. I had practised that* ***test*** *five times, and I just couldn't consistently do it in the* ***required time****. With his coaching, I was finally able to do* ***it*** *in the* ***right amount of time*** *every time we practised and on the final test.*

Here is the third example:

Besides encouraging me during actual tests at school, John *cheered me up when* ***my dog*** *died. My dog,* ***Boots****, was my companion for ten years. When he* ***died****, it was like losing a family member. John sympathized with me and encouraged me during my grieving time by listening to me reminisce about* ***Boots****. His* ***encouragement*** *helped me a great deal.*

There are several things to note about these three examples:

- All three examples have been placed in the same paragraph because they support the same topic: encouragement.
- Each one has a sentence to introduce it. These are underlined in the examples.
- Each example is approximately the same length. The first one is six typed lines; the second is four lines; and the third is five typed lines.
- Transitions link the ideas together in the body of the paragraph to create coherence. The transitions are in ***italics and bolded*** in the above examples. Transitions are the words that join the ideas or link them together. Transitions come in a variety of forms:
    - repeated words: e.g., "my dog" in one sentence = "Boots" or "my dog" repeated in other sentences
    - synonyms: e.g., "required time" in one sentence = "right amount of time" in another sentence
    - time indicators: e.g., "Let's look at a time" and "another time"
- The examples are in logical order. The author gives two examples about tests and then writes about the dog's death. The author doesn't write about the psychology test, then the dog, and finally the P.R.E.P. test. This would create an illogical order.
- Each example has a statement to end it before going on to the next example. The concluding sentences of each example are underlined.

The Concluding Sentence

This is the bottom layer in the example above.

Because of John's encouraging words in many situations, I value him as my friend.

1. Does it repeat the topic?
   Yes. The words "encouraging words" repeat the topic of encouragement.

2. Does it conclude the paragraph?
   Yes. It brings the paragraph to a close. The words "many situations" sum up all the examples, and the words "value him as my friend" bring a sense of finality to the topic.

THE OUTLINE

Before you write a paragraph, you should make an outline so that you can organize your thoughts. Here is the outline made for the sample paragraph, above.

Topic: *My Friend John*

Introductory sentence's topic: *friend, John = encouraging*

Attention-getter: *stating John's name and the fact that he is encouraging*

Supporting details:
- *encourages me when I do well*
- *example: when I got the 68 on the multiple choice test*
- *encourages me when I am trying to do something that is hard for me*
- *example: when I couldn't do the P.R.E.P. Test in the required time*
- *encourages me when I am sad*
- *example: when my dog died*

Conclusion: *encouraging words of John = friend*

Exercise 3.1 Breaking Down the Paragraph

Read the following paragraph from the December 2003 issue of Blue Line magazine. The numbers in brackets [ ] before the sentences will assist you in answering the questions that follow.

[1] Police in West Vancouver who were trying to make a positive identification on a con-artist found a made-in-Canada solution. [2] Officers checked for a tattoo on file for the man: a tattoo on his buttocks that read "Made in Canada." [3] The 55-year-old Quebec man was wanted on a Canada-wide arrest warrant revoking his parole for fraud-related offences in Quebec, Ontario, and Alberta. [4] He was arrested in West Vancouver for using fake cheques to buy pizzas. [5] Police said the man went by 22 different names and birthdates. [6] In order to make a positive identification, and with the co-operation of the suspect, police took a look at his buttocks for the tattoo.

Source: "Incredible." Blue Line Dec. 2003: 38.

1. What words in sentence 1 might capture people's attention?

   ____________________, ____________________, and ____________________

   ____________________.

2. What is the topic in sentence 1?

   ____

3. Write the outline for the body sentences (2–5). (Note that the body sentences do not include the introductory or concluding sentence.)

____

____

____

____

____

____

4. What are the three sets of transitional words or links between sentence 2 and sentence 1? (The first one has been done for you.)

   a) "Officers" in sentence 2 links to "Police" in sentence 1.

   b) ____________________ in sentence 2 links to ____________________ in sentence 5.

   c) ____________________ in sentence 2 links to ____________________ in sentence 1.

5. What are the transitional words or links between sentence 3 and sentence 2?

   ______________________________________ in sentence 3 links to

   ______________________ in sentence 2.

6. What are the transitional words or links between sentence 4 and sentence 3?

   ____________________ in sentence 4 links to ____________________ in sentence 3.

   ____________________ in sentence 4 links to ____________________ in sentence 3.

7. What words link the concluding sentence (6) to the introductory sentence (1)?

   Concluding sentence words:______________________________ link to

   Introductory sentence words: ______________________________.

LINKING PARAGRAPHS

You should be able to take a series of paragraphs and link them together into other forms of writing, such as magazine/newspaper articles and essays. How to link paragraphs together to create essays will be discussed in detail in later chapters. For examples of paragraphs flowing together in essays, see Chapters 5, 6, 7, and 10, and Appendix E. Below is an example of three paragraphs linked together in an article that provides a logical, coherent, unified account of a police incident.

Two RCMP officers were hospitalized in October [2003] with broken bones and other injuries after a man stole one of their cruisers and ran into them with it. Cst. Fleming Kaastrup, 38, of the Leduc detachment, and Cpl. Steve Daley, 43, from the Beaumont detachment—both south of Edmonton—had pulled over a camper-van after receiving a phone call about a suspicious vehicle.

While the officers were dealing with two of the van's three occupants, the remaining man jumped into one of the officers' cars and after hitting them, sped north where the car was found abandoned a few kilometres away. About 20 police officers were called in on a manhunt for the suspect. Several hours later, they converged on a residence near Fort Saskatchewan where a man had barged into the home while the occupants, a woman and a child, fled. After several hours of negotiation, a suspect surrendered peacefully.

Police did not confirm whether the man apprehended was the same man sought in the wounding of the police officers, but they said a truck stolen from the Beaumont area was found near the Fort Saskatchewan home.

Source: "Incredible." Blue Line Dec. 2003: 38.

Exercise 3.2 Writing Exercise

1. Choose a topic from the list below and, on the lines provided, write

   a) an outline, and

   b) a 5–6 sentence paragraph (Draft #1).

2. Exchange your paragraph with another student and mark each other's writing for spelling, punctuation, grammar, and sentence structure. Also, compare the content of each other's paragraph against the criteria for a paragraph listed in the summary at the end of this chapter.

3. Have your proofreader sign his or her name on the line provided at the end of your draft.

4. Rewrite your paragraph with all corrections and submit it to your teacher as your final copy.

5. Record the corrections of all spelling errors in your personal spelling list (Appendix D).

Possible Topics:

- The Main Reason Why I Chose This Course
- An Officer Needs to Be ________________ (Fill in a characteristic.)
- A Safe Driving Tip for Winter Driving
- My Favourite TV Show (Explain why.)

Outline

Topic: ____

Introductory sentence: topic: ______________________________________

attention-getter: ______________________________

Supporting details: ____________________

____

____

____

____

____

____

Concluding sentence: repeat topic: ____________________

conclude: ____________________

Paragraph: Draft #1: 5–6 sentences

____

____

____

____

____

____

____

____

____

____

____

____

Proofreader's signature: ____________________

Paragraph: Final Copy: 5–6 sentences

____

____

____

____

____

____

____

____

____

____

____

____

Exercise 3.3 Paragraph Criteria

1. Look in one of your textbooks, a journal, or a novel for a paragraph that is eight to ten sentences in length.

2. Examine the paragraph to see if it meets all the criteria listed in the summary for this chapter.

3. Write a critique of the paragraph, clearly stating whether it does or does not meet the criteria of a paragraph and explaining why.

Title of textbook, journal, or novel: ______________________________

Author of the paragraph: ______________________________

Page number: ____________

Your critique of the paragraph:

____

____

____

____

____

____

____

____

____

____

Summary

Check all your paragraphs to make sure that they meet the following criteria:

- The first sentence contains the topic.
- The first sentence has an attention-getter.
- The body sentences develop, discuss, and support the topic sentence.
- The transitions link the sentences and examples together in the body of the paragraph.
- The concluding sentence sums up the topic and brings it to a close.

Elements of the Essay

Learning Objectives

After students have learned the content of this chapter, they should be able to do the following:

- Define the words "essay" and "thesis statement."
- Write a thesis statement.
- Know all the parts that make up a five-paragraph essay.

Learning Benefits

Your teachers will often instruct you to write an essay based on a general topic or answer a test question in essay style. An employer may ask you to write a two- to three-page essay on why you want a particular job. A recruiter of a police force or law enforcement agency may ask you to write an essay as part of the application process. All of these situations, and many more, require that you write an essay. Knowing exactly what is meant by an "essay" will ensure that you write a piece of work that uses a solid thesis statement as its main focus.

WHAT IS AN ESSAY?

An essay is a piece of writing that starts off with a specific point of view and then develops and supports that point of view. It typically consists of an introductory paragraph, followed by the body of the essay, which is usually at least three paragraphs long and provides the argument or "evidence" to support the point of view in the thesis statement. Finally, a conclusion is written to wrap up the essay's argument.

The point of view mentioned in the introduction is expressed in a thesis statement, which controls the content of the essay. It is important to note that it is the inclusion of a thesis statement in a piece of writing that makes the piece of writing an essay.

The Thesis Statement

A thesis statement is a sentence that contains the following:

- the topic of the essay;
- the author's opinion; and
- three points, or reasons, to back up this opinion.

Examples:

a) *My favourite TV show is Law & Order because I like the realistic characters, situations, and outcomes.*

b) *In order to succeed, students need to attend their classes, do their homework, and study for tests.*

c) *Using the drug ecstasy can cause serious physical, mental, and emotional changes that could result in sudden death.*

Exercise 4.1 Thesis Statements

Let's examine the above examples. Complete the following chart for thesis statements (b) and (c).

Example	Topic	Opinion	Three reasons/points
a)	Law & Order TV show	It's my favourite program.	• characters • situations • outcomes
b)			
c)			

How do you write a thesis statement?

Step 1: Write out your topic.
Step 2: Freewrite. (That is, write every idea you can think of that fits your topic.)
Step 3: Examine the list of ideas for ones about which you feel you can write the most.
Step 4: Narrow the ideas down to three points/reasons.
Step 5: Decide which order to use to list your points (usually from weakest to strongest).
Step 6: Write the thesis statement, including the topic, the opinion, and the three points/reasons.

Here's an example of the process used for writing a thesis statement:

Step 1: Topic

Characteristics Needed to Be a Leader in Law Enforcement

Step 2: Freewriting

assertive	*responsible*
confident	*educated*
energetic	*passionate*
thorough	*focused*
willing to serve	*caring*
self-controlled	*competent*
self-disciplined	*knowledgeable*
committed	*self-starter*

Step 3: Examine list for ideas about which I feel I can write the most interesting (or persuasive) essay.

assertive, thorough, self-controlled, responsible, educated, competent, knowledgeable

Step 4: Narrow the ideas down to three points/reasons.

thorough, self-controlled, competent

Step 5: Decide on an order: from weakest to strongest.

thorough, competent, self-controlled

Step 6: Write the thesis statement.

In order to be considered a leader in law enforcement, an officer must display thoroughness, competence, and self-control.

Things to note about this thesis statement:

- It is one sentence.
- The sentence contains the following:
    - The topic: *In order to be considered a leader in law enforcement*
    - An opinion: *must show*
    - The three reasons:
        1. *thoroughness*
        2. *competence*
        3. *self-control*

Parallelism in the thesis statement

Note that the three reasons are written in parallel structure. This means that the number and type of words in each point in the series is balanced. The number of words in each point between the commas in the list of reasons is the same and each point has the same grammatical construction.

In the example above, each one of the characteristics is one word and these words are nouns:

- *thoroughness* = one word, noun
- *competence* = one word, noun
- *self-control* = one word (although hyphenated), noun

The following sentence is **not parallel** because the number of words in each point in the series is not balanced, and the grammatical construction is not the same. Note that there are four words in the first and second points, and two words in the third point, and that the first two points contain a verb and a noun phrase while the third contains a verb and an adjective.

Incorrect: *In order to be considered a leader in law enforcement an officer must display a positive **attitude**, have a good **education**, and be **assertive**.*

The **bolded words** are the three points that will be discussed in the essay, and they, like any words in a series, need to be parallel. This sentence would not be a grammatically correct thesis statement because of its lack of parallelism.

Other examples of parallel structure in thesis statements

a) *My favourite TV show is Law & Order because I like the realistic **characters**, **situations**, and **outcomes**.*

Explanation: "Characters," "situations," and "outcomes" are the three points being introduced here. Each has one word in it, and each word is a noun.

b) *In order to succeed, students need to **attend** their classes, **do** their homework, and **study** for tests.*

Explanation: Each of the three points contains a verb to start the point and a linking word to join the verb to the noun that follows it; each point also consists of three words.

attend	*their*	*classes*	= 3 words
^	^	^	
verb	linking word (adjective)	noun	
do	*their*	*homework*	= 3 words
^	^	^	
verb	linking word (adjective)	noun	
study	*for*	*tests*	= 3 words
^	^	^	
verb	linking word (preposition)	noun	

c) *Using the drug ecstasy can cause serious **physical**, **mental**, and **emotional** changes that could result in sudden death.*

The three points are that the changes are "physical," "mental," and "emotional." Each one of those words is an adjective modifying the noun "changes," and each example is one word.

For more examples, and for practice writing parallel sentences, see Chapter 1 ("Spelling, Grammar, and Punctuation").

Things to avoid in your thesis statement

Your thesis statement **should not** do the following:

1. It should not just **restate your topic**.

   e.g., *This essay is about the characteristics of a leader in law enforcement.*

2. It should not simply state a fact.

   e.g., *Citizens look for leadership qualities in law enforcement officers.*

3. It should not lack the three points/reasons.

   e.g., *In order to be considered a leader, a law enforcement officer must have certain characteristics.*

4. It should not just **state your opinion** about the topic.

   e.g., *Law enforcement officers need leadership qualities.*

The Importance of the Thesis Statement

The thesis statement is the statement that says to the reader, "This is an essay. This is not a story, a description, a list, a letter, a memo, or a report."

Your thesis statement must contain the three components described above (the topic, the opinion, and the three points/reasons) in order to be considered a thesis statement. If the sentence does not meet these criteria, it fails as a thesis statement. Furthermore, according to Thom Sunega, author of Know More Writing from Paragraphs to Essays, "If the thesis statement fails, the essay will fail" (305).

So, what does this mean to you? It should mean a lot to you as a student, because if you are asked to write an essay and the piece of writing does not contain a thesis statement, then the piece of writing is not an essay. This means that you have not met the criteria of the assignment and that the work you have handed in cannot be marked because it does not meet the required criteria.

It should also mean a lot to you if you are an individual who has been asked to write an essay as part of the application process for a job in law enforcement. The recruiters will be looking for the thesis statement in the first paragraph. Without the thesis statement, there is no essay. You will have ruined your chances of getting that job.

The same thing can be said for officers seeking promotion. Often, officers are asked to write an essay as part of the promotion process. The superiors will be looking for the thesis statement as the controlling part of the essay.

In plain words, if you are asked to write an essay—any kind of essay—and the work that you submit does not contain a proper thesis statement, then your writing may not be marked or you may end up with a very low grade.

No thesis statement

=

No essay

=

No marks

Therefore, work hard to make sure that all your essays contain thesis statements. Doing so will ensure that your essays will be marked by the teachers or seriously considered during the application or promotion process. Give your readers or employers what they want: an essay with a thesis statement that controls the content.

Exercise 4.2 Proper Thesis Statements

1. Put a check mark (√) on the line to indicate if each group of words is an acceptable thesis statement that meets all the criteria discussed in this chapter.
2. At the end of each entry that is not a thesis statement, explain briefly why it is not acceptable.

(The first one has been done for you.)

______ 1. Officers need to write notebook entries, supplemental reports, and statements. {**The third point is not parallel to the other two.**}

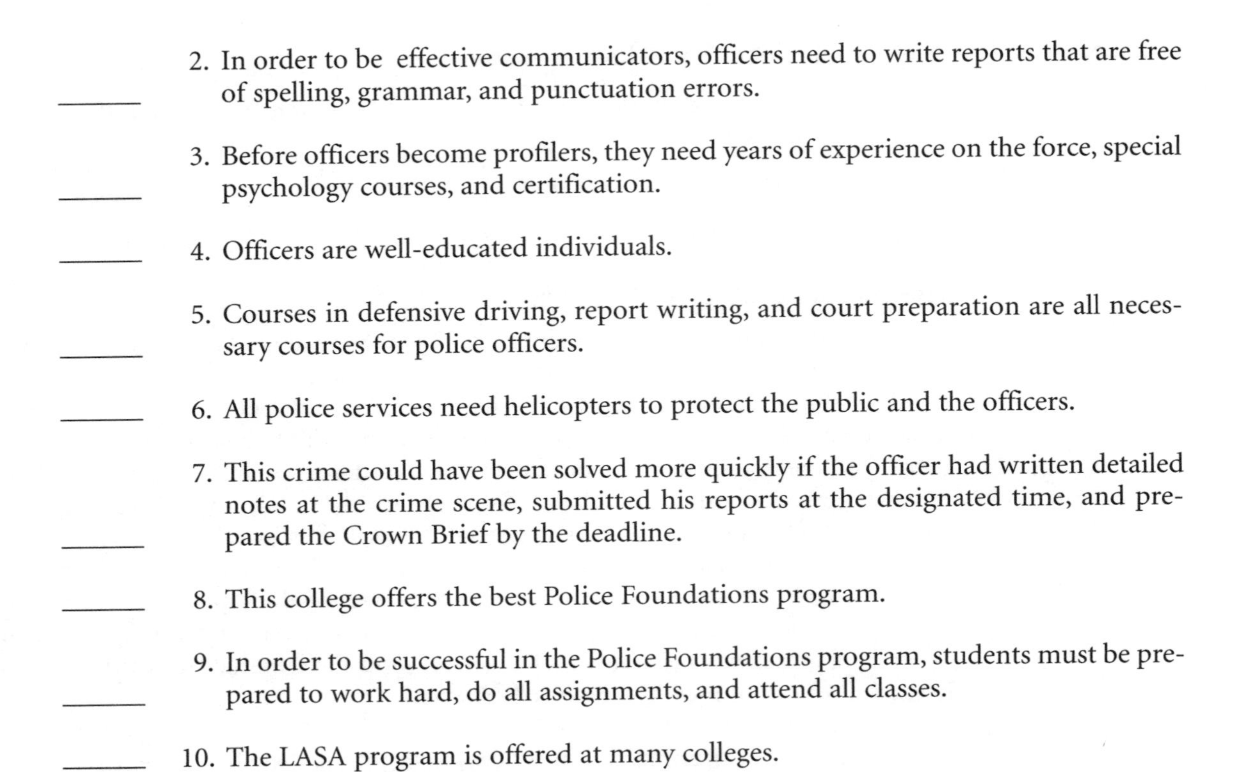

______ 2. In order to be effective communicators, officers need to write reports that are free of spelling, grammar, and punctuation errors.

______ 3. Before officers become profilers, they need years of experience on the force, special psychology courses, and certification.

______ 4. Officers are well-educated individuals.

______ 5. Courses in defensive driving, report writing, and court preparation are all necessary courses for police officers.

______ 6. All police services need helicopters to protect the public and the officers.

______ 7. This crime could have been solved more quickly if the officer had written detailed notes at the crime scene, submitted his reports at the designated time, and prepared the Crown Brief by the deadline.

______ 8. This college offers the best Police Foundations program.

______ 9. In order to be successful in the Police Foundations program, students must be prepared to work hard, do all assignments, and attend all classes.

______ 10. The LASA program is offered at many colleges.

Exercise 4.3 Writing Exercise: Group Work

In groups of three, choose one of the topics below and develop a thesis statement according to the steps outlined in this chapter. (The steps have been repeated below for your convenience.) The first topic has been done for you.

Once your group has completed the exercise, write your group's thesis statement on the board.

Once all the thesis statements on the board have been discussed and corrected, write them in this book under the corresponding topics. At the end, your class will likely have produced at least six good examples of thesis statements. (The instructor may assign the topics to the groups so that all of the topics are covered at least once).

Review: How to Write a Thesis Statement

1. Choose a topic or look at the one that the teacher has assigned to your group.
2. Freewrite. Write every idea your group members can think of that fits that topic.
3. Examine the list of ideas for ones about which your group members feel they can write the most.
4. Narrow the ideas down to three points/reasons.
5. Decide which order to use to list the points: usually weakest to strongest. Number the points.
6. Write the points in parallel form.

7. Write the thesis statement, including the topic, the opinion, and the three points/reasons in parallel form.

Topics

Topic 1: Reasons I Like Spring

Freewrite:

I don't have to wear all those heavy clothes.
Winter is over.
We have more sunshine.
The days are longer.
No more slush, freezing rain, and icy roads
School is out for the year.
Everything is in bloom.
There's new grass.
I enjoy celebrating the Easter holiday.

Three reasons (and their order) =

Winter is over. 1
School is out for the year. 3
Everything is in bloom. 2

New order and parallel form. (Note the similar grammatical construction of each item on the list):

Winter is over.
Everything's in bloom.
School is finished.

Thesis statement:

I prefer spring to any other season because winter is over; everything's in bloom; and school is finished.

Topic 2: Why I Chose This College

____

____

____

____

____

____

____

____

____

____

Topic 3: Why I Enrolled in the Law and Security/Police Foundations Program

Topic 4: How To Be A Good Police Officer

Topic 5: Why Officers Should Maintain Their Physical Fitness Levels

Topic 6: Techniques to Relieve Stress on the Job

Other Parts of the Essay

An essay has other parts that also make it an essay, but as we've been discussing in this chapter, no part of the essay is more important than the thesis statement.

The essay has the following parts:

1. introduction
2. body
3. conclusion

1. What goes into the introduction of an essay?

The introduction is the first paragraph of the essay, and contains the following elements:

- an "attention-getter"

and

- a transition that links the attention-getter to the thesis statement.

2. What goes into the body of an essay?

- In a short, five-paragraph essay, the body consists of three paragraphs that develop the three points of the thesis statement.
- These paragraphs are linked together with transitions that appear in the first sentence of each new paragraph.
- There is usually one paragraph per point.
- The points are discussed in the same order as they are stated in the thesis statement.
- Therefore, there are usually three paragraphs in the body of a five-paragraph essay: one for each point.

3. What is the conclusion of an essay?

The conclusion is the last paragraph of the essay, and it typically does the following:

- starts with a transition;
- revisits the thesis statement;
- concludes the essay; and
- links the conclusion back to the introduction.

When you put this all together, you have what is called the **five-paragraph essay model**, which will be discussed in greater detail in Chapter 5.

Summary

The essay is a piece of writing that contains the following:

- An introductory paragraph that gets the reader's attention and contains the thesis statement.
- A body of at least three paragraphs: one to support each point in the thesis statement.
- A conclusion, which wraps up the essay, revisits the thesis statement, and links the topic back to the introduction.

Remember: the thesis statement is the main focus of the essay. Without a thesis statement, the piece of writing is not an essay.

The Five-Paragraph Essay Model

Learning Objectives

After students have learned the content of this chapter, they should be able to do the following:

- Define the term "five-paragraph essay."
- Explain the analogy of bricks and mortar in relation to the body of the five-paragraph essay.
- Write an outline for this type of essay.
- Choose an appropriate tone for the audience of an essay.
- Write a five-paragraph essay.

Learning Benefits

Learning about the format of the five-paragraph essay is important, as this format will serve as your basis for all essays. Using this format correctly will enable you to write logical, coherent essays.

With the help of the analogy developed in this chapter—that of stacked bricks for the body of the essay—you should have no trouble applying the content of this chapter to every essay that you write. The sample outline and the sample essays can also be used as good examples for you to follow.

THE FIVE-PARAGRAPH ESSAY

The five-paragraph essay model consists of a piece of writing that contains five paragraphs. The thesis statement found in the introductory (first) paragraph is supported and developed in the second, third, and fourth paragraphs. The fifth paragraph contains a conclusion and a revisit of the thesis statement. The thesis statement is the controlling statement of the five paragraphs (as discussed in Chapter 4). Table 5.1 shows this structure.

Table 5.1: The Five-Paragraph Essay Model

Paragraph 1	Introduction: contains the thesis statement
Paragraph 2	First of three body paragraphs
Paragraph 3	Second of three body paragraphs
Paragraph 4	Third of three body paragraphs
Paragraph 5	Conclusion: revisits the thesis statement

Length of Paragraphs

You should note and remember the following characteristics of this type of essay:

1. There are five parts to the essay.
2. All the parts are **not** the same length. Paragraph 1 (the introduction) and paragraph 5 (the conclusion) are about the same length and are definitely shorter than paragraphs 2, 3, and 4 (the body), which are all about the same length. (The introduction and conclusion are generally about half the length of the body paragraphs.) For example, if you are asked to write a short five-paragraph essay, your first and fifth paragraphs would be about 2–3 sentences long with each body paragraph about 5–7 sentences long each.

Table 5.2 gives some approximations for lengths of the paragraphs in three essays of various sizes. All of this depends, of course, upon how long the essay is expected to be when it is finished. The length of the first paragraph tends to determine the length of the body paragraphs.

Table 5.2: Length of Paragraphs in a Five-Paragraph Essay

Paragraph #	Essay Example 1	Essay Example 2	Essay Example 3
	# of sentences	# of sentences	# of sentences
1	2-3	3-5	4-6
2	5-7	6-9	9-12
3	5-7	6-9	9-12
4	5-7	6-9	9-12
5	2-3	3-5	4-6

You don't want to end up with an off-balanced essay with, for example, ten sentences in the first paragraph, four in the second paragraph, six in the third, eight in the fourth, and one in the last. Balance the length of the first paragraph with the fifth one, and make the three body paragraphs the same length.

Now that we've had a look at the overall structure of the essay, and the relative size of each part of the essay, let's examine each paragraph in detail.

PARAGRAPH 1: THE INTRODUCTION

What to Include

What has to be in the first paragraph?

You need to include the following:

- an attention-getter in your first sentence;
- a link or transition from the attention-getter to the thesis statement; and
- the thesis statement, which states the three points that will be discussed in the body paragraphs (paragraphs 2, 3, and 4).

What should I use as an attention-getter to get the reader's attention?

Use one or more of the following attention-getters.

- a story (anecdote)
- a definition
- an example
- a description
- a controversial statement
- a relevant quotation
- interesting statistics about the topic
- a question
- a headline

Example of a good first paragraph:

Do you want to be considered a leader in law enforcement? If this is your desire, then you need to be a motivator, a participant, and an initiator.

What should I not use as an attention-getter?

Avoid statements like these:

- This essay will explain . . .
- I am going to tell you about . . .
- I am going to explain . . .
- The topic I have chosen to write about is . . .
- This essay is about [topic stated]. I am going to tell you three things about it. They are . . .

These statements should be avoided because they contain redundancies. For example, the reader should know that the writing is an essay as soon as he or she reads the thesis statement; therefore, you don't have to say that it is an essay, or that it is going to explain something.

Exercise 5.1 Attention-Getters

Answer these questions about the above example of a good first paragraph.

1. What technique was used to get the reader's attention?

   ____

2. What two words would capture an officer's attention?

   ____

3. What is the thesis statement?

   ____

4. What words link the thesis statement to the attention-getter?

   ____

Where should the thesis statement be located?

It should be located in the first paragraph, and it is usually the last sentence of that paragraph.

Why should it be in that location?

- The reader expects to find out from the beginning what the body of the essay is going to discuss.
- Clarity is established immediately.
- The reader knows the three points at the beginning. In other words, if you do this, your reader will not need to say, "Get to the point!" You will be telling the reader up front what you are going to talk about.

PARAGRAPHS 2, 3, AND 4: THE BODY

The Parts of the Body

In the body of the essay, all three points of the thesis statement are introduced, discussed, developed, concluded, and linked back to the thesis statement.

Each point receives one paragraph in which to do all this. Each paragraph starts off with a topic sentence that includes the following:

- a transition

  and

- the topic of the point for that paragraph.

The points are discussed in the same order as they are stated in the thesis statement.

It helps to think of the body of the essay as resembling three bricks stacked vertically, connected with mortar. Consider them to be the middle three of the five "building blocks" in your five-paragraph essay, and the "mortar" that joins them represents the transitional words or phrases (see Figure 5.1).

Figure 5.1 The Body of the Essay

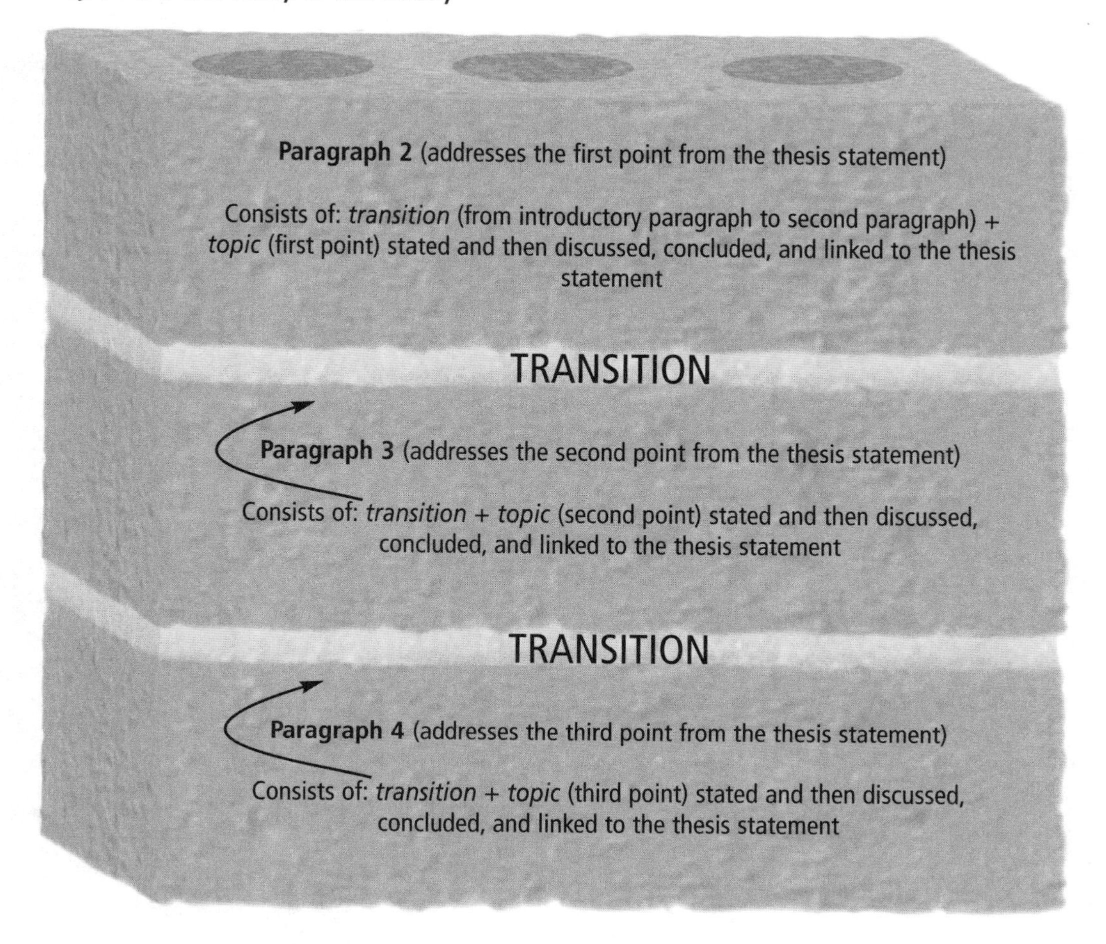

You may wonder how you can link the topic of each paragraph back to the thesis statement. In the last sentence or two of the paragraph, include the following:

- a summary statement of the point;
- a transition;
- the topic; and
- the order of that point in the thesis statement.

Example:

His encouragement helped me a great deal. Because of my friend's supportive words in many situations, encouragement is just one aspect I look for in a friend.

In the example above, the summary statement of the point is "His encouragement helped me a great deal."

The transition is "Because of my friend's supportive words in many situations."

The topic, "encouragement," is repeated twice.

The order of the points is referred to by the use of "one" in "one aspect."

See the essays near the end of this chapter (pages 71–76) for more examples of how to link the topic back to the thesis statement. This is usually done in the last one and/or two sentences.

Figure 5.2 on the following page provides an example, based on "Leadership in Policing" (see page 75), showing all five "bricks" in the essay.

Figure 5.2 Example of the Essay

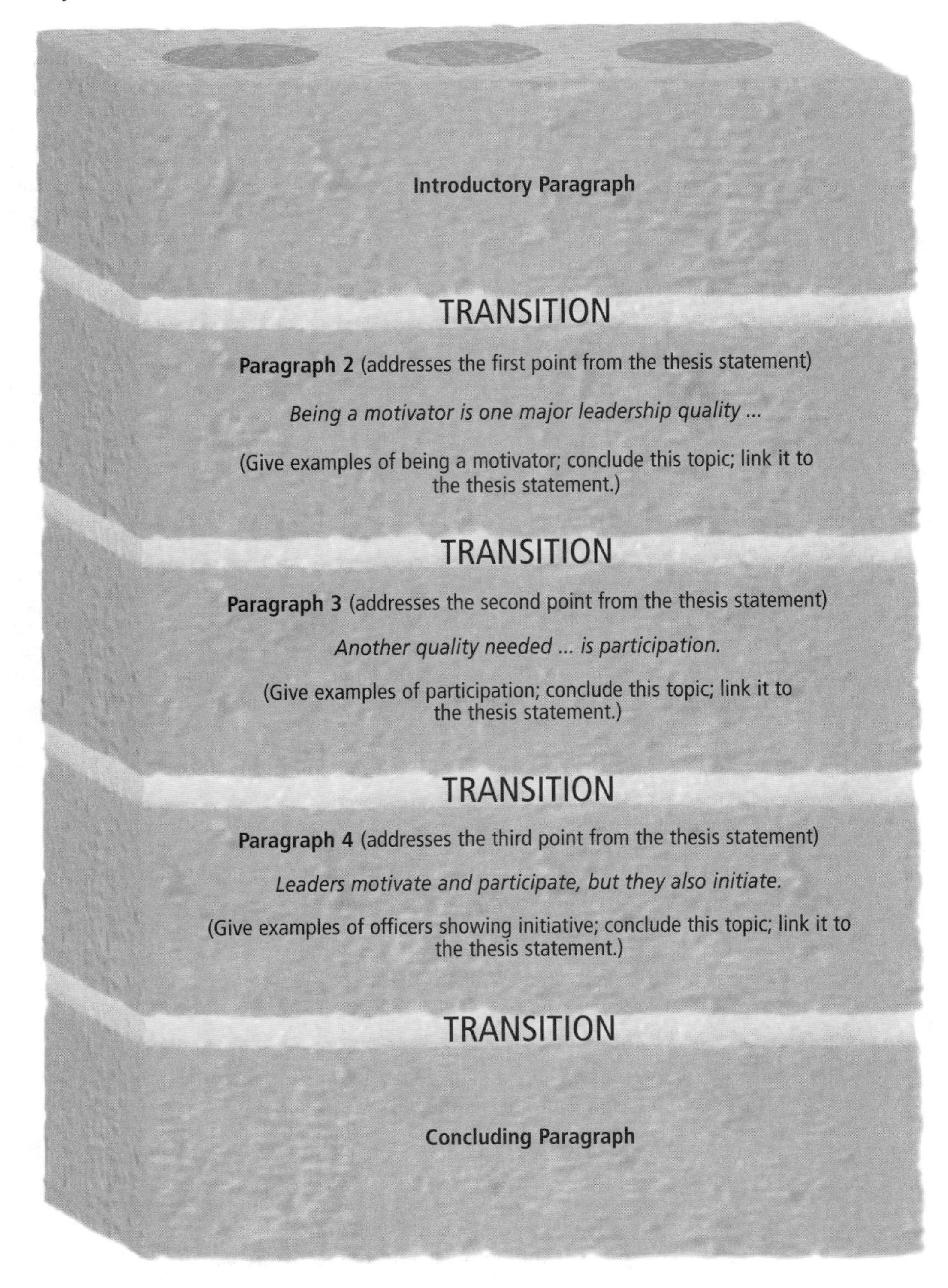

PARAGRAPH 5: THE CONCLUSION

The conclusion must include the following four elements: a transition, a thesis restatement, a link back to the introduction, and a definite conclusion.

Transitions

Transitions are needed to start the last paragraph and to link all the ideas in this paragraph together.

To start the final paragraph, you might use these transitions:

Finally, to sum up, in conclusion, therefore, etc.

To link the ideas together, you might use any number of transitional words to make the ideas flow.

Example:

For an essay about the TV show Friends, you might write something like this for the final paragraph:

Now, if anyone asks me to name my favourite TV show, I would have to say that it is Friends because I like the hilarious situations, the comedic characters, and the relevant plotlines. For these reasons, Friends is a show that I wouldn't miss for anything, even for getting my research paper done on time!

Note: The underlined words in the example above are the transitions. They are the words that link the ideas together so the writing flows logically and coherently. Also note that Friends appears underlined because it is the title of a television show (see the guide to MLA documentation style in Appendix B).

Thesis Restatement

The conclusion must also include a **restatement of the thesis** in new words. For example, here is a thesis statement from the introductory (first) paragraph from an essay entitled, "Why Friends Is My Favourite TV Show."

Friends is my favourite TV show because I like the humour, the characters, and the plots.

In the concluding (fifth) paragraph, you would restate the thesis statement in new words.

The hilarious situations, the comedic actors, and the relevant plotlines make watching Friends the highlight of my week.

Notice that the three points in the original thesis statement consist of two words in each reason; however, in the restated thesis, the three points are stated in **three new words** that mean the same things. Also note that in both versions, the listing of the points is parallel, and is therefore grammatically correct.

Link Back to the Introduction

To bring a final conclusion to the essay, link the conclusion to the introduction by mentioning the attention-getter again. For example, let's say that in your essay entitled "What Makes a Good Friend," you write the following as your attention-getter in the first paragraph:

What types of characteristics does someone need to be a good friend?

A question is a good way to get anyone's attention, even in an essay. Now, in the conclusion, you need to return to the question. You might do this by saying the following in the conclusion:

Now when someone asks you about the character traits that someone needs to be a good friend, you can tell them ...

Notice that the words in this sentence are not exactly the same as the words in the introductory sentence. You should not repeat the same words; use new words.

(Note that the three dots (. . .), called an "ellipsis," at the end of the example sentence above mean that more would be added to the statement.)

Thus, the term "characteristics" in the question in the introductory (first) paragraph and the words "character traits" in the conclusion (fifth paragraph) serve as the links between these two paragraphs.

A Definite Conclusion

Your essay's last paragraph should conclude the topic definitively. Sometimes this is done in the revisited thesis statement. When your reader comes to the last line of your essay, he or she should **not** want to turn the page to see what comes next or wonder what's missing.

What should not be in the conclusion?

Do not end your essay with a question because you should have brought your opinion, your topic, and your three points to a close by this point.

Incorrect: *Now that you know what my favourite show is, what is yours?*

Also, do not introduce a new topic into your conclusion. Your essay is finished, and it should have delivered everything that it promised from the start. So, for instance, you would not want to end an essay on Friends like this:

Incorrect: *Not only is Friends my favourite TV show, but West Wing is a close second favourite.*

Example of a good conclusion:

To sum up my thoughts on the characteristics of a friend, I would say that my definition of a friend is a person who encourages others, thinks of others, and tells the truth. I am very glad that I have one person in my life who has these characteristics.

OUTLINE FOR A FIVE-PARAGRAPH ESSAY

Before writing anything, you need to be prepared; this is similar to getting all your tools and materials ready to make a retaining wall before you actually start making it.

Before you write an essay, you would be well advised to develop an **outline**. Form 5.1 shows what an outline looks like.

Form 5.1 Outline for a Five-Paragraph Essay

Topic: ____________________

PARAGRAPH #	CONTENT
1	attention-getter: ____________________
	transition: ____________________
	thesis statement:
	topic: ____________________
	opinion: ____________________
	three points:
	1. ____________________
	2. ____________________
	3. ____________________
2	transition: ____________________
	first point: ____________________
	supporting details:
	____________________
	____________________
	____________________
	____________________
	link to thesis statement: ____________________
	conclude first point: ____________________
3	transition: ____________________
	second point: ____________________
	supporting details:
	____________________
	____________________
	____________________

____

link to thesis statement: _______________

conclude second point: _______________

4 transition: _______________

third point: _______________

supporting details:

____

____

____

____

link to thesis statement: _______________

conclude third point: _______________

5 transition: _______________

revisit thesis statement: _______________

conclude: _______________

link to introduction: _______________

Example of a Completed Outline

Topic: How to Be a Friend

PARAGRAPH CONTENT

1 attention-getter: ***What is the definition of a "friend"?***
transition: ***I am fortunate enough to have a special person in my life …***
thesis statement
topic: ***A friend,***
opinion: ***to me, is someone who is***
three points: ***encouraging, selfless, and honest.***

2 transition: ***To begin with,***
first point: ***a friend is encouraging.***
supporting details:
• encourages me when I do well
example: when I got that 68 on the psych test
• encourages me when I am trying to do something that is hard for me
example: when I couldn't do the P.R.E.P. Test in the required time

• ***encourages me when I am sad***
example: when my dog died
link to thesis statement and conclude first point: ***This is just one aspect of what I look for in a friend.***

3 transition: ***Second,***
second point: ***selfless***
supporting details:
• ***doesn't always want his own way***
example: choosing which movie to watch—action movie vs. "chick flick"
• ***lets others have things that he wants***
example: one piece of his favourite cake left, younger brother wanted it, let him have it
• ***gives up his spare time for others***
example: volunteers at nursing home where his grandmother lives
link to thesis statement and conclude second point: ***Therefore, not always thinking about him- or herself is another trait I look for in a friend.***

4 transition: ***The most important trait***
third point: ***honesty***
supporting details:
• ***never lies***
example: stayed out all night, mother asked him what time he got in, told her the exact time, 6:30 a.m., even though he knew that he would lose car privileges
• ***always keeps his word***
example: said that he'd take his little brother to the movies, and did take him even though his friends asked him to go to their cottage for the day
• ***never cheats anyone***
example: clerk at a convenience store gave him too much change and he gave back the extra amount
link to thesis statement and conclude third point: ***This is the most important characteristic someone must have to be my friend.***

5 transition: ***To sum up,***
restate thesis statement: ***a person who encourages me, thinks of others, and tells the truth***
link to introduction: ***is my definition of a friend***
conclude: ***I'm glad I have such a person in my life.***

Exercise 5.2 The Outline

After reading the above outline, answer the following questions by circling the correct answer or filling in the blanks.

1. Why was the point about a friend being encouraging (the first point) discussed in the second paragraph?

   It was the (third point / first point / second point) in the thesis statement. Therefore, it goes in the first paragraph of the body. The body starts in the (second / third / first) paragraph.

2. Why was honesty (the third point) discussed in the fourth paragraph and not the third?

   The (first / second / third) point of the thesis statement goes in the (second / third / fourth / fifth) paragraph of the essay, which is the third paragraph of the body.

3. Does the transition that starts a new point go at the end of the previous paragraph or at the start of the new paragraph that discusses the point?

   The transition goes at the (end / start) of the (previous / new) paragraph.

4. Is the thesis statement restated word-for-word in the last paragraph?

   (yes / no)

5. What is done with the original words of the thesis statement in the conclusion?

   They are replaced with (different / the same) words.

6. What words link the attention-getter in the first paragraph with the final paragraph?

   "__________" and "___________"

7. How many supporting details are there for each body paragraph?

   (three / one / two) for each detail

8. How many examples are there in each body paragraph?

   (three / one / two) for each detail

9. Why does this outline have so many details?

   a) to make it easier to __________ the essay

   b) to help the writer get __________

   c) to help the writer meet the ___________ of a developed essay

   d) to keep the_______ _______________ up front

   e) to make sure the paper is an essay

   f) to make sure all _____ points are discussed in a _______ order and equally

AUDIENCE AND TONE

You are now ready to move on to the next step, but before beginning the actual writing of the essay, as a writer, you must take into consideration two issues:

- the audience;
  and
- the tone.

Identifying Your Audience

"Audience" refers to the people who are going to read the essay. Generally speaking, you, the writer, decide which group of people you want to read your essay. This is your **target group**.

Your essay is supposed to make a point and have an opinion, so you aim its contents at a particular group of people.

Here are some audience characteristics you should consider when you are making up the profile of your target group:

age
gender
background:
- cultural/linguistic
- religious
- educational
- knowledge of the topic

their wants and goals
their attitudes
their expectations

What Is "Tone"?

"Tone" refers to the level of formality of the writing. After defining your audience or target group, you decide which of the following three tones would best suit that audience for the specific topic of the essay.

Casual tone

- uses the pronouns "*I*," "*my*," and "*you*"
- uses contractions: e.g., "*isn't*"
- uses slang or "in" words
- does not use swear words unless they are used in a dialogue and serve a point
- uses mainly simple, assertive, natural order sentences
- uses the occasional compound sentence

Informal tone

- uses the pronouns "*I*," "*my*," and "*you*"
- uses contractions: e.g., "*isn't*"
- does not use slang
- uses common everyday language
- does not use swear words
- uses some sentence variety; has more compound sentences than the casual tone and a few complex sentences

Formal tone

- does not use "*I*," "*my*," and "*you*"
- refers to people generally
- uses "longer" words with more than one syllable. e.g., "*particular*" instead of "*one main*"
- does not use slang
- does not use contractions
- does not use swear words
- uses a variety of sentences; e.g., compound and complex sentences appear frequently throughout the essay

Below are some examples of introductions and thesis statements, all written for the same topic, but using different tones:

My Favourite Season: Winter

Casual Tone

You know what guys? I really get into the winter scene thing. The snow covers the ground and looks like vanilla ice cream. The thermometer drops into that frigid zone, and that winter sun is just a-blazing for all it's worth. This has got to be the best time of year! Do you know why? The answer is simple. During this awesome season, I get to do cool things like go snowboarding, downhill skiing, and skidooing.

Informal Tone

What season is my favourite of them all? Winter is the one I like the best. The snow-covered land, the cold temperatures, and the winter sun make my life enjoyable because I love to snowboard, downhill ski, and skidoo.

Formal Tone

Most people prefer one particular season for a variety of reasons. Why one season is preferable over another depends upon personal likes and dislikes. Many people, when asked which is their favourite season, would respond that winter with its snow-covered landscapes, freezing temperatures, and clear days is their favourite because it affords them the opportunity to participate in active outdoor sports, such as snowboarding, downhill skiing, and skidooing. These sports fill their long winter months.

Exercise 5.3 Writing Exercise (To be completed in groups or individually.)

Choose one of the topics listed below or a topic assigned by your teacher.

1. On the lines below, write out three reasons to support your opinion and number them in the order in which you are going to discuss them.
2. Write out a three-point thesis statement for this topic.
3. Now write an introductory paragraph for this topic for a five-paragraph essay, using a casual tone.
4. Repeat steps 2 and 3, above, and use the informal tone for the same topic.
5. Repeat steps 2 and 3, above, and use the formal tone for the same topic.
6. Read your work to the class.

Topics:
My Favourite TV Show/Song
Why People Steal
Who Will Win the Grey Cup/Stanley Cup/Super Bowl?
Why ________ Should Be Inducted into the Hockey/Baseball/Basketball Hall of Fame
Star Wars vs. Star Trek: Which Will Be Popular the Longest?
University Isn't for Everyone
Another topic approved by your teacher

Topic: ______________________________

Three points:

1. ______________________________

2. ______________________________

3. ______________________________

Three-point thesis statement (remember to make your three points parallel):

____

____

____

____

Introductory paragraph using the **casual** tone:

____

____

____

____

____

____

____

____

Introductory paragraph using the **informal** tone:

____

____

____

____

____

____

____

____

Introductory paragraph using the **formal** tone:

____

____

____

____

____

____

____

____

STARTING TO WRITE

You're now ready for the next step. After writing the thesis statement, the outline, profiling your audience, and deciding on the appropriate tone, you can begin to write your essay.

Samples of Five-Paragraph Essays

To help you get started, some sample five-paragraph essays follow, written from the previously presented outlines.

A Friend
by
Katrina Donaldson

Katrina Donaldson Donaldson 1

Professor Doughty

Comunications 1

30 September 2004

A Friend

What is the definition of a friend? I am fortunate to say that I have a special friend in my life who reveals everything that my definition says. A friend, to me, is someone who is encouraging, selfless, and honest.

To begin with, my friend, John, is one of the most encouraging people I know. He doesn't hesitate to encourage me when I have done something well. Let's look at the time when we got back our second psychology test. This was a very hard test because it was based on six chapters, and the questions were all multiple choice. John knew that I often did not do well on multiple choice tests and didn't like them, so when I got back my mark, and it was a 68, he told me that I had done well because I had improved my percentage on multiple choice questions. This made me feel good! Another time, John kept coaching me when we were preparing for the P.R.E.P. Test. I had practised that test five times, and I just couldn't consistently do it in the required time. With his coaching, I was finally able to do it in the right amount of time every time we practised and on the final test. Besides encouraging me during actual tests at school, John cheered me up when my dog died. My dog, Boots, was my companion for ten years. When he died, it was like losing a family member. John sympathized with me and encouraged me during my grieving time by listening to me reminisce about Boots. His encouragement helped me a great deal. Because of John's supportive words in many situations, I value him as my friend.

Second, selflessness is a characteristic I look for in a friend. My friend, John, doesn't always want his own way. If we are trying to decide which movie to rent, we alternate between my choice and his choice. That means that we watch either what he

Donaldson 2

calls a “chick flick” or an action movie. He is the one who came up with this plan. This selfless attitude impresses me. Also, I have witnessed him letting others have things that he wants. One time when I was at his house, there was one piece of lemon cake left from dinner. John just loves lemon-flavoured sweets! He was just about to help himself to it, after he had offered it to me and I had refused it, when his eight-year-old brother came in from hockey practice. His brother asked if he could have the cake, and my friend let his brother have it. This also showed me how selfless John is. Furthermore, he shows this wonderful side to his nature by volunteering at the nursing home where his grandmother lives. Every Sunday, John rents one of those old Bing Crosby/Fred Astaire movies, goes to the nursing home, sets up the video, goes around to all the rooms to invite the residents to the movie, helps get them all settled in the lounge, and supervises the residents while they watch, enjoy, and sing along. The residents seem to wait all week for John to show up. They seem to be having such a wonderful time because of his selflessness. Therefore, not thinking always about oneself is another trait that I look for in a friend because of John’s example.

The most important trait that I look for in a friend is honesty. John has proven his honesty by never lying, always keeping his word, and never cheating anyone. Here are some examples. Once he stayed out all night and got home at 6:30 in the morning. When his Mom asked him in the morning what time he got home, he told her the exact time even though he knew that he would lose car privileges for not being home by 3:00 a.m., the time he and his Mom had agreed would be reasonable if he was using her car. There was also an incident that happened last summer. John kept his promise to take his little brother to the movies one Saturday afternoon. On the agreed-upon day to go to the movies, John received an invitation to go to someone's cottage for the day to do some wakeboarding. Although it was hard for John to turn down the day of wakeboarding, he did and spent that afternoon in a theatre filled with eight-year-olds watching the latest Walt Disney movie! Finally, John's honesty has shown up at the cash registers as well. He always counts his change after a purchase. I have seen him let the cashier know that too much money has been given to him. He always gives the money back if he has been given too much change. This sense of honesty is the most important characteristic someone must have to be my friend. I admire this the most.

To sum up my thoughts on the characteristics of a friend, I would say that my definition of a friend is a person who encourages others, thinks of others, and tells the truth. I am very glad that I have one person in my life who has these characteristics.

Leadership in Policing
by
David McNeil

David McNeil McNeil 1

Professor Doughty

Communications 1

30 September 2004

Leadership in Policing

What does it take to be considered a leader in policing? If it is your desire to be viewed as a leader, then you must be a motivator, a participant, and an initiator.

Being a motivator is one major leadership quality that you must have for others to consider you a leader. Being a motivator includes showing concern and care for fellow officers by encouraging them from time to time. Saying something like, "I know that you'll do a good job of it," acts as a motivating statement to a fellow officer. Also, taking the time to recognize what others have done is another example of being a motivator. For instance, if an officer's notebook entries were very detailed, you might compliment that officer by saying, "The details in your notebook entries will help you when the case comes to court." By saying things like this to others, you will be considered a motivator and a leader.

Another quality needed in leadership is participation. Others must see you as someone who joins in the activities and leads by example. If you are leading a physical fitness session, there is no better way to show your leadership attributes than to do all the exercises with the participants. Participating actively yourself is not the only way to show leadership. Taking extra courses through your local college or university shows that you are a participant in the journey of learning that never ends. Therefore, leading by example and participating in courses are two more ways to demonstrate to others that you are a leader.

Leaders motivate and participate, but they also initiate. So, you need to show that you can create new ideas to help your fellow officers or the public if you want people to see you as a leader. For example, if you have an idea about how to make something

McNeil 2

better, you would write a proposal and take it to your superior officer. The idea may be about anything that would make an officer's job easier, such as changing the black pens used by your service to another brand of black pen because these pens have waterproof ink and these newer pens work very well in the vertical position. Furthermore, you could develop a proposal with ideas of how to prevent so many accidents from occurring at a particular stretch of the road. Any ideas you present would show that you have initiative, which is a great quality for a leader.

In summary, do others see you as a leader? Ask yourself these questions: Am I a motivator? Do I participate? Do I take the initiative? If you answered "yes" to all of these questions, then people might just look to you as a leader. Congratulate yourself! You have reached your goal.

Exercise 5.4 Writing Exercise (To be completed in groups or individually.)

Go back to Exercise 5.3 on page 68.

1. Choose either your informal or formal introductory paragraph with its thesis statement.
2. Write an outline for the essay that this paragraph would begin on the page provided following these instructions (Form 5.2).
3. Write the essay on the pages provided (Form 5.3). This is Draft #1.
4. Have a classmate proofread Draft #1. Ask that person to sign his or her name on the line following the essay.
5. Correct the essay and write your final copy on the pages provided (Form 5.4).
6. Submit it to your teacher for marking.
7. Once you get the essay back, write all the spelling corrections in your personal spelling list (Appendix D).

Summary

Each of the five paragraphs in a five-paragraph essay has a specific purpose.

The first paragraph:

- introduces the topic
- gets the reader's attention
- states the thesis statement

The second, third, and fourth paragraphs:

- have transitions that introduce each point and link the ideas within the paragraphs to make them flow
- introduce points 1, 2, and 3 of the thesis statement in order
- develop, support, and discuss each point
- link each point back to the thesis statement
- conclude each point in its separate paragraph

The fifth paragraph:

- concludes the essay
- revisits the thesis statement
- links back to the introduction

Keep your audience in mind and write in a tone that they would enjoy and that is appropriate both for them and for your subject matter.

Form 5.2 The Outline for a Five-Paragraph Essay

Topic: ______________________________

PARAGRAPH # CONTENT

1 attention-getter: ______________________________

transition: ______________________________

thesis statement:

topic: ______________________________

opinion: ______________________________

three points:

1. ______________________________

2. ______________________________

3. ______________________________

2 transition: ______________________________

first point: ______________________________

supporting details:

____

____

____

____

link to thesis statement: ______________________________

conclude first point: ______________________________

3 transition: ______________________________

second point: ______________________________

supporting details:

____

____

____

____

link to thesis statement: ______________________________

conclude second point: ______________________________

4 transition: ______________________________

third point: ______________________________

supporting details:

____

____

____

____

link to thesis statement: ______________________________

conclude third point: ______________________________

5 transition: ______________________________

revisit thesis statement: ______________________________

conclude: ______________________________

link to introduction: ______________________________

Form 5.3 Draft #1

Proofreader's signature

Form 5.4 Final Copy

The Process Essay

Learning Objectives

After students have learned the content of this chapter, they should be able to do the following:

- Define the term "process essay."
- Break a series of tasks into three distinct stages/steps.
- Write a thesis statement for a process essay.
- Write a process essay based on the five-paragraph essay model.

Learning Benefits

During your regular day, there are many times when you have to explain to someone what to do or how to do something. When you are giving these instructions, you are actually explaining a process. In order for the person to follow your directions, you have to state the directions in a clear, concise, correct, and chronological way. This is exactly what you do in a process essay.

In this chapter, you will learn how to group these kinds of process directions into three steps or stages, write a thesis statement about the process, and then write about the process within the framework of the five-paragraph essay model.

Whether your goal is a career in policing, day care, computer programming, or business, knowing how to write a process essay will benefit you in many ways. In policing, in particular, the entire investigation of an incident is a process, and there are certain steps to follow throughout that process. Furthermore, knowing how to write something down in chronological order is essential in policing.

THE PROCESS ESSAY

A process essay is a five-paragraph essay that explains how to complete a task through a step-by-step, logical, chronological progression. Usually, each step builds on the previous one. You can't successfully start step two until step one is completed, and so on.

Being able to write a process essay is an important preparation step for students who desire to work in law enforcement. The process essay requires that the writer break down the steps into a beginning, a middle, and an end. This step is then followed by the writing of the information in a logical, coherent, and chronological order. As an officer, you will do the same thing when you write narrative reports describing incidents. In these reports, which are called "supplementary/narrative reports," officers tell the story of who did what, to whom, when it happened, and where it occurred. Therefore, learning how to write the process essay correctly will be a preparation for future writing in your career.

1. What does "chronological order" mean?

   "Chronological order" means that you write out the information in the ***time*** *order in which the details take/took place, from the beginning to the end.*

2. What are some examples of processes?
   a) a recipe
      e.g., how to cook spaghetti and meatballs
   b) a set of instructions
      e.g., the manual that comes with your DVD player and shows you how to set up the different functions
   c) a set of directions to a location
      e.g., directions to your school from your home or place of residence

3. What must the explanation of a process contain? It must contain the following:
   a) every single detail;
   b) chronological order—first step to last step; and
   c) transitional words that link the steps and create an order that is to be followed.

Exercise 6.1 Giving Directions

Be sure to read all instructions before attempting this exercise!

1. In groups of two, tell your partner how to get from the school to your house. Your partner will draw a map of what you tell him or her in the box below.
2. Your partner may not ask questions while you are giving the directions, and you may not look at your partner's response.
3. After you are finished, look at what your partner has drawn. Tell him or her any corrections that are necessary.

Switch roles so that both of you do this exercise.

List what you learned about giving directions:

____

____

____

____

____

4. Can you use recipes or directions to a location as the main topic of the process essay?

   No! These examples were used to introduce you to the definition of a process.

   Recipes and directions are very simple forms of writing, and are too short for the five-paragraph essay model. An essay has more depth to it than simple instructions or directions. Also, when you gave the directions, you most likely did not give a three-point thesis statement. This thesis statement is absolutely necessary for the process essay.

5. What is the purpose of the process essay?

   The purpose of the process essay is very simple: The author wants the reader to be able to perform this process correctly after reading the essay. The reader should be able to read the essay once and then do whatever process is described in it.

   The author is the expert. The author is passing knowledge to another person in the hope that this person will be able to follow the process described without any difficulty.

6. Do I still need to put a three-point thesis statement in this essay?

   Yes! It is an essay. A piece of writing without a thesis statement is not an essay.

Early Stages of Writing the Process Essay

7. What is the first step in writing a process essay?

   The first step is choosing your topic. This is the first step you take when you write any essay.

   To choose your topic:

   a) Brainstorm ideas on how to do something if you are not given a topic.
   b) Try to think of things that you do well. A good rule for writers to follow is to write from their own experiences. Chances are that you are an expert in at least one thing, if not more. Draw on your expertise now.

   ____

   ____

   ____

____

____

c) Narrow your ideas down to one topic.
d) Write your topic here: ________________________

8. I've got my topic now. What is the second step?
   a) The second step is to list the tasks involved in your chosen process. Make a list of every single task that you would need to do in order to perform this process. Start a new line for each new task.

____

____

____

____

____

____

____

____

____

____

   b) Go back and number the tasks in chronological order. Put in numbers 1, 2, 3, 4, etc. in the margin of your paper beside the tasks.
   If you realize that you have left some tasks out, then put them at the end of the list and number them like this:
   2a – if the task was to go between #2 and #3
   4a – if the task was to go between #4 and #5, etc.
   c) Rewrite the tasks in the correct order.

____

____

____

____

____

____

____

____

____

____

9. What is the third step?
   a) Examine the tasks in their chronological order and see how you can divide them into three steps/stages.
   b) Bracket [ ] all the tasks in 8c) above that would be included in step 1, step 2, and step 3.
      Step 1 = what you would do at the beginning
      Step 2 = what you would do in the middle
      Step 3 = what you would do at the end
      or
      Stage 1 = how to start
      Stage 2 = how to continue
      Stage 3 = how to stop/complete/finalize

   There you have it!

   The three steps/stages become your three points for your thesis statement in the process essay.

   c) Now write the three-point thesis statement.
      For example, after listing all the things you need to do before, during, and after class to do well in school, you might write this as your thesis statement:

   To do well in school, you have to prepare for classes, attend your classes, and review your notes.

Things to note about this thesis statement:

1. The steps are logical, moving from the beginning of the process to the end of the process.

   First *prepare*

   Second *attend*

   Third *review*

2. The process is chronological: before class, during class, and after class.
3. The three points are written in parallel form.
4. The three points are contained in one sentence.
5. The topic of the essay is in the statement.
6. Your opinion is in the statement.

This thesis statement meets the criteria of the five-paragraph essay.

Write your thesis statement here:

____

____

10. What is the fourth step?
    a) Write the outline for the process essay.
       Follow the outline format used for the five-paragraph essay (see Chapter 5). Keep in mind the image of bricks and mortar for the body of the essay. Figure 6.1 shows the format for the outline. Figure 6.2 shows a completed outline.

Figure 6.1 Outline for a Process Essay

Topic: ______________________________

PARAGRAPH # CONTENT

1 attention-getter: ______________________________

transition: ______________________________

thesis statement:

topic: ______________________________

opinion: ______________________________

three points (or steps):

1. ______________________________
2. ______________________________
3. ______________________________

2 transition: ______________________________

first point (step): ______________________________

supporting details:

____

____

____

____

link to thesis statement: ______________________________

conclude first point: ______________________________

3 transition: ______________________________

second point (step): ______________________________

supporting details:

____

____

____

____

link to thesis statement: ______________________________

conclude second point: ______________________________

4	transition: ______________________________
	third point (step): ______________________________
	supporting details:
	______________________________
	______________________________
	______________________________
	______________________________
	link to thesis statement: ______________________________
	conclude third point: ______________________________
5	transition: ______________________________
	revisit thesis statement: ______________________________
	conclude: ______________________________
	link to introduction: ______________________________

Figure 6.2 Example of a Completed Outline for a Process Essay

Topic: How to Do Well In School

Paragraph	Content
1	attention-getter: ***So, you want to be on the Dean's List.*** transition: ***This is an easy task if you just follow my tried and true expert advice.*** thesis statement topic: ***To do well in school and get your name up on that important list,*** opinion: ***you must*** three points (steps): ***be prepared for classes,*** ***attend your classes,*** ***and review your notes.***
2	transition: ***The first step to success*** first point: ***be prepared for classes***

supporting details:

- *the night before, read your timetable*
- *see what classes you have and in which order*
- *do all the homework for those classes in the order of your timetable*
- *study for any test that will be held on the next day*
- *review your notes from today's classes*
- *refer to your subject outline's order of sequence to see what you will be covering the next day*
- *read the chapters for each subject as outlined in the subject outline*
- *make notes from your readings on one side of a piece of paper*
- *leave the other half of the sheet empty for extra notes from class*
- *when all of this is done, pack up your backpack with all the books and supplies that you will need for the next day*
- *remember a pencil if you're having a scantron test*
- *make your lunch*
- *decide what you're going to wear*
- *set the alarm*
- *double check it*

link to thesis statement and conclude the first point (step): ***Now you're prepared to be successful.***

3 transition: ***The second success strategy***

second point (step): ***attend your classes***

supporting details:

- *arrive at school at least a half-hour early*
- *get a parking spot*
- *go to your locker*
- *review your timetable when you get to school*
- *empty your backpack of everything you don't need*
- *pack your backpack again*
- *double check to see that you have that pencil for the scantron test*
- *go to the classes*
- *don't be tempted to skip class just because you're tired, etc.*
- *attend every class*
- *stay for the duration of each class*
- *add extra notes to the ones you already have*
- *ask questions*
- *offer answers*
- *participate in discussions*

link to thesis statement and conclude the second point: ***This second step should add greatly to your success.***

4 transition: ***the final step***

third point (step): ***review your notes***

supporting details:

- *as soon as possible after each class, review your notes*
- *rewrite them if they're too messy*
- *reorganize them*
- *highlight points mentioned in the book and by your teacher*
- *make summaries*
- *make up questions and answers for yourself*
- *if possible, do extra research; check out the TV guide: maybe a course-related documentary on The History Channel, or an edition of Biography or 20/20*

- *start memorizing facts from the course*
- *tell someone at least one thing you learned in each class*

link to thesis statement and conclude the third point: ***This final step should not only help your memory but also put you at the top of the class when your papers are marked.***

5 transition: ***Therefore,***

revisit thesis statement: ***you need to do some work before class, be sure to be in class, and go over your notes regularly.***

conclude: ***I've used these techniques throughout my Grade 12 year and this year, and I can vouch that they do work. I am on the Dean's List at college for the second time.***

link to introduction: ***If your dream is to have your name on the coveted Dean's List outside the doors of the School of Justice's office, . . .***

Final Stages of Writing the Process Essay

a) Write the first draft of the essay from the outline. Notice that if you created a detailed outline like the one above, the essay is almost written.
b) Double-space the essay to make it easier to read. Also, your final submission must be double-spaced, so start off with it in this format.
c) Put it through the spell checker and grammar checker at least two times.
d) Save any changes you make based on these checks.
e) Print out your essay.
f) Read it again and proofread it again. Remember, the spell checker and grammar checker do not pick up every error.
g) Make the corrections on your computer.
h) Save the changes.
i) Put the essay through the spell checker and grammar checker again.
j) Save the changes.
k) Print out the essay.
l) Leave it alone for at least one hour. The longer you leave it, the more errors you will find.
m) Proofread it again.
n) Correct the errors on your computer.
o) Save the changes.
p) Print out your final draft.

Exercise 6.2 Writing Exercise

(To be completed in groups of two or three, or individually.)

1. Choose one of the following topics for a practice process essay.

______ How to Change a Car Tire

______ How to Improve Your Golf Score

______ How to Wallpaper/Paint a Room

______ How to Control Your Temper

______ How to Annoy Your Parents

______ How to Ask Out that Special Someone

______ How to Choose your Timetable

______ How to Choose the College Program That's Best For You

2. On separate sheets of paper, list all the tasks, in any order, that someone would need to do in order to complete the process easily, efficiently, and in a timely manner. Put one task on one line, like point-form notes. Remember to double-space your work. Even triple-spacing is good.

3. Review the tasks and number them in the order that they should be done.

4. Add any tasks that were left out and put them into the empty spaces left by the double/triple-spacing.

5. Put special numbers on them: 2a, 3a, 3b, etc.

6. Rewrite the tasks in the correct order.

7. Divide the tasks into three steps/stages. Use brackets, [ ], to show the distinct steps/stages.

8. Name the steps. Don't just call them steps 1, 2, and 3. See the Example of a Completed Outline for a Process Essay, in Figure 6.2.

   Note: The steps must show a definite progression, e.g., first to last. If there is no obvious progression, then what you have written is not suitable for a process essay.

9. Fill out the following outline for your practice process essay.

Form 6.1 Practice Process Essay Outline

Topic: ______________________________

PARAGRAPH # CONTENT

1 attention-getter: ______________________________

transition: ______________________________

thesis statement:

topic: ______________________________

opinion: ______________________________

three points (or steps):

1. ______________________________

2. ______________________________

3. ______________________________

2 transition: ______________________________

first point (step): ______________________________

supporting details:

____

____

____

____

link to thesis statement: ______________________________

conclude first point: ______________________________

3 transition: ______________________________

second point (step): ______________________________

supporting details:

____

____

____

____

link to thesis statement: ______________________

conclude second point: ______________________

4 transition: ______________________

third point (step): ______________________

supporting details:

____

____

____

____

link to thesis statement: ______________________

conclude third point: ______________________

5 transition: ______________________

revisit thesis statement: ______________________

conclude: ______________________

link to introduction: ______________________

Exercise 6.3 Writing Exercise (To be completed in groups or individually.)

1. Write the essay for the outline you developed in Exercise 6.2.
2. Please double-space your work and label it Draft #1.
3. Have someone proofread your essay and ask that person to sign your essay indicating that the proofreading has been done.
4. Rewrite the essay, double-spacing it and making the corrections that your proofreader pointed out. Label this second copy as your final copy.
5. Submit the final copy to your teacher for marking.
6. Write the corrections for all spelling errors in your personal spelling list (Appendix D).

Sample Process Essays

Below is a selection of sample process essays. The first three essays were written by college students, and cover some general topics. The last one, written by a police officer, explains how parents can keep their children safe at the mall when Christmas shopping. Each essay is a good example of a process essay.

How to Get Your Parents to Lend You Their Car
for the Weekend to go to a Friend's Cottage
by Joe Sandham

Joe Sandham

Sandham 1

Professor Doughty

Communications 1

30 September 2004

How to Get Your Parents to Lend You Their Car

for the Weekend to go to a Friend's Cottage

"There is no way! Don't ask such stupid questions!" Are these a few of the answers you get when you ask your parents if you can borrow their car for the weekend to go to a friend's cottage? If so, don't lose hope! Follow these steps to get your parents' car for a fun-filled weekend: do extra chores around the house; compliment your parents; and give them money.

First of all, do extra chores around the house. Wash the dishes without having to be asked; Windex the windows and the mirrors until they sparkle; wash the floors on your hands and knees. Those are just a few of the everyday chores that you can do to get into your parents' "good books." Then again, if these everyday chores do not impress your parents, then tackle the most despised room in your house to clean: the bathroom. Clean the disgusting brown ring off the bathtub; scrub that toilet clean, both inside and out; wipe off the shower stall's pesky soap scum; Windex the bathroom's mirror, window and pictures; and, most importantly, replenish the toilet paper and all the towels. When all this is done, you've completed the first step towards getting the keys to the car for the weekend.

Now you must complete the second step: throwing a few compliments to your parents at just the right moment. What parent does not like a compliment from time to time? You don't have a lot of time though, so you must keep pouring out the compliments, "Geez Mom! Have you lost weight? No? Oh, it looks like you did! That dress suits you perfectly! Mom, did I ever tell you that you are the best mother in the world?" Those compliments always get a smile and a kiss from your mom. Even though you don't like being kissed by your mom, you have to make some sacrifices in order to get the car. After swooning over your mom, move on to your dad. Just say, "Those glasses make you look smart. Out of all my friends' dads, I think you are the best looking." Your dad will become more confident with himself if you tell him those two compliments. You'll get a smile and a handshake, rather than a kiss. There, you've completed two-thirds of your mission.

Now you may move on to the final and most expensive step. What parents don't like money given to them, especially from a child who has a part-time job? There is one important thing to remember; you must give one parent some money when the other is not around. Go up to your mom and give her thirty bucks and say, "Here is some money to pay for the gas for the car, Mom. Please try to convince Dad to let me have the car this weekend." Your mom, being thrilled with the thirty dollars for gas, will happily oblige your request. Now, give your dad another thirty dollars and say, "Here's some money to contribute to the gas for the car. Please try to convince Mom to let me have the car for the weekend." Your father, proud that he raised you the right way, will happily oblige as well. Now, when you approach your parents for the last time about having the car, they will both happily agree to let you have the car for the weekend.

You have been successful! You are going to your friend's cottage for the weekend in your parents' car! It was easier than you thought. Just by working on house chores, complimenting both your parents, and giving your parents money, you now have a weekend of fun to look forward to in their car.

Source: Joseph Sandham, "How to Get Your Parents to Lend You Their Car for the Weekend to go to a Friend's Cottage." Reprinted with permission.

How to Haggle
by Ben Lenaerts

Ben Lenaerts

Professor Doughty

Communications 1

30 September 2004

How to Haggle

Have you ever been car shopping, found the perfect car, looked at the price and then said to yourself, "How am I going to afford that?" There is a way that you can afford that car or anything else you might want: haggle until you get down to the price you can afford to pay. The first step to haggling is to not seem too interested; the second is to create a high-pressure situation; and the third is to use verbal trickery and speed.

When you first approach the vehicle you desire, you must do so in an easy-going manner. You do not want to stand there and suddenly scream, "There it is!" and run frantically across the lot to get to the vehicle. This would tell the salesperson that you are going to pay whatever it costs for that item. You might lose any leverage over the salesperson that you might have had. A good approach is to casually examine the vehicle next to the one that you want, and then proceed to casually examine the vehicle you do want. This tells the salesperson that you are just browsing; thereby, it gives you adequate time to look at the price tag. It's that easy! You have just completed step one.

Step two is a little more difficult. In order to be successful in completing this step, you must be able to create a high-pressure situation. For example, you may need to tell a "little white lie" here by saying that you have an appointment in fifteen minutes, and keep looking at your watch. A popular theory that car dealers adhere to is that the longer a person waits, the more likely he or she will realize that the price is not going to go down; consequently, a person will spend more money on a desired car. So, play the dealer's game and create the high-pressure situation in order to allow the dealer to think that there is very little time to close the deal. You are now calling the shots. If the dealer takes you into the office or starts talking about a price, you have accomplished step two.

The final step, which is also the most difficult, occurs when the salesperson thinks that he or she is in control. Salespeople will only bring up the cost of something when they think they will be able to take advantage of you. By speeding up your speech and talking about the cost, you are causing two things to happen. The salesperson's alertness will be heightened, and his or her heart rate will increase. This is the time to start haggling full speed ahead. Simply start discussing numbers with the salesperson. Always remember to start very low; meanwhile, the salesperson will start lowering the price from the original. Increase your price by uneven increments. This will cause confusion. Confusion will make the dealer go lower than he or she normally would. When you reach a price you are happy with, yell out, "Deal!" You've now gotten the car for the price you can afford.

In conclusion, the tricks to haggling and subsequently getting a good deal are showing lack of interest, creating a high pressure situation, and using craftiness and speed. If you can master these skills and use them in that order, you will surely get the price you can afford to pay for whatever you buy. Use these skills whether you are buying a fourteen-thousand dollar car at a dealership or a fourteen-cent book of matches at a yard sale. With this said, I bid you happy haggling!

Source: Ben Lenaerts, "How to Haggle." Reprinted with permission.

How to Make a Championship Team
by Jeremy Bird-Dawson

Jeremy Bird-Dawson

Bird-Dawson 1

Professor Doughty

Communications 1

30 September 2004

How to Make a Championship Team

Have you ever wondered how a football team is built into a winning team or how a team can go from last place in its respective division only a year ago to a top contender the year after? A team can go from last place to first place by organizing the team makeup in three ways: getting a diversified, talented coaching staff; getting the players ready to play; and adopting a positive mental team approach. By following these steps, your football team is sure to be in the playoffs.

First, getting a good coaching staff is essential to starting the process of building a championship team. The coaching staff must be composed of individuals who have specific qualities that, in the end, will come together to build the complete coaching staff package. To begin with, the potential coaches must have a football background to ensure knowledge of the game. Also, there must be a coach for each position to ensure that the players are getting the proper coaching for their individual positions. Furthermore, the coaches must be firm, fair and unbiased. Finally, the coaches must be patient and understanding, for not every player is going to be an all-star. Building a coaching staff that works is the first and right step towards building a championship team.

Second, the players are the ones out on the field, so they need to be ready to play. Practices start during training camp, or "Hell Week," when the coaches get their first looks at their new players. The players must be in top physical shape to play, so they must push themselves harder each day. After training camp is over, the playbook is introduced, and all the players learn the plays. As the season approaches, during practice, the plays are polished and practised to ensure they run smoothly. When the players are ready to play, the coaching staff knows that they have completed the second phase to building a championship football team.

Third, a positive mental approach is the most important element to winning a championship. The players, as well as the coaches, must believe in themselves and the job they are doing. The team must adopt the attitude that losing is not an option. They also must have complete faith in each other. A team that believes that they can play ball together will achieve success. As well, the players must be ready to sacrifice their own bodies for the good of the team and to win each game. When a team has the right mental approach, it is truly ready to walk onto the field and become a championship team.

In conclusion, a coaching staff made up of various gifted individuals, players who are physically performing at their highest peak, and a team that has a "We will win" mentality are the essential components needed when a championship football team is being built.

Source: Jeremy Bird-Dawson, "How to Make a Championship Team." Reprinted with permission.

How to Survive the Holidays
by Officer Brendan Kennaley

Brendan Kennaley

Kennaley 1

Professor Doughty

Communications 1

30 September 2004

How to Survive the Holidays

Webster's dictionary definition of the word "holiday" suggests that it is "a period of rest from work." Yet, I think that most of us dread the hustle and bustle caused by the annual Christmas holiday. Perhaps it is the countless parties, family socials, the crowded parking lots, the out-of-stock signs, or the kids home from school that cause the stress that can at times be overwhelming, both emotionally and financially. Yet, some very simple steps can be followed when going shopping with your children to limit these stresses for both you and your children and make this year's holiday a safe and happy one while going to the mall, upon arriving at the mall, and while shopping at the mall.

The first step to a safe shopping trip with your children is for you to accept that the drive to the mall and the search for that close parking spot will simply take longer than at other times of year. This is essential to avoid a case of road rage on your part. Plan to leave a little earlier than usual and do take the time to ensure that your children are properly fastened in your automobile. This will greatly limit the possibility that they may get hurt in the event of a collision. Whether they object or not, always use the required safety equipment, even if it's only a short trip to your favourite mall. If you have to stop off at another store on the way to the mall, never leave them unattended in the car while you make that brief visit inside to pick up that one item. It would be better for you to pick up those items on your way to or from work when you don't have the kids with you, rather than during your trip to the mall with them. Furthermore, travel at the posted speed and leave plenty of room between you and the car in front of you while driving and when stopping. All of these safety tips on the way to the mall should get you and your children there safely.

Kennaley 2

Your second step to ensuring a happy and safe shopping expedition with the children is discussing some "being at the mall safety tips" with your children. Before you get out of the car, remind or explain to your young children that the lots are busier at this time of year and that because of this, they must be more careful and ensure that they walk with you rather than ahead of you. Remind them that they may see an approaching vehicle, but that the driver may not actually see them. Also, before you leave your car in the parking lot, avoid leaving bags, parcels, presents, phones, or the like in your vehicle where the thief casing the lot for that easy score can see it. Place these items in your trunk and always lock your vehicle. A quick look back as you walk to the store will help you remember the location of your car when you return to it. Taking the time to complete this second step will help to ensure a less stressful and safe time for you and your children as you arrive safely at the mall.

Once inside the mall, similar rules to the parking lot rules should be enforced. Having your children walk with you in the mall, instead of ahead of you, is a good safety measure. Furthermore, whether it's in the lot or in the store, never lose sight of your kids. A quick mental note of what your child is wearing will assist store employees, mall security, or the police in locating any kids that do get lost. A recent photo of your child that you keep in your wallet and is readily available to investigators will assist them greatly. If your kids are older, have a prearranged meeting place and time. Ensure that they understand that punctuality is essential, and if they are not at the agreed-upon place at the arranged time, call security immediately. Keeping your eyes on your children and having your children keep their eyes on you will help to ensure a safe experience for all during this holiday season.

There you have it: three easy steps to take to be safe this season while shopping with your kids. It is during this festive time that we all need to remind ourselves to simply slow

Kennaley 3

down and be patient. Remember that your kids are irreplaceable and the last two weeks before Christmas should be an opportunity to share some very precious moments with them. Do your part and make the holiday a safe and happy one.

Source: Officer Brendan Kennaley, "How to Survive the Holidays." Reprinted with permission. Officer Kennaley is a Collision Reconstructionist for the Durham Regional Police Service Traffic Services Branch. He has been a member of the D. R. P. S. for the past fifteen years.

Summary

Use the following checklist to ensure that your process essays meet all the requirements discussed above.

Your process essay must be

- based on a topic relating to how to do something;
- written in chronological order; and
- based on the five-paragraph essay model style.

The first paragraph must

- include an introduction to the topic;
- include an attention-getter; and
- have a three-point thesis statement that contains the three steps/stages necessary to complete this process.

Body paragraphs must

- discuss the stages in the order that they are stated in the thesis;
- use transitions in the first sentence of each body paragraph to show a progression of time;
- use appropriate words to show that each step must be taken in order to complete the task; and
- be written clearly, concisely, chronologically, and correctly so that anyone reading the essay will be able to follow the sequence of steps in order to complete the task.

The concluding paragraph must

- bring the topic to a close;
- include a revisit to the thesis statement in the first paragraph; and
- link back to the introduction.

The Research Essay Part 1: Getting Started

Learning Objectives

After students have learned the content of this chapter, they should be able to do the following:

- Recognize that the research essay uses the five-paragraph model as its template.
- Know how to choose a topic for the research essay.
- Start a preliminary list of works cited (bibliography) for a research essay with the help of resource sheets.

Learning Benefits

Within the first week of classes, you may find out that you will be required to write up to five research essays during the term. If you are like most students, you hate writing essays, particularly research essays. They require so much time! So, what are you going to do? Why not just jump in and learn how to do them properly? This chapter starts you off on the three-step process for writing research essays. The first step is discussed in this chapter, and the second and third are discussed in Chapters 8 and 9. It is a long process, but if you start early and follow each step, you should be able to produce what the teacher requires.

If an officer is trying for a promotion, quite often one of the major requirements for the selection process is the submission of a research paper. Furthermore, if policing is your chosen career, you definitely need to learn research skills because they are a major part of the investigation process.

THE RESEARCH ESSAY

A research essay is, first of all, an essay. Therefore, it is a piece of writing that contains all the aspects of the five-paragraph essay, including the thesis statement, which controls the discussion in the body of the essay. Furthermore, it also contains evidence of research in the form of direct quotations as well as paraphrases and summaries of other authors' works (articles/books). This research is included in the essay to support and develop the three points in the thesis statement. This research is also acknowledged throughout the essay through documentation, such as the use of quotation marks and references to the authors' works at the end of all direct quotations, paraphrases, or summaries. You basically prove your thesis statement with the help of what other writers have written about your topic or supporting points. After the conclusion of your essay, you include a list of works cited, a bibliography, of all the resources that you used in the essay.

All of the components mentioned above make up a research essay.

Referencing: MLA Style

In this book, the **Modern Language Association (MLA)** style of referencing and documentation is used. As you look at the essay examples and the content of the chapters dealing with the research essay, you will note that footnotes or endnotes are not used to indicate the sources of quoted, paraphrased, or summarized information. Instead, immediately after the quotation, paraphrase, or summary, there are parentheses, (   ), with specific information in them.

Information about the MLA style is included in these chapters about the research essay (Chapters 7–9), but detailed information is also provided in Appendix B.

Review of the Five-Paragraph Essay Style

Just like the other essays in this book, the research essay is also written within the framework of the five-paragraph essay model discussed previously. This style acts as the template for all essays.

Here is a review of it.

Paragraph 1

- introduction
- attention-getter
- transition to a . . .
- three-point thesis statement

Paragraph 2

- transition to a . . .
- topic sentence that states the . . .
- first point in the three-point thesis statement,
- followed by supporting details and a . . .
- concluding statement, which concludes the first point and links back to the thesis statement

Paragraph 3

- transition to a . . .
- topic sentence that states the . . .
- second point in the three-point thesis statement,
- followed by supporting details and a . . .
- concluding statement, which concludes the second point and links back to the thesis statement

Paragraph 4

- transition to a . . .
- topic sentence that states the . . .
- third point in the three-point thesis statement,
- followed by supporting details and a . . .
- concluding statement, which concludes the third point and links back to the thesis statement

Paragraph 5

- transition to a . . .
- revisited thesis statement, followed by a . . .
- concluding statement, which links back to the introduction

WHAT IS MEANT BY "RESEARCH"?

Now that the style or format of the essay is established, you need to consider what goes into the essay for it to be considered a research essay. You need to do some research on what other authors have said about your topic.

1. What is research?

Basically, research is finding out information about a topic from someone else or something else (i.e., a book, an article, etc.). Research involves going to the library, onto the Internet, or somewhere else to obtain written material about the subject. It also involves interviewing experts about the topic.

2. What if I know a great deal about the topic before I start the essay?

That is good, but you still must do research for your topic and include that research with your essay. Not only do you have to do the research, you must include proof in the essay that you have done research about your topic.

3. How do I show proof that I have done research?

You will do this in eight ways in the essay, according to the MLA style of documentation:

i) Include the **names** of the authors or people interviewed in the essay.
ii) Include the **titles** of the articles, books, and written material in the essay.
iii) Include **short direct quotations** (one word to four typed lines) from authors, with quotation marks around the words that you are quoting or copying.
iv) Include **long direct quotations** from authors. Long direct quotations are copied words that take up five or more lines of typing. Do not put quotation marks around these words; start a new paragraph for the quotation and indent all lines in the quotation 2.5 cm from the margin.
v) Put **references** in parentheses, (   ), directly after the quoted words. The information to be included here varies. The details and rules about what needs to be included are discussed in Chapter 8 and in Appendix B.
vi) Include **paraphrases** (rewritings of the authors' words using your own words and using approximately the same number of words) plus the references for the paraphrases in parentheses, (   ), immediately after the paraphrases.
vii) Include **summaries** (brief synopses of the authors' ideas) plus references for the summaries in parentheses, (   ).
viii) Include a **list of works cited**, a list of all the resources you used in the essay, as the last page of the essay. In other styles of referencing, this list is called a "bibliography."

4. What happens if there is no proof of research in the essay?

Then, you have not written a research essay. Furthermore, if there is no proof of research in the essay, then **plagiarism** has occurred, and the essay will receive a failing grade. Not only that, but plagiarism is considered a very serious academic offence, and punishment at most schools is severe. So, always be sure to include proof of your research, and never try to pass off other people's writing as your own.

5. What happens if you just write your own ideas and points that you already know?

Then, you have not written a research essay.

6. Let's say I am doing an essay on Wayne Gretzky, and I know everything there is to know about The Great One. Do I still have to quote, paraphrase, and summarize what other people have to say even though I know that information too?

Yes, you **must** still use quotations, paraphrases, and summaries from other people. Otherwise, you would not be including research. You would simply be telling the reader everything you know about Wayne Gretzky.

Doing research means finding out more about a topic. No matter how much you know about someone or something, there is always more to learn. Besides, you will find that other people who are considered experts on the subject you are writing about have the same opinion as you do! By including their names in the essay, you bring credibility to your essay.

Hint: Sometimes it is better to stay away from topics that you know a great deal about because you can often be tempted not to do research.

SAMPLE RESEARCH ESSAYS

Sometimes, it is easier to achieve an understanding of what you are required to do at a general level—before you get into the details of the process. Therefore, for those of you who like to see the "whole picture" first, two good research essays written by college students have been included at this point in the chapter, before we go into further details about what is involved in writing a research essay. (There are more sample research essays in Appendix E for your reference.)

Things to look for in these essays:

- the five-paragraph essay style
- the three-point thesis statement found in the first paragraph
- the amount of research used in the essay
- the use of quotation marks around copied words that are one word to four lines long
- the absence of quotation marks around copied words that are five lines or longer
- the use of short quotations, long quotations, paraphrases, and summaries
- the MLA referencing used within the body of the essay to show the sources of the information; they are included in parentheses, (   )
- the use of transitions to make the information flow from one point to another
- the last sentence of each body paragraph (the second, third, and fourth paragraphs), which sums up the point of that paragraph and links the point back to the thesis statement
- the revisited thesis statement in the last paragraph
- the link back to the introduction in the last paragraph

Remember, with a little work, and by following the directions in this chapter, you too can write essays like these.

Whose Rights Are Paramount?
by
Chris Morris

Chris Morris

Morris 1

Professor Doughty

Communications 1

30 September 2004

Whose Rights Are Paramount?

Frank Boyle, an 85-year-old man, was found beaten to death during the summer of 1991, in his home in Likely, British Columbia (Leishman 1). All three of British Columbia's courts, which are under the jurisdiction of the Supreme Court of Canada, found there was enough evidence to convict Michael Feeney for the second-degree murder of Mr. Boyle (1). The Supreme Court heard an appeal from Feeney asking for protection under the "Canadian Charter of Rights and Freedoms" (R v. Feeney 1). During the appeal, the defense claimed police had entered, arrested, and searched Feeney's house without proper permission, and therefore, violated the right granted to Feeney under Section 8 of the "Charter" (1). Section 8 of the "Charter" states, "Everyone has the right to be secure against unreasonable search or seizure" (S.8). With this in mind, the Supreme Court overturned the lower Court's decision in the interest of guaranteeing the rights and freedoms of the previously convicted Feeney, essentially making Michael Feeney a free man. The Supreme Court's final interpretation of Section 8 in this case was not just, because it showed a disregard for the victim, societal values, and public safety.

To begin with, the court's decision showed a disregard for the rights of the victim, Frank Boyle. Justice is only preserved when there is a demonstration of "both fairness and reasonableness"("Justice" 468). Mr. Boyle's rights and freedoms were put to an abrupt halt on that summer night in 1991 (Leishman 1). There was no regard paid to this fact when the majority of nine judges voted to overturn Feeney's conviction (R v. Feeney 51), thus electing to preserve and protect the rights of a murderer. In the interest of the victim, it is neither reasonable, fair, nor just, that his murderer is not serving the prescribed penalty for his crime. Instead, Feeney is still enjoying the rights and freedoms of which he deprived his victim.

Secondly, from the days when only the Ten Commandments governed societal values, up until today, society on a whole has believed the act of murder to be unjust. In fact, the Supreme Court embraced this value over a murderer's rights as recently as 1986 in the case of R v. Landry (Leishman 2). Mr. Landry's case challenged the same breach of rights and freedoms under similar circumstances as R v. Feeney, but "[the court] simply ignored the legal precedent"(1). It is true that during the Feeney investigation, the police officers in charge were mistaken or used poor judgment, but they did not act like "lawless vigilantes" (L'Heureux-Dubé 51), nor did they purposely disregard Mr. Feeney's rights (Leishman 2). These officers acted in good faith, and it is reasonable and fair to assume in this particular case that society's values would warrant poor police work, rather than let a murderer go free (L'Heureux-Dubé 51-52) and ignore justice.

Lastly, the final conclusion in this case was decided without any sense of public safety. First and foremost, the Supreme Court ruling placed "a savage killer on the loose in the community" (Leishman 2) when it reversed the lower court's ruling and granted Feeney his freedom. Secondly, the case set a dangerous precedent for other cases and risked "having thousands of other convictions judicially overturned" (2). This will place even more criminals back on the street, with the ability to re-offend. As for future situations, "the ruling [will] cause[ ] concern among police and victims' groups, that public safety might be put at risk . . . [because] of the delay required to obtain a warrant" (Department of Justice 2). Therefore, this ruling was unjust since it demonstrated that it is more reasonable and fair to put an entire nation's safety at risk to guarantee the rights and freedoms of a savage murderer (Leishman 2).

In essence, when the Supreme Court granted an appeal to Feeney, he also received protection under Section 24(2) of the "Charter," rendering him a free man (R v. Feeney 1). All things considered, the "egregious ... ruling" (Leishman 1) by the Supreme Court judges did not serve justice for Mr. Boyle, nor did it appeal to the values of our society, and it showed a blatant disregard for public safety. In short, dissenting Justice L'Heureux-Dubé maintains that the search of Mr. Feeney's residence was reasonable and "the police felt obliged to act quickly in order to prevent any further violence in the community. For this foresight they should be commended" (199). With those points in mind, one can conclude that the decision to overthrow the previous ruling was unfair, unreasonable, and therefore by definition, unjust ("Justice" 468). "The . . . 'Charter' . . . guarantees the rights and freedoms set out in it, subject only to such reasonable limits...demonstrably justified in a free and democratic society" (S.1). Those reasonable limits were surpassed; as such, the appeal under Section 8 of the "Charter" should have been quashed in the interest of Mr. Boyle, society, public safety, and ultimately, justice.

Morris 4

Works Cited

"Canadian Charter of Rights and Freedoms." Martin's Annual Criminal Code 2004. Edward L. Greenspan. Aurora: Canada Law Book Inc., 2004. S.1 – S.24(2).

Department of Justice. "News Releases." Minister of Justice Tables Response to Feeney Case. 30 Oct. 1997. Updated 24 April 2003: 7 par., Short. 12 Jan. 2004 <http://canada.justice.gc.ca/en/news/nr1997/feprs.html>.

Leishman, Rory. "Chief Justice Should Explain the Egregious Feeney Ruling." The Montreal Gazette 9 May 1998: Short (Less than 1200 words). 11 Jan. 2004 <http://www.conservativeforum.org/EssaysForm.asp?ID=6147>.

L'Heureux-Dubé, Claire. "R v. Feeney." [1997] 2 S.C.R. 13. 1997 Vol. 2. 12 Jan. 2004 <http://www.lexum.umontreal.ca/csc-scc/en/pub/1997/vol2/html 1997scr2_0013.html>.

"Justice." Collins Dictionary. Second edition. Glasgow: HarperCollins Publishers, 2003. 468.

"*R v. Feeney*". [1997] 2 S.C.R. 13. Vol. 2.22 May 1997: 51p., Long. 12 Jan. 2004 <http://www.lexum.umontreal.ca/csc-scc/en/pub/1997/vol2/html 1997scr2_0013.html>.

How Cameras in Police Cruisers Will Impact Law Enforcement
by
Jeff Thibideau

Jeff Thibideau

Professor Doughty

Communications 1

30 September 2004

How Cameras in Police Cruisers Will Impact Law Enforcement

Almost anyone who has cable T.V. has seen the show, Cops. This show's premise basically revolves around the day-to-day duties and disputes that police officers deal with while recording everything with in-car cameras and cameramen. To most, the idea of video taping police interactions with the public is viewed as a good thing and something more police agencies should consider. On "February 17, 2004" (Mitchell 1), the Ontario Provincial Police (O.P.P.) initiated "a year long test program" (1) involving "22 provincial police cruisers in the Greater Toronto Area and 12 in Kenora, [that] will be equipped with high-tech digital cameras to record police interaction with the public" (Livingston 2). The installation of cameras in O.P.P. cruisers will provide concrete evidence for all traffic disputes, greater protection for officers and the public, and ensure that police conduct is appropriate.

First, the impact of this decision by the province to install cameras in the cruisers will help to settle traffic disputes in a courtroom setting because the disputes are recorded. The tapes can act as concrete evidence of the fact. One of the main hopes of the project is to "stop people from making 'frivolous defences' in court" (1). This would save the province money that would otherwise be used in wasted court proceedings. In addition to the video cameras recording any events that take place in traffic disputes, "officers will wear microphones to record conversations with stopped drivers and passengers" (Mitchell 1). The added bonus of being able to hear the audio element of the events filmed on camera will help to confirm whatever is seen on the tapes. With the ability to see and hear everything that has happened in a traffic dispute, the court would then be able to come to a fair and compelling decision in each case. Ontario Premier Dalton McGuinty stated that "anyone who's ever seen T.V. footage from cameras mounted on the dashboard on police cruisers will know that they can be a useful tool" ("Cameras in cop cars to get test run" 2). As long as the events being recorded are not in any way tampered with, the visual and audio recordings would prove to be very compelling evidence in any courtroom setting.

Furthermore, the in-car camera program will impact law enforcement for the better because it will provide greater protection for officers and the public. Corrections Minister Monte Kwinter made it clear that he firmly believes that the cameras will indeed "protect officers and the public" (Livingston 1). Kwinter also stated that "the project's designed to protect police officers, not target them" ("Cameras in cop cars to get test run" 2). "The cameras, one mounted in the windshield, the other focused on the backseat, begin to record if the [cruiser's] sirens or lights are activated, or if the [cruiser] is involved in a crash" (2). The overall design of this equipment is very effective in protecting both the officer and the public because the tape with its audio and visual representation of the incident will show exactly what was seen and heard throughout the incident. This works in everyone's favour. For example, if a male claims in court that he was denied his rights upon detention, the tape will show the truth, and the communication between the male and the officer will be honestly revealed. If the suspect is lying, the tapes will clearly show that the officer was not guilty of what he is being accused. As well, if the male is telling the truth about the denial of his rights, the recorded testimony will not only protect his case, but strengthen it as well. Therefore, as Kwinter said, "'[The video camera] protects the police officer, it protects the citizen [because] if there is a dispute, there will be a record of it'" (2). This program can only be of benefit to everyone.

Lastly, the in-car camera program is making an impact on law enforcement because the cameras will ensure that police conduct themselves professionally and appropriately in the line of duty. O.P.P. spokesperson Const. Sue Cain said that "'Kenora and Toronto were likely selected because they have diverse populations'" (qtd. in "Police in Kenora, Toronto get cameras" 1-2). "Installing video cameras in police cruisers is a legitimate way to combat allegations of racial profiling in Ontario" (1). The in-car program will act as a useful tool in determining whether or not police officers are representing themselves the way the province wants them to towards the public. Those who gave life to this program believe that it will "allow police to observe and evaluate police and citizen interactions in the community" (1). Premier McGuinty, elected in 2003, firmly believed that this new program would work for the long-term goals of the provincial police services. McGuinty stated, "'We've got a responsibility to do what we can to minimize (racial profiling), and ideally eliminate it'" (qtd. in "Cameras in cop cars to get test run" 1) after the "Ontario's Human Rights Commission recommended establishing a provincial body to combat the problem [of allegations of racial profiling]" (1). Therefore, the video cameras will have an impact on police conduct.

In conclusion, the message the provincial government is conveying by testing cameras in police cruisers is that recorded interactions of officers and civilians can possibly do more good than harm for the policing system. The use of these cameras in police cruisers will provide visual and auditory evidence of what happened at the scene, offer protection for officers and civilians who were at the scene, and verify that the police conduct at the scene was appropriate. Therefore, these cameras in police cruisers can prove to be an asset to everyone.

Thibideau 4

Works Cited

"Cameras in cop cars to get test run". The London Free Press 11 December 2003: 2, Short. 10 March 2004 <www.canoe.ca/NewsStand/LondonFreePress/News>.

Livingston, Gillian. "OPP pilot project to test video cameras in cruisers". The London Free Press 18 February 2004: 3, Short. 10 March 2004 <www.canoe.ca/NewsStand/LondonFreePress/News>.

Mitchell, Bob. "OPP test in-car cameras". The Toronto Star 17 February 2004: 2, Short. 18 February 2004 <www.torontostar.ca>.

"Police in Kenora, Toronto get cameras". The London Free Press 10 February 2004: 2, Short. 18 February 2004 <www.canoe.ca/NewsStand/LondonFreePress/News>.

Source: Jeff Thibideau, "How Cameras in Police Cruisers Will Impact Law Enforcement." Reprinted with permission.

STARTING THE ESSAY

1. When do I start the essay?

You should start it as soon as you get the assignment.

2. Why do I need to start so early?

It is a long project, and research takes time.

3. Can I do the research essay the night before it is due?

This is not a very good idea.

4. So, approximately how much time do I need to do a research essay?

A lot depends upon the required length of the essay. If you are required to write a three-page, double-spaced, typed essay, then it could take approximately fifteen to twenty hours to write the essay. The longer the length of the paper, the more time you will need to write the essay.

Yes, that is a lot of time for one assignment, but a research essay is usually worth a large proportion of your final mark. The many hours you put into the essay will pay off in the long run.

5. How long is this process?

There are twenty-one steps involved in the process.

6. What are the twenty-one steps involved in the development and writing of a research paper?

1. Choosing a topic
2. Composing a preliminary bibliography
3. a) Summarizing
   b) Taking notes from written sources and using direct quotations to avoid plagiarism
   c) Taking notes from videos
4. Examining your notes to find three points to discuss
5. Writing the preliminary thesis statement
6. Making more notes from other research material
7. Writing the second thesis statement
8. Finalizing the thesis statement
9. Getting the thesis statement approved by the teacher
10. Sorting through and throwing out some of the research
11. Cutting and pasting the research
12. Prioritizing the supporting details
13. Composing the outline
14. Writing the first draft
15. Proofreading the first draft
16. Writing the second draft
17. Writing the list of works cited
18. Allowing time to elapse
19. Proofreading the second draft
20. Writing the final copy
21. Preparing the essay to meet the submission requirements

Exercise 7.1 Preparing to Write a Research Essay

Consider your due date and answer the following questions.

1. What is your due date for your research essay? ______________________

2. What is the date today? ______________________

3. How many days are between those two dates? _____

4. What else, besides this essay, do you have to do between those two dates? Consider other assignments as well as your work schedule and major social activities. Include these dates in chronological order below.

   ____

   ____

   ____

   ____

   ____

   ____

During your busy time before the due date, you need to make time to do the following specific steps to complete the essay:

1. Choose a topic.

2. Check with the teacher that the topic is suitable.

3. Make sure that you have the correct number of resources required by your teacher.

4. Print out all your information from any Internet source that you are going to use. This information may not be on the Internet later on.

5. Preview any documentaries or videos that fit your topic. The libraries have a wide variety of topics.

6. Research for more information about your topic from the following sources:
   - the Internet
   - newspapers—current and back issues
   - magazines—current and back issues
   - books
   - interviews

7. Follow steps 2–21 of the process outlined earlier for writing a research essay.

Let's get started on the process of writing that excellent research essay!

STEP 1 IN THE RESEARCH ESSAY PROCESS: CHOOSING A TOPIC

1. Choose a topic that interests you. This is important for the following reasons:

- You'll like doing the work.
- You'll get involved with the topic.
- You'll write an interesting essay.
- Your reader will know that you know what you are talking about.
- You'll be following the writer's creed: "Write about what you know!"

2. Be flexible and willing to change.

If your first topic is not working, then change to another one.

Exercise 7.2 Your Interests

Let's examine your interests.

First of all, your teacher will probably give you a general topic to use as your overall topic.

a) Write that general topic here: ______________________________

b) In the first column of the table below, list at least five specific topics that fit into that general topic and interest you.

Then prioritize the topics in order of your preference by writing the numbers 1 through 5 in the second column of the table.

Topics	Preferences
1.	
2.	
3.	
4.	
5.	

c) Pick out your first, second, and third choices, and write them in the first column of the following table. Then read (d), below, for instructions on completing the second and third columns of the table.

Choices	Scores	Total
First Choice:		
Second Choice:		
Third Choice:		

d) Now you need to narrow your three choices down to one choice. To help you do this, answer the following questions and put your scores beside each topic above, in the second column of the table (under "Scores"). You will be adding a series of numbers: one for each of the five questions below.

i) Do I really like this topic? Rate it from 1–4, with 4 being the highest.

ii) Do I have the minimum number of resources required for this topic? No = 0; Yes = 3

iii) How many resources do I have for this topic? Give yourself a score to correspond with the number of resources.

iv) Have I already discovered three very good points to discuss? No = 0; Yes = 3

v) How many points do I have to discuss for this topic? Write the number in for each topic. Now, add up the scores for each topic, which you've written in the second column, and write the total for each topic in the third column (under "Totals").

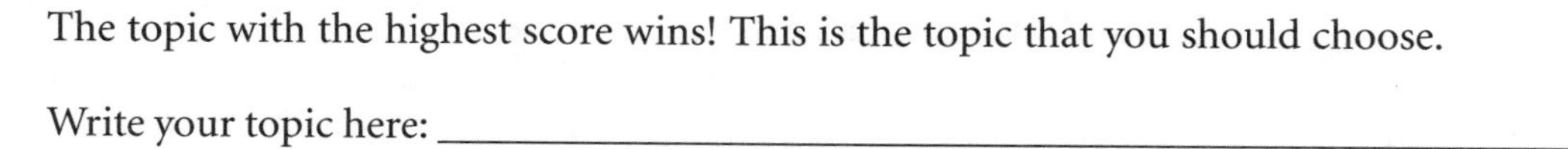

The topic with the highest score wins! This is the topic that you should choose.

Write your topic here: ______________________________

You should now have your topic for your research essay. Now it is time to collect your resources together. Your resources are all the articles, books, videos, and names of experts you have collected so far that have some information about your topic.

STEP 2 IN THE RESEARCH ESSAY PROCESS: COMPOSING A PRELIMINARY BIBLIOGRAPHY (LIST OF WORKS CITED)

1. What is a "bibliography"?

A bibliography is a list, included at the end of your essay, that tells your reader which resources you used and included in your essay.

2. What is a "bibliography" called in the MLA Style of bibliographic citation?

It is called the list of works cited.

3. What do the words "works cited" mean?

Works = the resources (videos, articles, books, etc.) used for the research
Cited = referred to, quoted from, etc.

Therefore, the list of works cited is a list of the resources you used in the essay.

4. What are examples of resources?

Resources can be any or all of the following:

a) an article on your topic;
b) videos or documentaries on this topic that you found in the audio-visual department in the library;
c) interviews;
d) surveys;
e) books; etc.

5. Why is this list a preliminary list?

Preliminary means "introductory." Therefore, a preliminary bibliography is your first list of the resources that you could use for your topic. It is created at an early stage in your research.

It is also preliminary because you may not use all of these resources in your essay, so you would later have to delete the ones not used. Also, once you start writing the essay, you may find that you don't have enough information for one of your points. You would therefore do more research and then add the new resources to your list of works cited. Keep in mind that your list of works cited will include **only** the resources that you actually referred to in your essay by using quotations, paraphrases, or summaries (i.e., it may not contain all the resources you included in your preliminary bibliography).

Example

Your Topic: The Impacts of D-Day

Let's say that in your preliminary bibliography, you have an article entitled "D-Day: The Most Important Day in the Twentieth Century," by John Albert Smith.

When you are doing your research, you write out some notes from the article, but then when you write your essay, you do not refer to Smith's article in the essay, nor do you use any of his information.

Consequently, you would **not** include Smith's article and name in your final list of resources, the list of works cited, at the end of the essay.

6. Where does this list of works cited go in the essay?

It goes on the last page, on a separate sheet, at the end of the essay.

7. How do you compose a preliminary list of works cited?

a) Use one copy of **Form 7.1 First Page: Resources** (see page 127) for each resource that you use. This form is called the "first page" because it becomes the first page of your notes for every resource that you use. There are extra copies of Form 7.1 in Appendix A. You may use them and photocopy more as you require them.
b) Fill in all the information on the First Page: Resources page that pertains to your source of information. Be sure to include additional information for Internet sources, videos, and interviews on the page as indicated. This information will be very valuable when it comes time to write your list of works cited at the end of the essay.
c) Use one First Page: Resources page for each resource.
d) Staple the pages together in alphabetical order according to the author's surname or the first word of the title if no author is listed with the source. Ignore the words "The," "A," or "An," at the beginnings of titles when organizing the resources in alphabetical order. In these cases, order the title based on the second word.
For example, one of the resources used for the research essay on Bernardo in Appendix E was an article entitled "The Homolka–Bernardo Murders." The "H" in Homolka was the deciding factor as to where to place this resource in the list, not the "T" in "The." Therefore, this article was second, after Davey's book and before Lavallee's song.
e) *When do I record the information about the resource?*
Record the information about each resource as you find it and take notes from it. It is too easy to forget about one of your resources later on.
f) *Where do I find this information?*
If you are referring to an **article**, the information is found in any one of four places, or in all of them:
   i) the **first page** of the article
   ii) the **cover** of the magazine, book, etc.

Form 7.1 First Page: Resources

Title of article/chapter/video clip (in quotation marks): ______________________

Name(s) of author(s): ______________________

Title of book/magazine/journal/newspaper/video (underlined): ______________________

Editor: ______________________ Edition: ______________________

City of publication: ______________ Publisher's name: ______________________

Volume number: ______________

Year/date of publication: ________ / ______ ______ ______
year only date month year

Page number(s): __________

For Internet/CD ROM resources only:

Starting page number of article: _____

Number of words/paragraphs/pages in article: __________
short/long? _____

Site/path/file address: ______________________

Date you visited the site: ______ ______ ______
date month year

For interviews only:

Name of person interviewed: ______________________

Person's job title: ______________________

Date of interview: ______ ______ ______
date month year

For videos only:

Name of producer: ______________________

Production date: ______________

Date you viewed the video: ______ ______ ______
date month year

iii) the **copyright page** of the magazine, book, etc.
iv) the **inside title page** of the magazine, book, etc.

If you are referring to a **book**, the information is found in three places:
i) the **cover**;
ii) the **inside title page**; and
iii) the **copyright page** (located on the back of the title page).

Look for the little circled © for the copyright date: the year of publication in most cases.

g) *What if I can't find the name of the author?*
This happens sometimes, with Internet articles in particular. If the author's name is not provided, then don't fill in the line for the author's information. Just start with the title of the article, starting with the first word in the **title** of the article or book.
However, make sure you fill in all the other information from the Internet site very carefully and thoroughly on the rest of the page, including the site date—the date when you visited the site and got the information.

h) *What if I can't find the date of the resource?*
If there is no date, then put **n.d.** on the line for the date.
However, for Internet resources, always include the date that you visited the website (your site date or access date), in this order: date month year.

i) *How do I record the author's names if there is one author? Two authors? Three authors? Four or more authors?*
One author: reverse order of author's names, separated by a comma.
surname, first name
e.g., *Smith, Roger*
Two authors: first author's surname then first name (separated by a comma), followed by second author's first name then surname (i.e., regular order, with no comma between them).

Note: First author's name is in reverse order and second author's name is in regular order.
e.g., *Burns, Peter and Janice Burke*
Three authors: first author's surname, followed by a comma, then first name, followed by a comma, then second author's first name then surname, followed by a comma, then the third author's first name then surname.
Note: First author's name is in reverse order, second author's name is in regular order, and third author's name is in regular order.
e.g., *Lim, Tom, Mike Montgomery, and Susan Ankenmann*
Four or more authors: First author's surname then first name (separated by a comma), followed by "et al."

Note: First author's name is in reverse order, and the other authors are represented by "et al.", which means "and all the others"
e.g., *Roebuck, Roberta et al.*

j) *Can I change the order of the authors' names from the order that is indicated in the article or on the front cover of the book?*
No. Record the names in the exact order in which they are written on the article or in the book. The names are written in the order of the authors who wrote/contributed the most to the article or book. Therefore, Roberta Roebuck did most of the work in the above example for four or more authors.

k) *What if initials are used in the author's name?*
Treat the initials as if they were names, and include them. Examples:

One author:	Author's name:	*T. Shawn Edmonson*
	Recorded as	*Edmonson, T. Shawn*
	Author's name:	*Sally J. Rollins*
	Recorded as	*Rollins, Sally J.*
Two authors:	Authors' names:	*B.J. Parker and Chin M. Lee*
	Recorded as	*Parker, B.J. and Chin M. Lee*

l) *How many entries or resources should I have in my list of works cited for a research paper?*
Check with your teacher and the assignment information package or handout. Generally, you are required to have a minimum of **three** entries or resources in your list of works cited.

Be careful that you meet your teacher's requirements. Some teachers require that you use a variety of media for your resources. For example, you might not be allowed to get all of your resources from the Internet. You might be required to have resources from books or actual hardcopies of articles from magazines, journals, or newspapers.

Note: At this point, you are just recording the information for each resource onto your First Page: Resources pages. Later on, when you have finished the essay and know which resources you actually used in your essay, you will write the list of works cited from the information on these pages. More detailed information about the rules for writing the actual list of works cited is explained in Appendix B: MLA Documentation Style.

Summary

To get yourself off to a good start to writing a research essay, you should do the following:

- review the five-paragraph essay style;
- choose a topic that suits the general topic stated by the teacher and one that can be researched; and
- find a minimum of three resources for your topic and start a preliminary list of works cited by filling in the First Page: Resources page for each resource.

You have now finished Part 1: Getting Started, in the three-part process of writing a research essay. This part (Chapter 7) includes Step 1 in the Research Essay Process: Choosing a Topic and Step 2 in the Research Essay Process: Composing a Preliminary Bibliography. These are the first two steps in the twenty-one step process. You are now on your way to doing the second part in the three-part process of writing an essay: summarizing and taking notes from written resources and videos. This information will be discussed in Chapter 8.

The Research Essay Part 2: Summarizing, Quoting, and Note Taking

Learning Objectives

After students have learned the content of this chapter, they should be able to do the following:

- Summarize a piece of written information.
- Use direct quotations in their essays.
- Take notes from a video and use them in their essays.
- Apply MLA style rules when documenting summaries and direct quotations so that they will not plagiarize the information in their essays.

Learning Benefits

It is extremely important to know how to summarize and include direct quotations from another author's work so that you can include them in your research essays, your oral presentations, your workshops, or just in your daily life as you share with others some information that you have learned.

There are many documentaries and educational videos available now for students to use. Knowing how to take notes efficiently and correctly from these media sources will enable you to save time and use these valuable sources in your essays. Taking notes correctly before you write your essays will eliminate the chance of you misquoting or not knowing where you received the information.

By using the MLA style of documentation in your essays for all of your summaries and direct quotations from written sources and other media, you will avoid being charged with plagiarizing the information. Whenever you use another author's work, you must reference it. You must "give credit where credit is due," as the saying goes. Knowing how to do all this in your written work will make your work credible.

Summarizing, quoting, and note taking are also important skills to have in a career in policing. Officers may summarize a witness's statement, for example. They use direct quotations when they are on the stand and refer to the exact words that a witness or suspect has said. Furthermore, referencing is a major part of an officer's life. Learning the MLA style of documentation will aid an officer when he or she writes an essay for a promotion opportunity or a research report as an assignment.

Step 3a in the Research Essay Process: Summarizing

Summaries are shortened versions of a variety of things, such as written works, movies, TV shows, or your daily events. You use summaries on a daily basis in your life when you tell your friend what you did last night, relate a brief synopsis of a movie or TV show that you watched, or share the general story of a book. Summaries are written or said in your own words and are shorter than the original work. They are always referenced. You need to let your reader know from whose work you got the information.

You will use summaries of other authors' words in your research essay to inform your reader about what other authors have to say about your topic. Rather than write out pages and pages of long quotations from other authors' work, you can simply condense what they say in your own words and use a reference to tell the reader where you found the information.

Example

After reading a 365-page book called The Concrete Blonde, by Michael Connelly, you might tell your friend the following:

I read an interesting book called The Concrete Blonde by Michael Connelly. It was about this detective called Harry Bosch, who not only solved the murder of a Californian woman buried in concrete but also discovered the killer of four other women who were murdered by The Follower. The book also dealt with Bosch's own court case and his relationship with his girlfriend, Sylvia.

Things to note about this summary:

- It's shorter than the original: 5 lines instead of 365 pages.
- It's in the summarizer's words, not the words of the original author, Connelly.
- It includes the references: the title of the book and the author.

Exercise 8.1 Writing Exercise

1. On the following lines, write a summary of a movie or TV show that you have seen recently. Include the title of the movie or TV show and underline it.
2. Read it to a partner.
3. Listen to your partner's summary.

____

____

____

____

____

____

Why Do I Need to Learn How to Summarize?

You may be asked to write a book report, a synopsis of a guest speaker's presentation, or a critique of a video. All of these include summaries.

You may also be asked to write a research essay. When you write that research essay, you will be doing a lot of reading about your topic. You should not include in your essay everything you have read or heard about the topic; you should instead summarize what others have said about the topic and reference the sources.

Sample Summary

Before we see an actual summary, let's first look at a complete article so that you can compare the full-length article to the summary. Below is an article from the May 1998 issue of Blue Line magazine. The author's name was not given with the article. Read the entire article first, and then read the summary that follows it.

Sidearms Taken Away from RCMP Auxiliaries

RCMP auxiliary officers in British Columbia had their right to carry sidearms revoked in early April. The decision was announced by the RCMP following a review by the force and the province's Attorney General's Ministry, RCMP spokesman Sgt. Russ Grabb said.

B.C. is the only jurisdiction where the RCMP has allowed auxiliaries to carry a sidearm, a practice that has been in place since 1986.

Grabb said the decision to allow them to carry a weapon would have been made by the Attorney General's Ministry of the day.

But the decision to take the sidearms away is only an interim one with final recommendations to be submitted to the Attorney General's Ministry in September.

Grabb said the decision is in line with some of the recommendations made in the 1994 Oppal Report on policing in the province.

"What we're doing is abandoning the old command- and control-based, paramilitary system in favour of one that focuses on community-based policing," he was quoted as saying.

The decision to prohibit B.C.'s 1,100 auxiliaries from carrying a gun didn't result from one incident in which a weapon was discharged by an auxiliary, but there have been cases of such, Grabb said.

"There have been incidents and concerns raised and there's quite a number of them, but it's not just incident driven," he was quoted as saying.

The order to suspend the auxiliaries' right to carry a sidearm was issued very suddenly, said Terry Deacon, president of the Prince George auxiliary association.

Deacon said there was no consultation or any mention of what incidents involving auxiliaries might have triggered the decision prior to the ban being imposed.

Source: "Sidearms Taken Away from RCMP Auxiliaries." Blue Line, May 1998, p. 37.

Now, here is that same article summarized and referenced:

According to an article entitled "Sidearms Taken Away from RCMP Auxiliaries" in the May 1998 issue of Blue Line magazine, as of April 1998, British Columbia's auxiliary officers are no longer allowed to carry any sidearms. The RCMP reviewed the issue of carrying the firearms with the Attorney General's Ministry and took into consideration the change to community-based policing as one of the reasons for this decision. This decision is also in keeping with recommendations from the Oppal Report written in 1994 (37).

As you can see, the long article has been reduced to a smaller size, written in different words, and referenced by the inclusion of the article's title, the magazine's title, and the page number.

Steps in Writing a Summary

Step 1: Get organized

1. What do I need for this first step?

a) a pen or a pencil
b) a copy of Form 7.1 First Page: Resources
This is the page on which you write all the information that you will need to reference an article from which you quote or summarize and when you write the list of works cited at the end of the essay. You have already seen this page in Chapter 7. You should complete one of these pages before you take notes from an article or other source of information for your essay. This becomes the first page of your notes for every resource that you use.
If you have not read the information in Chapter 7 covering how to compose a preliminary bibliography and how to fill in Form 7.1, go back and complete that section of Chapter 7 before you go on in this chapter. It is important to write down the vital information about your article before you take notes. (Extra copies of Form 7.1 are included in Appendix A for your use.)
c) a copy of Form 8.1 Second Page: My Notes
d) additional copies of Form 8.1 if more notes are required (see Appendix A)
e) a copy of the written work, e.g., the article, the book, etc., that you are planning to use in your essay

2. What is Form 8.1 Second Page: My Notes?

This is the page on which you will write the first page of your notes before you actually write the summary or the exact words in your essay. This form is called the "second page" because it is the second page of information about this particular source of information. Form 7.1 First Page: Resources is the first page for this particular source of information.
When you finish all your notes from one source, attach them together in this order:
❒ Form 7.1 First Page: Resources
❒ Form 8.1 Second Page: My Notes (however many pages you used; remember, extra copies are in Appendix A)
This will ensure that you have all the notes from one source together.

Step 2: Reading

1. Can I start the notes yet?

No, not yet. First, read the written work (e.g., the article) without writing anything.

2. Why can't I read and take notes at the same time now?

Reading without taking notes when you read the article for the first time allows you to do the following things:
a) read without interruption to see the flow of the article and the main idea and
b) understand the written information.

Form 8.1 Second Page: My Notes

Notes taken from:

Title: ____________________

Author(s): ____________________

Page number(s): __________

Question	My Notes: Direct Quotations	My Words

Step 3: Directed reading with note taking and quoting

1. What does "directed reading" mean?

"Directed reading" means that you should complete the following steps:
- Read the passage again.
- Look for the answers to specific questions.
- Record the answers by directly quoting from the source.

2. What are the specific questions?

- Who? (Who is doing/saying something? i.e., Who is the article about?)
- To/For/About whom? (To whom or about whom are they speaking?)
- What? (What is happening/going to happen?)
- When? (When will this occur?)
- Where? (Where will it happen?/Is it happening?)
- Why? (Why is this occurring?)
- How? (How will this be done/is this being done?)
- How much? (What will this cost?)
- Any extra information required?

3. What does "directly quoting from the source" mean?

It means copying the words from the passage and putting quotation marks around them.

4. Is there any easy timesaving way to do this?

Yes. Using Form 8.1: My Notes will make this process quicker and easier.

5. What do I do first?

On Form 8.1, fill in the title of the article or book on the correct line at the top of the page. Put quotation marks around the title if it is the title of an article; underline the title if it is the title of a book.

6. What do I do next?

Fill in the names of the author(s) just as you did on Form 7.1 First Page: Resources, in the proper order, on the correct line at the top of the page.

7. What's next?

Fill in the page numbers from which you got the information.

Be honest! If you used only pages 23–25 of a book, then record only pages 23–25.

Internet printouts containing parts of books or articles will most likely not be numbered according to the page numbers of the original source. They will be numbered from 1 to the end.

For example, if the Internet source has been taken from pages 123–178 in a book, the numbers 123–178 will not usually be on the printout. Page 123 will become page 1; page 124 will be page 2, etc. You will use the new page numbers of the printout in your reference.

8. What goes in the left column of the chart?

Start by writing "Who?" in the left column, then read the example that follows in number 9, below. After that, read the article again to find out "who" is the main person or group of people discussed in the article.

9. What goes in the middle column?

The answer to the question "Who?" goes in the middle column in point form. Copy the exact words from the article and put quotation marks around them. The middle column should contain the following:

- the main points of the article that answer this particular question, copied in the exact words from the article, with
- quotation marks around the words, and
- the page numbers of the article in parentheses, ( ), if the article is more than one page.

10. Why do I put quotation marks around the copied words?

You do this to avoid **plagiarism**. Remember, you're quoting someone when you use his or her words. You want to make sure that you're acknowledging that the words are someone else's.

11. Do I put the parentheses in with the page numbers after every quotation?

If the article is only one page long, you don't have to do this because you've recorded that one page number at the top of Form 8.1. However, if your article is more than one page, you need to put all the page numbers on which each quotation appears in the parentheses after the quotation.

12. Why should I put the page number in parentheses?

When you go to insert the summary or a direct quotation into your essay, you need to know on what page(s) you found this information. This information about the page numbers gets recorded after each quotation or summary when you write the essay.

13. What goes in the right column at this point?

Nothing goes in there for now. Just write the directly quoted answers for all the main questions, one at a time.

14. What's next?

- Leave 2–3 lines.
- Put the words, To/For/About Whom?, in the left column.
- Fill in the answers to that question in the middle column.
- Repeat this procedure for all the rest of the questions:

  What?
  When?
  Why?
  How?
  How much?
  Extra information?

15. Why don't I just put all the eight questions down the side of one page at the same time and fill in the blanks?

One page may not be enough. You may need more spaces for the answer to one question than you have allotted. Do one question at a time. If you discover that you have left something out, you can go back and put it in at the correct location. Note in the Example of Form 8.1 on page 138 that some of the answers to the questions use up more lines than others.

What if . . .?

What if the article doesn't answer a question directly?

- Don't write anything in the middle space.
- Leave three to four lines blank.
- You may need to infer an answer. This does not mean that you should guess at the answer. This means you read carefully to see the meaning, which may not be obvious at first.

Example:

The sample article says, "Alberta police officers must follow new guidelines" (37). There is no specific date given in the article, but you can infer from the words "must follow"(37) that it is happening now or in the very near future, since the article was in the May 1998 issue.

How to write notes for a summary: using the first two columns of Form 8.1

Let's look at an example. Below is an article written by Morley Lymburner from the May 1998 issue of Blue Line magazine, page 37.

An example of how to begin the summary of this article, using the first two columns of Form 8.1, follows the article. The summary notes are not completed yet; this sample shows only Step 3: directed reading with note taking and quoting.

Alberta Introduces Pepper Spray Guidelines for Police to Follow

Alberta police officers must follow new guidelines when using pepper spray. Police can't spray an individual more than once or target anyone known or suspected of having respiratory problems, the Law Enforcement Review Board ruled in March.

The restrictions follow a complaint by a taxi driver who claimed a Medicine Hat officer wrongfully sprayed him while attempting to break up a fight between youths and his passengers on Jan. 31.

While the board dismissed the complaint and cleared the officer involved, recent controversies over the use of pepper spray have led the board to impose the new rules.

Two Canadian men have died over the past two years as a result of excitation delirium after being sprayed by police, the board said.

A Calgary man with a history of mental illness died in June 1996, after he was sprayed more than once. An inquiry, which cleared the officer, ruled further study on the use of pepper spray was necessary.

An Ontario man died a year earlier in a similar incident.

Kelley Gordon, an Edmonton police spokesman, said pepper spray is one of the most useful non-lethal weapons officers have.

Gordon said the force will look over the review and restrictions before forming an opinion.

"Under certain circumstances, I don't know how you could tell if someone has a breathing problem," Edmonton police Sgt. Brad Manz was quoted as saying.

Manz also said police don't normally blast someone with pepper spray a second or third time if it proves ineffective on the first attempt.

While police are taking a wait and see approach, the president of the Alberta Federation of Police Associations says he is opposed to the new regulations.

"Any sort of reticence on our behalf in dealing with violent offenders isn't good for the public, isn't good for the police officer," the local press quoted Jon Netelenbos as saying.

Netelenbos said police may choose to use physical force instead of the spray because of the board's decision.

Source: Morley Lymburner, "Alberta Introduces Pepper Spray Guideline for Police to Follow." Blue Line, May 1998, p. 37. Reprinted with permission.

Figure 8.1 Example of Form 8.1: My Notes

Notes taken from:		
Title: "Alberta Police Officers Must Follow New Guidelines"		
Author(s): Lymburner, Morley		
Page number(s): 37		
Question	My Notes: Direct Quotations	My Words
Who?	"Alberta police"	
To/For/About Whom?		
What?	"must follow new guidelines when using pepper spray" "police can't spray an individual more than once" ". . . can't . . . target anyone known or suspected of having respiratory problems"	
When?	"ruled in March" by "the Law Enforcement Review Board"	
Why?	"recent controversies over the use of pepper spray" "have led the board to impose new rules" "complaint by a taxi driver who claimed a Medicine Hat officer wrongly sprayed him while attempting to break up a fight between youths and his passengers on Jan. 31." "the board dismissed the complaint" "cleared the officer involved"	

(continued)

Why?	"Two Canadian men have died over the past two years as a result of delirium excitation after being sprayed by police" "A Calgary man with a history of mental illness died in June 1996, after he was sprayed more than once" "inquiry, which cleared the officer, ruled further study on the use of pepper spray was necessary" "An Ontario man died a year earlier in a similar incident"
How?	
How Much?	
Extra Info	"Kelley Gordon, an Edmonton police spokesman, said pepper spray is one of the most useful non-lethal weapons officers have" "'Under certain circumstances, I don't know how you can tell if someone has a breathing problem,' Edmonton police Sgt. Brad Manz was quoted as saying. Manz also said police don't normally blast someone with pepper spray a second or third time if it proves ineffective on the first attempt." "[Jon Netelenbos] the president of the Alberta Federation of Police Associations says he is opposed to the new regulations" ". . . police may choose to use physical force instead of the spray because of the board's decision"

Questions about the Notes in the Example of Form 8.1

1. **Why were the single quotation marks, ' ', used?**
   The single quotation marks, ' ', were used because regular (double) ones, " ", were used in the original.
   This is an example of a quotation within a quotation.
2. **Why were the three dots (. . .) used?**
   Three dots (called an "ellipsis") indicate that words have been left out of the original in the quotation.
3. **Should I use abbreviations when I am writing my notes?**
   Use the conventional ones, such as &, $, #, and @.
   If you make up an abbreviation, you may forget what the abbreviation means later on.

Step 4: Rewriting the copied (quoted) words using your own words

1. Do I just rewrite into a paragraph all the direct quotations I've copied to write a summary?

No—that would be quoting. You want to **summarize** the information, not quote it.

2. So, what do I do now?

a) Look at your notes in Form 8.1.
b) You will now rewrite the direct quotations, using your own words, in the right hand column. These are the words that will be used in your summary. See Figure 8.2 for an example of the rewriting of the quotations from "Alberta Introduces Pepper Spray Guidelines for Police to Follow."

Figure 8.2 Example of Form 8.1 with Rewriting of My Notes

Notes taken from:		
Title: "Alberta Introduces Pepper Spray Guidelines for Police to Follow"		
Author(s): Lymburner, Morley		
Page number(s): 37		
Question	My Notes: Direct Quotations	My Words
Who?	"Alberta police"	Police services in Alberta
To/For/About Whom?		
What?	"must follow new guidelines when using pepper spray" "police can't spray an individual more than once" ". . . can't . . . target anyone known or suspected of having respiratory problems"	Have to adhere to new use of pepper spray rules Rule #1: Only one spray per person allowed Rule #2: Don't spray anyone who you suspect has difficulty breathing
When?	"ruled in March" by "the Law Enforcement Review Board"	in March of 1998 . . .

(continued)

Figure 8.2 Example of Form 8.1: My Notes *(continued)*

Why?	"recent controversies over the use of pepper spray"	The Law Enforcement Review Board passed this rule because of controversial issues about pepper spray use.
	"have led the board to impose new rules"	
	"complaint by a taxi driver who claimed a Medicine Hat officer wrongly sprayed him while attempting to break up a fight between youths and his passengers on Jan. 31."	There has been one claim of wrongful use of pepper spray by an Albertan. The officer was not charged.
	"the board dismissed the complaint"	
	"cleared the officer involved"	
	"Two Canadian men have died over the past two years as a result of delirium excitation after being sprayed by police"	Two Canadians have died after being sprayed.
	"A Calgary man with a history of mental illness died in June 1996, after he was sprayed more than once"	
	"inquiry, which cleared the officer, ruled further study on the use of pepper spray was necessary"	
	"An Ontario man died a year earlier in a similar incident"	
How?		
How Much?		
Extra Info?	"Kelley Gordon, an Edmonton police spokesman, said pepper spray is one of the most useful non-lethal weapons officers have"	Kelley Gordon, a person who represents the police in Edmonton, stated that officers use pepper spray as a non-deadly tool.
	"'Under certain circumstances, I don't know how you can tell if someone has a breathing problem,' Edmonton police Sgt. Brad Manz was quoted as saying. . . . Manz also said police don't normally blast someone with pepper spray a second or third time if it proves ineffective on the first attempt."	Sgt. Brad Manz questioned how an officer can know about a suspect's breathing ability and said that, usually, if pepper spray is used, it is only sprayed once.
	"[Jon Netelenbos] the president of the Alberta Federation of Police Associations says he is opposed to the new regulations"	
	". . . police may choose to use physical force instead of the spray because of the board's decision"	

Step 5: Writing the summary

1. Now, can I write the summary?

Yes, write the author, title, source, date of the article, and the main topic in the first sentence of the summary. Then take the rest of the words from the right column and write them in sentences to compose your summary.

At the end of the summary, before the final period, insert parentheses, with the page number(s) in them.

The period will be the last punctuation mark, after the parentheses.

2. Key points to remember about summarizing

A summary must meet the following criteria. It must:
a) be in your own words;
b) include references: author and/or title;
c) be shorter than the original;
d) not necessarily be told in the same order;
e) not include double quotation marks; and
f) include the parentheses, at the end of the summary with the page number(s) in them.

The reference information will **always** include the page number(s) of the source. The reference information may include the surnames of the author(s), depending upon whether or not they were used in the summary. If the author's name is in the summary, do not put the name in the parentheses.

Example of a finished summary

An article entitled "Alberta Introduces Pepper Spray Guidelines for Police to Follow," in the May 1998 issue of Blue Line, states that the Alberta Law Enforcement Review Board passed a rule that Alberta police services now have to adhere to new pepper spray rules:

1) An officer can spray only one spray of the pepper spray at a suspect.

2) An officer can't spray anyone who the officer suspects of possessing problems breathing.

This new ruling was made because of controversial issues about former pepper spray use. There has been one claim of wrongful use of pepper spray by an Albertan; the officer was not charged. Two Canadians have died after being sprayed. In response to the new rulings, Sgt. Brian Manz questioned how an officer can know a suspect's breathing abilities and stated that usually, if pepper spray is used, it is only sprayed once. Furthermore, Kelley Gordon, a person who represents the police in Edmonton, supported pepper spray as a useful non-deadly tool for officers (37).

Exercise 8.2 Summarizing

Answer the following questions about the above summary:

1. What references occur in the first sentence?

   a) the title of the ______________

   b) the title of the ______________

   c) the date of the ______________

(Circle the correct answers.)

2. Where does the main topic occur?

   In the (second / first) sentence

3. What do the rest of the sentences contain?

   supporting (thesis statements / details)

   important (details / information)

4. Which words in the summary are the same as the original?
   a) people's (addresses / names)
   b) names of (cities / schools)
   c) names of (organizations / computer programs)

5. What is the other reference in this summary?

   the (last sentence / parentheses) with the

   (page numbers / words) in them at the end of the last sentence,

   before the period

6. What does each part of "(37)" represent?
   a) The parentheses, ( ), are used because they are required by the (APA / footnote / endnote / MLA) style of documentation to indicate the parenthetical referencing for that summary
   b) The number, 37, indicates the (page number / line number / paragraph number) of the article in the magazine, Blue Line.

7. Do I have to include the page number? (yes / no)

   According to MLA style rules, without the page number, the referencing (would / would not) be complete.

8. What if I leave out "(37)"?
   - You (have / have not) referenced properly.
   - The page number must be immediately (after / before) the summary, (outside / within) the parentheses, and (after / before) the period.

9. Why isn't "page" or "p." written before "37" in the parentheses?

   In the MLA style, you (do / do not) include the word or abbreviation for "page."

Writing the summary using MLA documentation

Now you are ready to write summaries of each source of information you found for your essay and any other time that you need to do a summary. When writing your summaries, make sure to do the following:

1. Write in sentences in paragraph form.
2. Use your words and not the author's words.
3. Put the following in the first sentence:
   a) the title of the article in quotation marks;
   b) the title of the source (magazine/book) with the title underlined;
   c) the date of the source;
   d) the main topic of the article; and
   e) the author's name if given.
4. Include the main points of the article in your words in the rest of the sentences.
5. Write enough information so that a person reading the summary will know what the article is about without having to read the article.
6. Link the ideas together with transitions so that the points flow logically and coherently.
7. Keep the meaning of the original words.
8. Use fewer words than the author did.
9. Do not include double quotation marks around the words.
10. End the summary with parentheses, before the last period.
11. Include the page number(s) from which you got the information inside the parentheses.
12. Don't plagiarize by forgetting to include the parentheses with the correct information at the end of the summary.

Exercise 8.3 Writing Exercise

1. Read the article from Blue Line that follows these instructions.

2. Complete the Form 8.1 Second and Following Pages: My Notes that follows, in order to write a summary of that article. (There are more copies of this form in Appendix A.)

3. Write a summary on the page provided (Form 8.2). Don't forget to reference the source with the page number in parentheses.

4. Use the list above to check that you've met all the criteria for a summary.

Officer Puts Wheels on a Safe Skating Program

In-line skating has become one of the trendiest and fastest growing activities in North America. Accordingly, the popularity of this mode of transportation has become a concern to public safety officials for many years. One member of the Ontario Provincial Police, after recognizing a solution to the problem, decided on his own initiative, to put his wheels on to save lives.

Constable Dan Marshall of the Kingston Detachment of the O.P.P. developed a handout pamphlet and training video, complete with popular music played by a local rock band, as the centre piece for his in-line skating safety program simply entitled "Safe Skate."

The Safe Skate program has proved so popular that many agencies across Canada have requested the video and accompanying material. Further recognition was received when Marshall became the recipient of the 1997 National Police Award for Traffic Safety.

"In 1995 I decided I should devote more attention to safe in-line skating," Marshall explains. "Recognizing the huge popularity of the skates in my community, I attempted to

obtain materials and any information I could so I could deliver it to area students. I had been skating myself for around eight years and was both surprised and discouraged at the lack of information geared to this activity. I came to realize that more and more people were being attracted to this sport with little or no direction."

Marshall got to work researching the issues involved and the safety concerns of skaters, pedestrians and motorists. After compiling his information and developing a training program, he then turned his attention to the community to see how the program could be distributed, expanded and financed. Eventually, a tri-fold pamphlet was produced and a short video accompanied by an interactive and short classroom demonstration.

Ten Kingston area schools were initially targeted as test schools for the prototype of the Safe Skate program. The presentations were delivered in a single day at each of the schools with five presentations each day. Over 5500 students were exposed to the material in a grueling ten-day period. By listening to feedback the program was refined further and the final presentations were ready for maximum impact and program broadening.

During the initial presentations it was found that over 80% of the students owned in-line skates. A much smaller percentage had all the proper safety equipment and an even smaller group of students wore the equipment on a regular basis. The ratios of usage of safety equipment have dramatically increased since the lecture series and the program was deemed a tremendous success by both teachers and students alike. The Safe Skate program is presently being used by over 16 police agencies across Canada and is being used and promoted by 20 safety councils and organizations.

Marshall points out that a lot of credit for the success of the Safe Skate program goes to local community groups, companies and individuals who saw the benefits of this initiative and sponsored and supported him; also, he had the help of a local school teacher and three enthusiastic students in the communications technology department. Material and financial support was given by a local Canadian Tire store and publicity was received from local radio, television, newspapers and cable companies. A local graphics company and boards of education in the area gave financial and other material support to the program as well.

In spite of all this community support, the real credit for the Safe Skate program belongs to the individual with the drive and determination to investigate, coordinate and initiate the program from concept to completion. Constable Dan Marshall was the person with the vision and drive to encourage people to skate safely.

Upon receiving the National Police Award for Traffic Safety last year, Commissioner Tom O'Grady stated that Marshall's "personal initiative and contribution to traffic safety and public education will have a lasting effect for many young in-line skaters in the future."

Source: Morley Lymburner, "Officer Puts Wheels on a Safe Skating Program." Blue Line, May 1998: 6. Reprinted with permission.

Form 8.1 Second and Following Pages: My Notes

Notes taken from:

Title: ____________________

Author(s): ____________________

Page number(s): __________

Question	My Notes: Direct Quotations	My Words

Form 8.2 My Summary of ____________________

Summary of How to Summarize

Summaries meet the following criteria:

- They are shortened versions of an original piece of writing.
- They are written in your words.
- They are written in sentence form.
- There are no double quotation marks, “ ”, around any words because the words used are your words, not the author's.
- They include the main topic and all the key points of the piece of writing being summarized.
- They keep the same meaning as the original.
- They are referenced to avoid plagiarism: title of article, title of magazine, date of publication, author(s), and page number.

To write good summaries, do the following:

1. List all the references.
2. Take notes by directly copying the answers that answer these questions: Who? To/For/About whom? What? When? Where? Why? How? How much?
3. Rewrite the answers in your own words.
4. Write the summary, meeting all the above criteria for summaries.

STEP 3B IN THE RESEARCH ESSAY PROCESS: TAKING NOTES FROM WRITTEN SOURCES AND USING DIRECT QUOTATIONS TO AVOID PLAGIARISM

In your essay, you will be using summaries and direct quotations to support your points.

1. What are direct quotations?

Direct quotations are the words that you copy from another author or source and use in your essay.

2. Should an essay include direct quotations?

Yes, a research essay should have direct quotations in it to show:
- that you have done research to back up your points;
- that the information is not just your ideas or opinions; and
- that you have not plagiarized.

Many times, it is much easier and better to use the exact words of another author than to try to put that author's words into your own words.

3. How do you include these direct quotations in your essay?

You use the same method that was discussed in the previous section of this chapter regarding how to summarize, but instead of writing the author's words in your own words, you use the **exact words** of the author.

4. Do you have to do something special to the copied words to show that these words have been written by someone else?

Yes, you do. It all depends upon the length of the direct quotation (or copied words). There are two kinds of direct quotations:

i) short quotations: one word to four typed lines of the original author's words
ii) long quotations: five or more typed lines of the original author's words

Short Quotations

5. How do you include the short quotations in an essay?

When using the MLA (Modern Language Association) style of documentation, there are four ways to do this.

6. Do the four ways have anything in common?

All four ways include the following things:

a) the direct quotation (the copied words);
b) quotation marks around the copied word(s) if the quotation is one word to four lines in length;
c) parentheses at the end of the quotation marks;
d) the page number from which the quotation came, in the parentheses;
e) a reference to the author or the title either in the same sentence as the direct quotation or in the parentheses at the end according to the MLA style;
f) integration: the direct quotations fit into the flow of the essay; and
g) a period at the very end of the sentence. (The parentheses are considered part of the sentence.)

7. What are the four ways, or methods?

i) Author's name included in the sentence
Include the **name of the author** in the sentence that contains the quotation. If the author and quotation both appear in the sentence, don't put the author's name in the parentheses at the end of the sentence. Put only the page number(s) in the parentheses.

Example:
According to Scott Rintoul, "Not all rave-goers participate in drug abuse" (48).

ii) Title of article/book included in the sentence
Include the **title of the book/article** in the sentence that contains the quotation. If the author is known, include the author and the page number in the parentheses.
However, if the author is not known, just put the page number(s) in the parentheses.

Example:
The article Raves and the Social Order states that "[n]ot all rave-goers participate in drug abuse" (Rintoul 48).

Question: Why were the square brackets, [ ], used?
You use the square brackets to show that you have **changed** something from the original. In this case, the word "Not" was capitalized in the original article. In order

to include "Not" in this sentence and have it integrated, grammatically correct, and spelled correctly, the capital would have to be changed to the lower case.

You would **not** write this:
. . . states that "Not all rave-goers participate in drug abuse " (48).

The word "Not" would not need a capital in this sentence; therefore, change it to fit the spelling of the sentence, but use the square brackets, [ ], to indicate the change.

Question: Where are the square brackets located on the computer keyboard?
This is a commonly asked question. The square brackets are found on the right side, just slightly to the left of and up one row from the ENTER key. Don't hold down the "Shift" key when using these keys.

iii) Author's name and title of article/book both included in the sentence
Include both the **author's name** and the **title of the article or book** in the sentence that contains the quotation. If you write both the author's name and the title of the article or book in the sentence, don't include them in the parentheses. Put only the page reference number(s) in the parentheses.

Example:
In the article entitled Raves and the Social Order, Scott Rintoul states that "[n]ot all rave-goers participate in drug abuse" (48).

iv) Neither the author's name nor the title of the article/book included in the sentence
Include **only the quotation** in the sentence (i.e., without the author's name or the title of the article/book). In this case, you include the surname(s) of the author(s) and the page number(s) in the parentheses. You do this because there is no mention of the author or the title in the sentence that contains the quotation.

Example
Some people think that everyone who goes to a rave is using drugs, but "[n]ot all rave-goers participate in drug abuse" (Rintoul 48).

Quoting in Succession

8. How do you reference a series of quotations, paraphrases, and/or summaries from the same source? For example, how would you reference two quotations from the same source that follow each other?

There is also a rule for writing two or more quotations in a row from one author. This is called quoting in succession.

9. How does quoting in succession work?

This rule makes your life very easy. If you summarize or quote words from the same author more than once **in a row**, all you have to put in the parentheses of the second one is the **page number** from which you got the quote.

Example:

Some people think that everyone who goes to raves is using drugs illegally; however, "[n]ot all rave-goers participate in drug abuse" (Rintoul 48). It seems that there are some people who want to make raves an "[o]rganized safe environment with the absence of drugs . . . to attempt to gain public approval and support of these events" (48).

10. What are the key components of using short quotations?

Here is a review of how to use short quotations in an essay.

- Use the copied words (quotations) in sentences.
- Use quotation marks around the copied words.
- Use parentheses immediately after the quotation.
- Always include the page number in the parentheses.
- Do not include the word or abbreviation for the word "page" in the parentheses.
- Put the proper information in the parentheses, according to the method that you used (i.e., based on what information you've included about the source within the sentence).

11. Do I have to include the parentheses, containing the author's surname (if necessary) and the page number, at the end of every quotation?

Yes. Without the parentheses and the necessary information in them, you will have **plagiarized**. The same rule applies for summaries. When you are quoting or summarizing, failing to include the necessary information in the sentence and/or within the parentheses is plagiarism, which is a serious offence.

Plagiarism

12. What is "plagiarism"?

According to the Canadian Oxford Dictionary, to plagiarize is "to pass off (the thoughts, writings, inventions, etc., of another person) as one's own " (1108).

To avoid plagiarism, do not use anyone else's words unless you put quotation marks around those words if those words are considered a short quotation and/or use the special format for long quotations and indicate where you found those words.

When you use or copy someone else's words, you are quoting that person or writing a direct quotation.

13. What are the four most important things to remember to avoid plagiarism when including short quotations?

1. Always put quotation marks, "   ", around all the words that you have copied from another person, even if it is only one word.
2. Always put parentheses, (   ), after each quote or summary.
3. Always include the correct information in the parentheses, depending upon which method you used.
4. Always include the page number(s) in the parentheses.

Long Quotations

14. What are long quotations?

Long quotations are quotations that take up **more than four** typed lines in your essay

Here is an example of a long quotation in a piece of writing:

What effect did the Great Plague have on the population of Great

Britain and Europe? According to Charles R. Swindoll, the Great Plague

> *stretched across the Old Country like a thick, drab blanket. It came as a thief in the night . . . unannounced, treacherous, silent. Before it left, 25 million people on the Isles and in Europe had died. The mortality rate was astounding. In May of 1664, a few isolated cases were reported and quietly ignored. Exactly one year later, 590 died that month. By June, it was 6, 137; July, over 17,000; August, over 31,000. Panic struck. More than two-thirds of the remaining population fled from their homes to escape death. (42)*

15. What are the key points to remember when integrating a long quotation into your essay?

a) Start a new line for the quotation regardless of how many words are on the line before it.
b) Double-space the quotation.
c) Do not place double quotation marks, " ", around the quotation.
d) Indent the quotation on both sides.
e) Integrate the quotation into the sentence.
f) Put a period at the end of the quotation and before the parentheses. This is opposite to the order used in short quotations.
g) Reference it according to the MLA Style.

In the above example of a long quotation, two things were done to show the references:

1. The author's name was included in the sentence that introduced the quotation.
2. The page number from the book was included in the parentheses.

Exercise 8.4 Quoting

1. Read the following piece of writing based on an article entitled "Coping with Shiftwork," by Sue Woolfenden, from the March 2004 issue of Blue Line.

2. Answer the questions that appear after it.

Poorly scheduled work schedules that require shift work can have an "impact on the quality of service, employee relations, job satisfaction and organizational costs" (Woolfenden 14).

> *A structured approach to scheduling will ensure that both organizational and employee priorities are not forgotten. Assess whether the schedule meets the community's needs and ensure*

> *more than just one shift pattern option is considered. Keep in mind people's health, welfare and views, as well as legal issues, and having designed a schedule, consider how it's going to be managed. (14)*

Questions about the first quotation in the example: *"impact on the quality of service, employee relations, job satisfaction and organizational costs" (Woolfenden 14).*

Circle the correct answers.

a) Was the correct format used for the direct quotation? (yes / no)

b) Why was this format used?

The quotation is less than (six / five / seven) lines of typing.

c) Are the quotation marks necessary? (yes / no)

d) Was the quotation integrated into the sentence? (yes / no)

e) Why were the parentheses placed after the quotation?

to include the (book's title / reference information)

required by the (MLA / footnote) style of documentation.

f) What would happen if you left them out? You would be penalized for (grammar errors / plagiarism).

g) What does the name in the parentheses represent? the author's (first name / surname)

h) Why is the name included in the parentheses? to (reference / delete) the quotation and tell the reader who said it

It's the (third / first) reference in the essay to that author's words.

i) What does the "14" represent? the (line / paragraph / page) number on which the quotation was found

Where does the period go? (after / before) the parentheses

Questions about the second quotation in the example, beginning with the words, *A structured approach to scheduling . . . .*

j) Was the correct format used for the direct quotation? (yes / no)

k) Why was this format used?

It is (more than / less than) four lines of typing.

l) Does it need quotation marks? (yes / no)

m) Was the quotation integrated into the sentence? (yes / no)

n) Where are the parentheses in relationship to the period?

(before / after) the period

o) What would happen if you left out the information in the parentheses?

You would be penalized for (plagiarism / lack of coherence).

p) Why is the author's surname not in the parentheses?

It is mentioned in the (sentence / parentheses), near the beginning.

This is the (second / first) reference to that author's words.

This is called "quoting in (consequence / succession)."

q) The quotation is (double- / single-) spaced.

r) Why was a new line started for the quotation even though the line before it was not completely used?

You always start the long quotation on (the same / a new) line.

s) What does the "14" represent?

It is the (page / paragraph / line) number on which the quotation was found.

16. So, how do I take my notes and not plagiarize?

It is very simple if you remember the following steps:

a) Use the forms in Appendix A: First Page: Resources; Second Page: My Notes, etc., to make your notes, just like you did for the summaries.
b) Fill in the left column with the questions and fill in the middle column with the words that you are copying from the author.
c) Put the copied words in quotation marks immediately as you write them in the middle column. This will save you wondering later if you copied the words or rephrased them in your own words. You may decide not to use these direct quotations later on, but for now, you know that the words are copied.
d) Put the parentheses after the copied words.
e) Fill in the page number from which you copied the words **every** time if the article is longer than one page. These page numbers will be invaluable to you when you write the essay.
f) Do **not** fill in the right column this time. You don't want to use your own words; you want to use the author's words.

Quotations within Quotations

17. How do you quote words that already have quotation marks around them in the original copy?

These are called quotations within quotations and are punctuated as follows:

Short quotations: … "'copied words that have double quotations around them in the original'" ( ).

Note the triple quotation marks.

Long quotations: … 'copied words that have double quotations around them in original …… .' ( )

Note the single quotation marks.

Example

In an article written by Elvin Klassen entitled "Tracking Hookers, Pimps and Johns Electronically," in the March 2004 issue of Blue Line, *Vancouver Police Department's Detective Oscar Ramos praised the database known as DISC (Deter Identify Sex-trade Consumers) (34), which he developed along with Detective Raymond Payette (34). According to Ramos, "'If you searched for a white male with a baseball cap driving a green van in PRIME [another database], . . . you would get three million hits. It is not focused. When you get into DISC, it is all about sexual predators and power'" (34). Payette added,*

> *'We can ask for a simple search such as how the john asks for an act in a certain way . . . PRIME is a great program and is built to do the data management system for a department and it does that well. DISC can search details . . . . The great success for DISC is that it gets all the cities together across Canada. That has never happened before. Focusing into sexual exploitation helps us change our thinking about what is really happening. It is not about sex.[I]t is about power.'(34)*

Summary of How to Use Direct Quotations in Essays

For examples of short quotations, long quotations, and summaries in essays, see the research essays in Chapter 7 and Appendix E to observe how these student authors integrated direct quotations, both short and long, and summarized to support and develop their thesis points. Take note that their method of referencing was the MLA style of documentation. Table 8.1 gives a summary of how to use direct quotations.

Table 8.1: Summary of Using Direct Quotations

Requirements	**Short Quotations** *(one word to four typed lines)*	**Long Quotations** *(five typed lines or longer)*
Quoted material integrated into essay's content?	Yes	Yes
Use double quotation marks?	Yes	No
Double-spaced?	Yes	Yes
Start a new line?	No	Yes
Indented from the rest of the content?	No	Yes
Referenced?	Yes	Yes
Use parentheses?	Yes	Yes
Where should the parentheses be placed?	Immediately after the end quotation marks: e.g., "copied words" ( )	After the period (usually): e.g., copied words. ( )
Where should the period be placed?	At the end of the entire sentence; not after the quotation unless it's the end of the sentence	Usually at the end of the long quotation if it is the end of the sentence

STEP 3C IN THE RESEARCH ESSAY PROCESS: TAKING NOTES FROM VIDEOS

Sometimes you may find a documentary video that fits your topic perfectly. Videos are very good sources of information. Taking notes from the videos can be a bit tricky, but the following information should help you take full advantage of these media resources.

1. How can I use a documentary video in my essay?

The documentary video could have valuable information that you can quote, paraphrase, or summarize in your essay. References to these videos can be used to introduce the topic, support a point in the body, or conclude the essay.

2. Where do you get a video for an essay topic?

Go to the library and access the card catalogue on the CD-ROM. Do a search for a video just like you would do a search for a book.

3. How many times should I watch the video?

Watch it a minimum of two times.

4. Why do I have to watch it that many times?

The first viewing allows you to get the main idea of the content and take a few notes. The second viewing allows you to take detailed notes.

First Viewing

The first viewing is like a preview of the video. You watch it and take notes without stopping the video.

Follow these steps:

a) Take lots of paper and pens or pencils with you.
b) Get organized in the room before you start the video.
c) Find the correct starting spot on the video for your particular topic. Some videos have a series of short clips.
d) Divide your paper into two columns: one for the first viewing and one for the second viewing, as shown in Figure 8.3.

Figure 8.3 Notes from Video

Title of Clip:	
Title of Video:	
First Viewing (Non-stop)	Second Viewing (Stop and Start)

e) Take another copy of **Form 7.1 First Page: Resources** from Appendix A and record the information about the video that you will need for your list of works cited (bibliography).
f) Now you are ready to start the First Viewing.
   You have the following:
   - the videotape set at the right starting point;
   - four to five pages set up for your notes, divided into two columns;
   - Form 7.1 nearby and filled out, along with a pen or pencil; and
   - the remote control.
g) Now watch the video clip without stopping it and make brief notes in the left-hand column on the note sheets.
h) As you take the notes, write on every second or third line because you want to leave room to fill in (during the second viewing) things that you missed during the first viewing. Remember: Don't stop the video during the first viewing. You are just trying to get the main points from the information.
   For examples, see the following figures, below:
   1. Figure 8.4, Notes from Video Taken During First Viewing, for the notes made during the first viewing of the video clip entitled "Raves: Dancing the Night Away."
   2. Figure 8.5, a copy of Form 7.1 First Page: Resources, filled in with the information needed about the video for the essay's list of works cited.

Figure 8.4 Notes from Video Taken During First Viewing

Title of clip: "Raves: Dancing the Night Away"	
Title of Video: CBC: News in Review, March 2000	
First Viewing (Non-stop)	Second Viewing (Stop and Start)
commentator: Knowlton Nash	
"started more than a decade ago"	
"own fashion" - white gloves - glow sticks - neon - tank tops	
"own philosophy" "all night party" "ravers getting a bad rap" "a celebration of love" "now death"	
drugs - "Special K" - "ecstasy" - cheaper	
easy to get drugs	
"nine people died" in 1999	
Nova Scotia - Port Hawksbury - Jamie Brittain - 4 pills - convulsions - collapsed (inside) - taken outside–died	
rave's name: "Temptation"	
ecstasy–drug - small pills	
"get the most out of the music and the light show"	

(continued)

Figure 8.4 Notes from Video Taken During First Viewing *(continued)*

effects - gastro - muscular rigidity - unresponsive - coma
"want to bring back raves to what they used to be" "Peace Love Unity Respect"

Source: Adapted from "Raves: Dancing the Night Away." CBC News in Review, March 2000 (video). Reprinted with permission.

Figure 8.5 Using Form 7.1 for Video
For a reminder of how to use this form, please see pages 126–129 in Chapter 7.

Form 7.1 First Page: Resources

Title of article/chapter/video clip (in quotation marks):

"Raves: Dancing the Night Away"

Name(s) of author(s): ____________________

Title of book/magazine/journal/newspaper/video (underlined):

<u>CBC: News in Review, March 2000</u>

Editor: ____________________ Edition: ____________________

City of publication: ____________ Publisher's name: ____________

Volume number: ____________

Year/date of publication:________ / ______ ______ ______
year only date month year

Page number(s): ____________

For Internet/CD ROM resources only:

Starting page number of article: _____

Number of words/paragraphs/pages in article: ________ Short/long? _____

(continued)

Figure 8.5: Using Form 7.1 for Video *(continued)*

Site/path/file address: ____________________

Date you visited the site: ______ ______ ______
date month year

For interviews only:

Name of person interviewed: ____________________

Person's job title: ____________________

Date of interview: ______ ______ ______
date month year

For videos only:

Name of producer: CBC

Production date: March 2000

Date you viewed the video: 14 May 2000
date month year

Let's examine what took place during the first viewing.

Exercise 8.5 First Viewing

Circle the correct answers in the questions below.

1. On which side of the sheet of paper did the notes get written for this first viewing?

   (left side / right side) only

2. Why were the notes written only in the left column?

   to leave room for the notes from the second viewing, which will go in the (left / right) column

3. Was the video stopped at all?

   (yes / no)

4. Why not?

   in order to get the overall picture and some of the (supporting / main) points

5. Were the notes in sentence form or in point form?

   (sentence / point) form

6. Why are there quotation marks, " ", around most of the words?

   These (were / were not) the exact words of the commentator or speaker on the video.

7. On Form 7.1 First Page: Resources, why does the first title have quotation marks around it?
   - The first title refers to the (complete video / video clip) that was taken from the entire video, which is CBC: News in Review, March 2000.
   - You (put quotation marks around / underline) short resources such as video clips, articles, songs, etc.
   - You (put quotation marks around / underline) longer resources such as an entire video, a book, a magazine, etc.

Second Viewing

1. Rewind the tape to the beginning of your clip.

2. Have the following ready on your desk:

   a) the note sheets from the first viewing—you will now record, in the right hand column, extra information about points that you wrote down during the first viewing of the video clip;

   b) about five extra blank sheets beside you to record information that you totally missed the first time;

   c) the remote control because you are going to stop and start the video as many times as you need to in order to write down all the information that you may need;

   d) pens/pencils; and

   e) a drink and snack might help too.

Figure 8.6 shows the note sheets with the first and second viewing notes completed.

Figure 8.6 Notes Taken During the First and Second Viewings

Notes from Video:	
Title of clip: "Raves: Dancing the Night Away"	
Video title: CBC: News in Review, March 2000	
First Viewing (Non-stop)	Second Viewing (Stop and Start)
commentator: Knowlton Nash	
"started more than a decade ago"	"started out as a teenage ritual of music, dancing, and love" "is [now] killing people" "almost every weekend in Canada" "almost every city across Canada" "thousands crowd the dance floor"

(continued)

Figure 8.6 Notes Taken During the First and Second Viewings *(continued)*

"rave organizers recognized its potential to draw large #'s of people to parties"	
"own fashion" - white gloves - glow sticks - neon - tank tops	
"own philosophy"	"do it for the music, the dancing, for the communal feeling of love"
"all night party"	"all night marathons of togetherness"
"ravers getting a bad rap"	
"a celebration of love"	
"now death"	
drugs - "Special K" - "ecstasy" - cheaper	make it in "bathtubs," Doctor stated "You may have been given Valium sold to you as E; therefore, the time you get the real stuff, it has adverse effects."
easy to get drugs	"getting easier to get drugs at them"
"nine people died" in 1999	"in Ontario" after taking ecstasy politicians want to close and stop raves
Nova Scotia - Port Hawksbury - Jamie Brittain - 4 pills - convulsions - collapsed (inside) - taken outside—died	will never be the same after Jamie's death Ecstasy—he took 2 before rave, bought more at rave all night party in Halifax—Exhibition Park
rave's name: "Temptation"	"promised to be the biggest all-night party Atlantic Canada had ever seen" "security checked patrons to make sure drugs didn't pass by the front doors" "a raver testified that it 'didn't matter how tight security was,' [she] always got it [ecstasy] through and 'dealt it straight out in the open'" after Jamie's death—most venues closed DJ said that there are now fewer "safe places to put on events"

(continued)

Figure 8.6: Notes Taken During the First and Second Viewing *(continued)*

ecstasy

- drug	- brightly coloured
- small pills	- illegal

"get the most out of the music and the light show"	3 a.m.–"3,000 people on the floor"

effects

- gastro	"neurological mechanisms which affect the heart"
- muscular rigidity	"feelings of intense well being and happiness"
- unresponsive	
- coma	-ravers think ecstacy = "harmless"

"want to bring back raves to what they used to be"

"Peace
Love
Unity
Respect"

Figure 8.6: Extra Notes

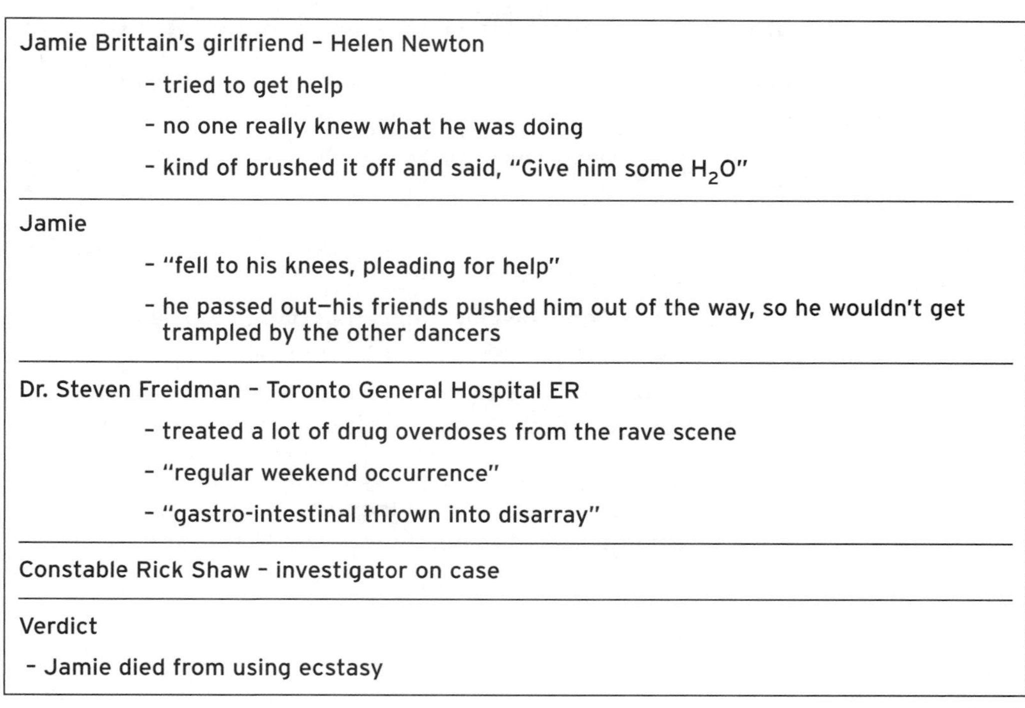

Jamie Brittain's girlfriend - Helen Newton

- tried to get help
- no one really knew what he was doing
- kind of brushed it off and said, "Give him some H_2O"

Jamie

- "fell to his knees, pleading for help"
- he passed out–his friends pushed him out of the way, so he wouldn't get trampled by the other dancers

Dr. Steven Freidman - Toronto General Hospital ER

- treated a lot of drug overdoses from the rave scene
- "regular weekend occurrence"
- "gastro-intestinal thrown into disarray"

Constable Rick Shaw - investigator on case

Verdict

- Jamie died from using ecstasy

(continued)

Figure 8.6: Extra Notes *(continued)*

Town of Port Hawksbury - "hit hard" - J. "one of town's favourite sons" - J. coached little league - played on local hockey team - he and other teammates had experimented with marijuana, but E was the new and exciting drug in town
Girlfriend - "I think he kind of did think they were harmless." - E new to Port Hawksbury - no one really knew what the effects were
D.J. - Chris Sheppard - held the 1st rave in TO in 1988 - his mantra—"Ravers love to repeat" - rave—"a celebration of love" - gathered together to "celebrate life, love, energy, compassion"
Marie Silcott - author <u>Raves in America</u>—book "everything about rave's culture greatly influenced by drugs"

Summary of How to Take Notes from Videos

In order to take good notes while watching videos that you will use in your essay, follow these steps:

1. Fill in one copy of Form 7.1 First Page: Resources from Appendix A.
2. Format your note sheets as indicated in Figure 8.3.
3. Watch the video the first time without stopping the video, but take notes on your note sheets in the left column.
4. During the second viewing, put extra notes in as needed in the right column and on extra pieces of paper. See Figures 8.5 and 8.6.
5. Put quotation marks around any words that are the exact words of the commentator or anyone speaking in the video, and write the speaker's name.

You have now completed Part 2, Step 3 in the three-part, twenty-one-step process of writing a research essay. Many of the steps in Part 3, explained in Chapter 9, are short, but they are important to do in order to write your research paper.

The Research Essay Part 3: Putting It All Together

Learning Objectives

After students have learned the content of this chapter, they should be able to do the following:

- Write a thesis statement for a research essay.
- Learn how to throw out the irrelevant information from their notes, prioritize their supporting details, and cut and paste their remaining notes.
- Proofread their drafts.
- Write a list of works cited.
- Submit a research essay that meets the submission requirements.

Learning Benefits

Learning how to write your thesis statement for your research essay will result in your research essay having a focal point throughout its entire length. It will also ensure that you have met the main requirement of a research essay and that the essay will be marked by the teacher. Being able to organize all the notes according to the thesis points will save you time when you start writing your first draft. Proofreading each draft will allow you to correct as many errors as you can so that the final copy will be clear and correct. Including your list of works cited as the last page will allow your reader to know all the sources of information that you used in the essay.

Writing a research essay is a long process, but if you take it one step at a time, start early, and use all the information in this book, you should find it a lot easier to write your research essays.

REVIEW

At this point, you have completed the following steps to writing a research paper:

Step 1: Choosing a topic
Step 2: Composing a preliminary bibliography
Step 3: Summarizing, quoting, and note taking

You can now move on to the next step, in which you will examine your notes to find three points to include in a thesis statement.

STEP 4 IN THE RESEARCH ESSAY PROCESS: EXAMINING YOUR NOTES TO FIND THREE POINTS TO INCLUDE IN A THESIS STATEMENT

Let's start by reviewing what makes up a thesis statement, so you'll know what to look for when examining your notes. The template in Figure 9.1 shows the components of a thesis statement. You can use this template to fill in these various parts.

As Figure 9.1 shows, in order to write your thesis statement, you need the following:

1. the overall topic;
2. the topic that you will use that relates directly to the overall topic; and
3. the three points that you are going to discuss in the essay.

Let's pretend that a student, Frances, wrote all the notes for the video on raves discussed in Chapter 7, in the section on Taking Notes from Videos. Let's also pretend that these are the only notes she has at this time. We will follow her through the process of writing her thesis statement for her essay based on the overall topic entitled "**A Newsworthy Event and How It Made an Impact**."

After reviewing the video, Frances decided to go with the death of the boy at the raves as her newsworthy topic.

Then, she looked over her notes that she made from the video about raves and Jamie Brittain's death and tried to find three things that were affected by his death either at the time of his death or after it occurred.

After reading her notes a few times, Frances felt that she had three impacts and listed them in her notes as follows:

Impacts of Jamie's Death

1. Jamie's death increased the public's awareness of the danger of ecstasy.
2. Jamie's friends formed the "Family".
3. Jamie's death increased ravers' desire to get raves back to the original drug-free parties.

Now, Frances has a topic and her three points that she is going to state in the thesis statement and discuss in the research essay.

These three points may change once she writes the thesis statement and/or does more research. However, this is a good starting point.

Exercise 9.1 Writing Exercise

Go back through all the notes that you have made for your topic so far. Write out the three points that you think you will discuss in your essay.

1. ____________________

2. ____________________

3. ____________________

Next, you will write a preliminary thesis statement using the Thesis Statement Template (Figure 9.1).

Figure 9.1 Thesis Statement Template

OVERALL TOPIC: ____________________

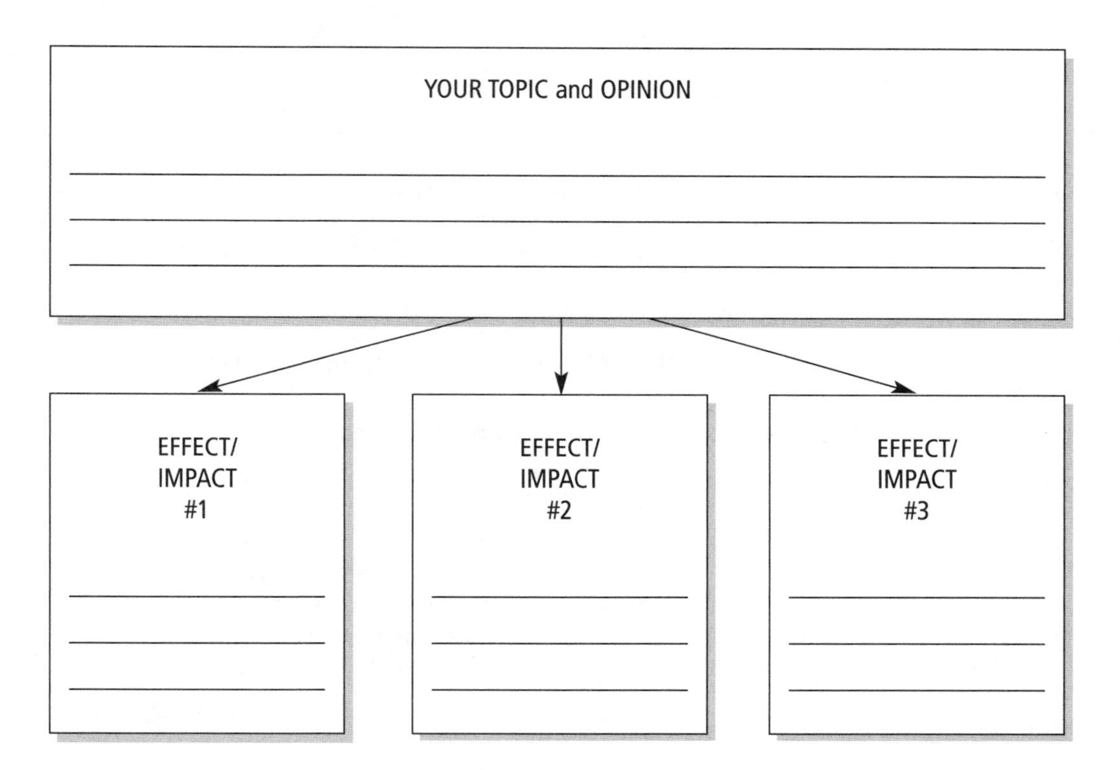

STEP 5 IN THE RESEARCH ESSAY PROCESS: WRITING THE PRELIMINARY THESIS STATEMENT

1. In the Thesis Statement Template represented in Figure 9.1, fill in your overall topic that was given to you as an assignment topic (on the top line in Figure 9.1, labelled "Overall topic"). Figure 9.2 shows the overall topic that Frances was given.

Figure 9.2 Thesis Statement Template with Overall Topic Included

OVERALL TOPIC: *A newsworthy event and how it has made an impact*

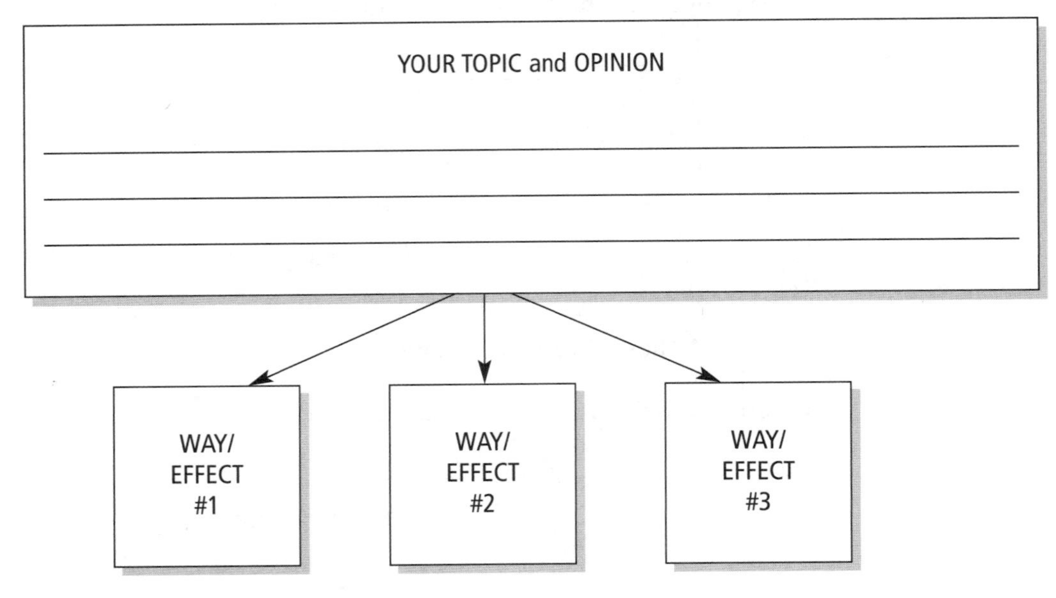

2. Fill in your own topic that directly relates to the overall topic in the top box of the Thesis Statement Template.
   As Figure 9.3 shows, Frances has chosen the death of Jamie Brittain at a rave as her topic.

Figure 9.3 Thesis Statement Template with Student's Topic Inserted

OVERALL TOPIC: *A newsworthy event and how it has made an impact*

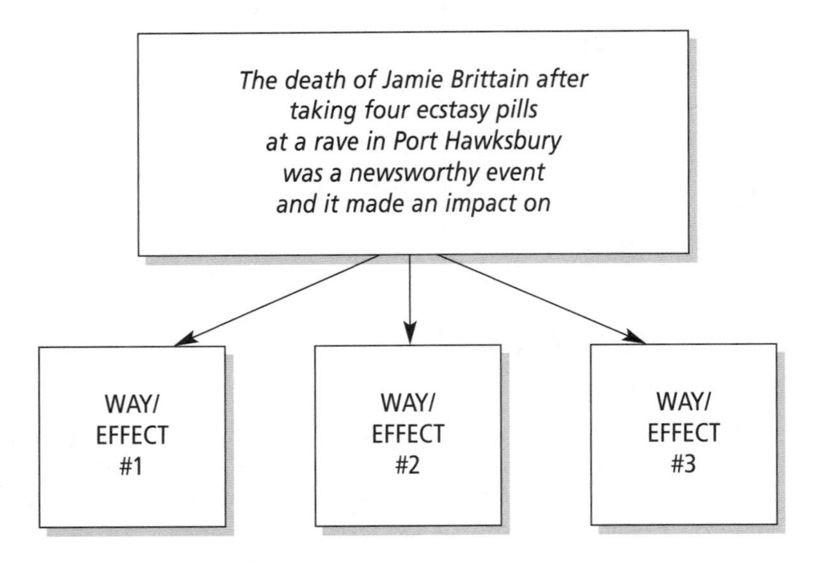

3. Now go back to Exercise 9.1 and look at your notes. Then, go back to the template (Figure 9.1) and fill in the three points that you think you might use for this essay. After viewing the video two times, Frances filled in her topic and the three points she feels she can discuss in the essay, as shown in Figure 9.4.

Figure 9.4 Thesis Statement Template with Three Thesis Points

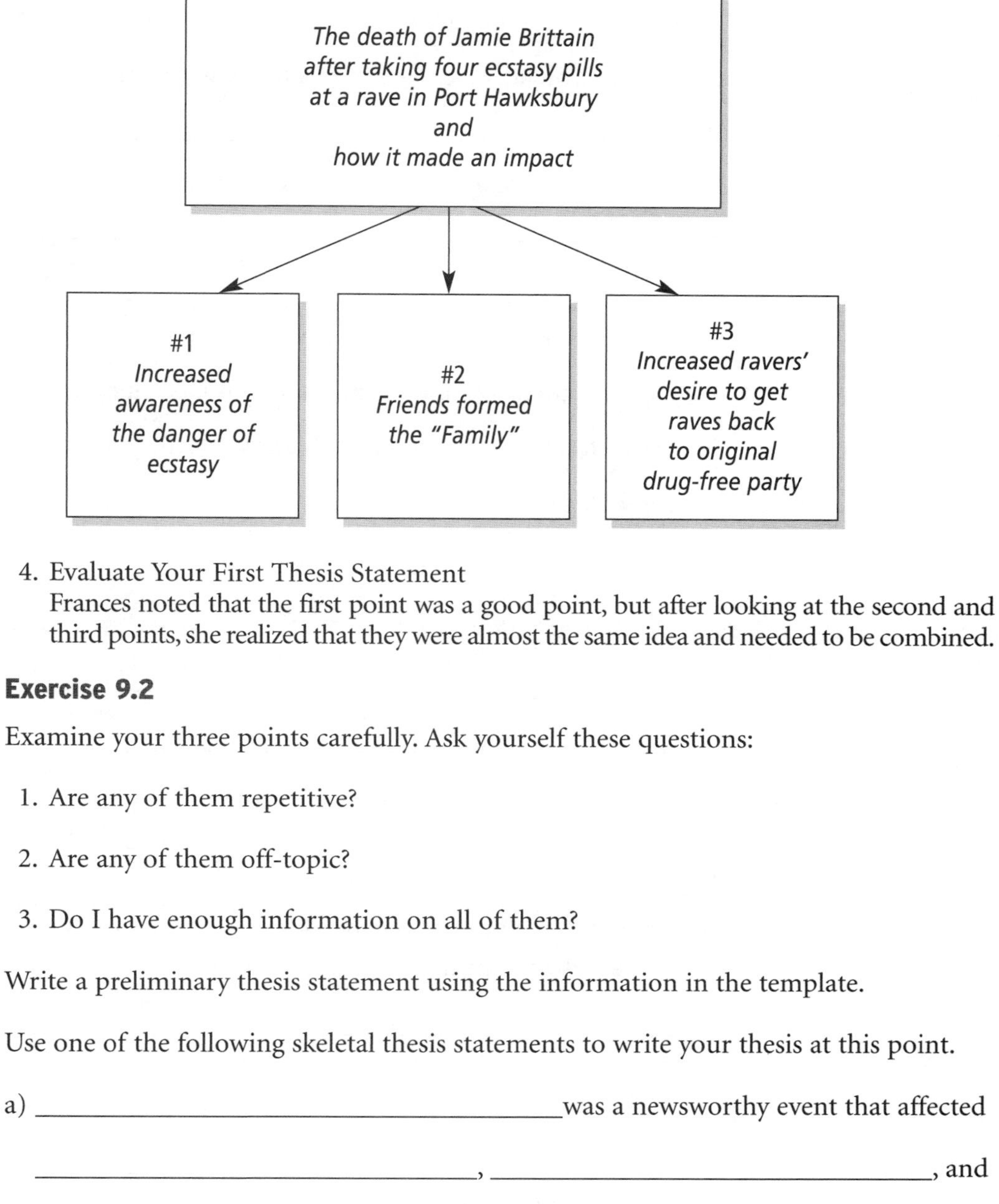

4. Evaluate Your First Thesis Statement
   Frances noted that the first point was a good point, but after looking at the second and third points, she realized that they were almost the same idea and needed to be combined.

Exercise 9.2

Examine your three points carefully. Ask yourself these questions:

1. Are any of them repetitive?
2. Are any of them off-topic?
3. Do I have enough information on all of them?

Write a preliminary thesis statement using the information in the template.

Use one of the following skeletal thesis statements to write your thesis at this point.

a) ______________________ was a newsworthy event that affected ______________________, ______________________, and ______________________.

b) ______________________ affected ______________________, ______________________, and ______________________.

c) any other variation. (Samples a and b are some of the easiest variations to use.)

At this point, Frances has a preliminary thesis statement that would read something like this:
The death of Jamie Brittain after taking four ecstasy pills at a rave in Port Hawksbury, Nova Scotia, has resulted in an awareness of the dangers of ecstasy, a desire to get raves back to their original time of love and peace, and ____________.

Exercise 9.3 Preliminary Thesis Statement

Let's examine this preliminary thesis statement.

1. How many sentences are there in this thesis statement? _____
2. What is the topic? ____
3. What are the two points in this thesis statement?

   a) ____

   b) ____

   (The third point is missing at this time.)
4. What are the three words that show that this is an opinion? _____ _____ _____

   Frances is stating her opinion that this boy's death has made an impact.

Exercise 9.4 Writing Exercise

1. Write your preliminary thesis statement here.

   ____

   ____

   ____
2. Give another student your thesis statement and ask him or her to read your thesis statement and write the answers to the following questions on the lines provided.

   a) Is your thesis statement one sentence? _______

   b) What is the topic? ______________________

   c) What are the points in the thesis statement?

   ____

   ____

   ____
3. Go back over the answers and make any necessary changes to your thesis statement.

   ____

   ____

   ____

   Frances has more work to do for her thesis statement because she needs three points.

STEP 6 IN THE RESEARCH ESSAY PROCESS: MAKING MORE NOTES FROM OTHER RESEARCH MATERIAL

Even if Frances had three points in her preliminary thesis statement at this time, she would still have to do more than watch one video to get her information for her essay. Remember that you usually have to have a minimum of three sources of information for your essay.

Therefore, now is a good time to do that extra research and obtain other resource material on your topic:

1. If you are using a video resource like CBC: News in Review, there are usually some articles in the Resource Package that accompanies each video clip. Take full advantage of these resources.
2. Look for other sources of information:
   Newspapers: Articles appeared in the newspaper when the event happened. Go to the major/local newspaper's Web site and search for the articles. You can also get back-copies of newspapers from most libraries. Ask the librarian how to search for the articles.
   The **Internet** may have some articles, too, on this topic. Remember! If you use an article from the Internet, you must **print it out**. First of all, your teacher may require that you include the article from the Internet with your essay. Secondly, because the Internet is a "fluid" source, this means that the article could be on the Internet today and gone tomorrow. Therefore, you may need a hard copy from which to take your notes.
   Magazines: Issues of Maclean's or Newsweek dated around the time of the occurrence would probably have an article on the topic. You can find copies of these magazines on the Internet, or, once again, ask the librarian to help you find back-issues.
   Other examples: books, people (experts, witnesses), pamphlets, etc.

Read the material and make notes by doing the following for **each** piece of resource material:

1. Fill in one copy of Form 7.1 First Page: Resources for each resource. (There are copies in Appendix A.)
2. Follow the guidelines previously covered in Chapter 8: quoting, summarizing, and note taking.
3. Double- or triple-space your notes so that you can cut and paste them together later under the separate points in your three-point thesis statement.
4. Write on one side of the paper.

If you are working from a printed source, such as the original article from the newspaper or a printout from an Internet source, you can simplify your work by underlining or highlighting the information that you think you might use. Use a different colour of highlighter for each point. This method saves you time because you don't have to keep including the referencing in parentheses after each note.

Example:

Let's go back to Frances and the writing of her thesis statement for her essay.

Remember, she had a thesis statement with only two points.

Now she researches other sources for supporting information.

Newspaper clippings:

Frances discovered that in May 2000, there were many articles written about raves and the problems associated with them. She was able to find the following articles:

Newspaper	Date	Title and Page Number
The Toronto Star	Wed., May 17, 2000	"Officer Likes Sound of New Raves Bill" A1, B4
The Toronto Star	Wed., May 17, 2000	" Dabblers in Ecstasy Told: Beware" B1, B4
The Toronto Star	Thurs., May 18, 2000	"Parent Wants Raves Banned" B5
The Globe and Mail	Thurs., May 18, 2000	"RCMP Seize $5-million Worth of Rave Drug" A21
The Toronto Star	Friday, May 19, 2000	"Ravers Need Facts, Inquest Told" B3
The Globe and Mail	Sat., May 27, 2000	"The Story of E" A16-17
The Globe and Mail	Sat., May 27, 2000	"It Can Kill But No One Knows How" A17
The Globe and Mail	Friday, June 2, 2000	"Raves Should Stay, Jury Recommends" A3
The Toronto Star	Friday, June 2, 2000	"Don't Ban Raves: Jury" A1, E5
The Globe and Mail	Wed., June 28, 2000	"Toronto Called Ecstasy Centre of North America" A17

Next, Frances went to the Internet and looked up some Web sites. She found four sites that were of interest to her after looking at about ten of them.

Caution: When researching from Web sites, you need to be very careful about who has written the articles on the sites. For example, Frances found that some of the articles written about the drug, ecstasy, were written by fourteen-year-old ravers who use the drug. There was interesting information, but none of it was grounded in medical or scientific knowledge.

After deciding which Web site articles to use, Frances printed them out and made notes on them in the same way she made notes when she quoted and summarized from her other sources.

Now, Frances has notes from the following sources:

1. the video on her topic;
2. the resource package that came with the video;
3. the newspaper clippings; and
4. the Web sites.

Frances is ready to go on to the next step.

STEP 7 IN THE RESEARCH ESSAY PROCESS: WRITING THE SECOND THESIS STATEMENT

After doing all this research, Frances read her original thesis statement again. She decided that she didn't like the thesis statement because she was not happy with the third point of her preliminary thesis statement.

Now that she has read the resource package provided with the video, the newspaper articles, and the Web site information, she has decided that she is going to change her focus from the death of Jamie to raves themselves because she thinks the topic of Jamie's death is too narrow. He was not the only young person to die from an overdose or use of ecstasy. Furthermore, she was able to find three points to discuss about the impact the publicity about raves has had on society.

Now she has enough to write a **second thesis statement**.

Frances' First Attempt at the Second Thesis Statement

Topic *Because raves*
Opinion *have become a focus of attention in the news, the general public is now aware of*
Three points
- *raves themselves,*
- *the drug, ecstasy, and*
- *the dangers of raves*

Reminder: Recall that **parallelism** was covered in Chapter 1.
Example:

*I like **apples** and **peaches**.*

The two items in the series, "apples" and "peaches," are both one word; they are both nouns; and, importantly, they are both plurals, which keeps them consistent with one another. Therefore, this sentence contains parallelism and is correct.

Evaluation of the second thesis statement, first attempt

☑ The topic fits into the general topic.
☑ There are three points now.
☒ The three points are not parallel.

Frances' Second Attempt at the Second Thesis Statement

Topic *Because raves*
Opinion *have become a focus of attention in the news, the general public is now aware of*
Three points
- *what goes on at raves*
- *where ecstasy fits in, and*
- *the results of using ecstasy*

Evaluation of the second thesis statement, second attempt:

☒ The three points are still not parallel.

Frances' Third Attempt at the Second Thesis Statement

This time, Frances will just work on writing the three points in parallel form.
It is easier if you list the central point of each:
- *raves*
- *ecstasy*
- *death*

Having done that, she can now put them into a parallel construction that gets her meaning across:
- *the rave phenomenon*
- *the drug, ecstasy*
- *the untimely deaths*

The three points are finally parallel!
At this point, Frances can write the final thesis statement.

Exercise 9.5 Writing Exercise

List your three points for your thesis statement, one underneath the other, on the following lines. Check to see if they are parallel. Review Chapter 1 and the information above. Rewrite your points as many times as you need to in order to get them parallel. Have someone check your final list for parallelism.

____

____

____

____

____

____

____

____

____

____

____

____

STEP 8 IN THE RESEARCH ESSAY PROCESS: FINALIZING THE THESIS STATEMENT

Frances now puts the topic, the opinion, and the three points together in one sentence that has parallelism in it.

> *Because raves have become a focus of attention in the news, the general public is now aware of the rave phenomenon; the drug, ecstasy; and the untimely deaths within the teen culture.*

It does not necessarily take that much effort to write your thesis statement. It all depends on the amount of research you do before you write the thesis statement and how much practice you have had writing them.

Exercise 9.6 Writing Exercise

Write your final thesis statement here.

____

____

____

STEP 9 IN THE RESEARCH ESSAY PROCESS: GETTING THE THESIS STATEMENT APPROVED BY THE TEACHER

If your thesis statement is not correctly written, then your essay is in jeopardy. Getting it approved by your teacher can ensure that you're on the right track. It does not take long to do this step.

1. Write out the thesis statement on a piece of paper.
2. Double- or triple-space the writing.
3. Arrange to meet with the teacher at a time and place that is convenient to both of you.
4. Take the following to your meeting:
   - the thesis statement;
   - the notes that you have taken from all your resources;
   - copies of any of your resources: books, newspaper articles, printouts from Web sites, etc.;
   - pen/pencil; and
   - your outline of the essay if it is done or partially done. This would be an added bonus to the discussion.
5. Meet with the teacher.

   If the statement you have written is a good thesis statement, then off you go to write the research essay. If the thesis statement needs some work, then you will get some advice as to what you need to do. Then, it is up to you to go and do more work and resubmit the thesis statement for the teacher's approval. The teacher is not going to write the thesis statement for you.

Caution: Don't be like the student, John, in the following scenario:

John's class was given the topic "A Canadian Who Made a Difference." John wrote a sentence about a woman and how she had made a contribution to society; he asked the teacher to see if he had done it correctly and to give him approval for it before he wrote the essay. This sentence was not approved as a thesis statement because it did not have three points written in parallel form, nor did it address the topic. John tried writing another thesis statement and came to the teacher. Once again, the thesis statement was not approved. Finally, after three tries and a lot of hard work by John, he had an approved thesis statement that responded to the topic and included three ways that the woman had contributed to Canadian society. John left the teacher's office with the approved thesis statement.

On the essay's due date, John handed in an essay that did not include the approved thesis statement; he had used parts of the first one he had submitted and some other information! There was only one point in the thesis statement, and the essay did not respond to the topic or type of essay. He had written a biography of the woman's life instead of stating three ways that this woman had made a contribution to society.

When John received a failing grade for his essay, he was very confused and upset. When he met with the teacher to discuss the mark, he told the teacher that he didn't like the thesis statement that had been approved, so he had asked his girlfriend to write one for him. The student chose to use the girlfriend's thesis statement after all the work that he had done to finally have an approved thesis statement. This choice resulted in a very low, failing mark because the writing was not an essay; it was a biography; and it did not have a three-point thesis statement that responded to the topic.

Upon completion of this step (i.e., getting your thesis statement approved by your teacher), you have now completed the following steps in the research essay writing process:

1. Choosing a topic
2. Composing a preliminary bibliography
3. a) Summarizing
   b) Taking notes from written sources and using direct quotations to avoid plagiarism
   c) Taking notes from videos
4. Examining your notes to find three points to discuss
5. Writing the preliminary thesis statement
6. Making more notes from other research material
7. Writing the second thesis statement
8. Finalizing the thesis statement
9. Getting the thesis statement approved by the teacher

You are off to a great start! You have a topic, your notes, and your approved thesis statement. Now it's time to get your notes organized before you write the essay. Let's move on to the next steps.

STEP 10 IN THE RESEARCH ESSAY PROCESS: SORTING THROUGH AND THROWING OUT SOME OF THE RESEARCH

This does not mean throwing out the teacher-approved thesis statement like John did in the above story. It means throwing out all the notes you have taken that do not directly support your three points, and it is one of the hardest things to do.

You have just spent hours researching and making notes. You have all this "great stuff" that you want to put into the essay. You feel that everything is important.

You have to keep two things in mind when doing this step:

1. the **length** of the paper that you are required to do

If the teacher says it is to be three double-spaced typed pages, then you need to stay within this framework.

2. the font and point (font) size required.

You are usually going to type in a font and point size identical to what the subject outline is typed in. This font is usually Times New Roman, point size 12 in Microsoft Word software; this is the font and point size that most computers automatically default to, and that is what the teacher will expect.

Some students who won't throw out some of their information and have too much information to fit into the required number of pages will reduce the point size to fit into the required number of pages. They change the point size to a size that is extremely small and very hard to read.

Other students haven't done enough research and haven't got enough to write about to fill the required length, so they change the point size to something that looks like a primary grade story book size or bigger, just to fill up the pages.

Most teachers will not accept essays that are typed in a point size that is smaller or bigger than that required for the assignment.

How to throw out

1. Read all your notes again.
2. Use a highlighter to highlight anything that does not relate **directly to or specifically support** one of your three points. Don't be tempted to put it into the essay.

Then, move on to Step 11, cutting and pasting the remaining notes onto sheets with the corresponding headings.

Step 11 in the Research Essay Process: Cutting and Pasting

The next step in the process involves cutting and pasting the research notes into the correct thesis statement points. You can cut, paste, and copy on the computer, but it is easier to work from printouts or the original copy.

Here is a suggested method for doing this. Have the following ready:

- a large table or working space—even the floor will do
- lots of scrap paper
- scissors
- tape or glue
- markers: three different colours—one for each point
- a file folder

Procedure

1. Label the file folder as "Extra Info" and put it to the side of the table.
2. Take three pieces of paper and write one thesis statement point on each one in **big bold letters** with the markers. Use a different colour for each point.

   Example
   For the essay on raves, there would be the following sheets of paper:
   - *one sheet with "The Rave Phenomenon" written on it*
   - *one sheet with "The Drug, Ecstasy" written on it*
   - *one sheet with "The Untimely Deaths" written on it*

   These pages are to help you stay focused on your three points and to act as headings or title pages for all the notes that you are going to add to the piles.

3. Place these three sheets of paper a little distance from each other on a large table or the floor.
4. Place a blank piece of scrap paper just below each of the three sheets of paper. These pieces of scrap paper act as the "catch basin" for the notes.
5. Take your notes from one of your resources (e.g., Form 8.6: the notes from the second viewing of the video about raves) and read each point.
6. Cut out each point with scissors and do one of two things with that point:
   a) Lay this point on top of the scrap piece of paper below the point that it will support.
   This is the "cut" part of this step.
   Don't paste or tape the points yet. That happens later.

OR

   b) Put this point into the file folder marked "Extra Info" because it doesn't relate to the points. These will be the ones you highlighted previously.
   This is the "throwing out" part. You are not actually throwing the information out; you are putting it aside. You probably won't use it, but just to be safe, you keep it for now.
   However, you keep these points away from your piles of the three thesis statement points and out of sight.

7. Do this for every point in every note that you have taken.
   If you have done your notes properly, you not only have the information, but you also have the references and page numbers recorded in your notes.
   If you don't have the page numbers and references recorded, put them onto each piece of paper **now**.
   Otherwise, you will not remember what the resource is later when it comes time to write your essay. Remember, the information in the parentheses is crucial to avoid plagiarism. Keep in mind that you **must also reference summaries**.
8. You should have four piles now: one for each of the three points and a pile of notes in your Extra Info file folder.

STEP 12 IN THE RESEARCH ESSAY PROCESS: PRIORITIZING THE SUPPORTING DETAILS

1. What does "prioritizing" mean?

putting information or tasks into the order of their importance

2. What do I prioritize?

the supporting details for each thesis statement point

3. How do I do that?

a) Go to the pile of notes that you have on the piece of paper below or near your first point.
   e.g., In the essay about raves, it would be the pile of notes Frances has under the title "The Rave Phenomenon."
b) Spread the individual notes for this point out so that you can see them all.
c) Read the notes again and consider whether or not **each one** can directly support the first point of the thesis statement.
d) Once again, put any that do not support the first point of the thesis statement aside into the file folder.
e) Take the remaining notes and put them into one of the following orders:
   i) the least important to the **most** important
   ii) an order that shows that the points are of equal value
f) Get some more pieces of scrap paper.
g) Tape or paste the notes from this thesis statement point onto the scrap paper in the order that you have decided to present them.
   This is the "paste" part of the "cut and paste" step.
h) You might want to number the notes in order once you have taped them down.
i) Number the pages of notes for point number one.
j) Staple all those scrap pages with the taped/pasted and ordered notes for point one to the piece of paper that has the words for point one written on it.
k) You now should have all the notes for point one stapled together and in the order that you want to present them.
l) Repeat this process for the second and third points in the thesis statement.
m) You should now have three sets of notes stapled together: one for each point.

STEP 13 IN THE RESEARCH ESSAY PROCESS: COMPOSING THE OUTLINE

Writing the outline involves the following process:

1. Refer back to Chapter 5: The Five-Paragraph Essay Model for information on the outline.

2. Use that same outline format to write the outline for the research paper.

3. Why should I use that same outline format?

The research paper is based on the five-paragraph essay model. You use the same outline for every essay.

4. Which part of the outline should I fill in first?

the **thesis statement**

5. Which part should I fill in second?

the revisited **thesis statement** in the conclusion

Example

For the essay about raves, Frances might use this for the revisited and restated thesis statement in the conclusion:

> *Since there was a great deal of publicity about raves in the media during the months of May and June 2000, the public is more knowledgeable about the all-night raves; ecstasy, the killer drug; and two teens' early deaths.*

Questions about this revisited thesis statement:

a) Were the same words from the original thesis statement used in the revisited thesis statement?

   No

b) Were the three points included?

   Yes

c) Are the points in this sentence parallel?

   Yes

Ask yourself these questions when you write your revisited thesis statement for your final paragraph. The answers to those questions about **your** thesis statement need to be the same as the answers above.

6. What do I do third?

Write the **body** in the outline for the essay.

- Fill in the key words for each thesis point.
- Point 1 goes in paragraph 2; point 2 goes in paragraph 3, etc.
- Write your notes for each point in the spaces for each of the three corresponding body paragraphs: paragraphs 2, 3, and 4.
- Remember that the more details you include in the outline, the better your final essay will be. It will also be much easier to write the essay.

This is the same thing that you did for the five-paragraph essay and the process essay.

7. What do I do fourth?

Now is the time to be creative. You write the **introduction** next. Decide how you are going to get the reader's attention. We discussed ways to do this in Chapter 5.

Examples:

Use a headline:

A headline in <u>The Toronto Star</u> *on Thursday, May 18, 2000, read as follows: "Parent wants raves banned" (B5). This was only one of the many headlines about raves during the months of May 2000 and June 2000 in the Toronto papers.*

Use a question:

What is a rave? What is this drug, ecstasy? Why did those two young men die at the raves? These questions may have been going through people's minds as they either watched the news or read the papers during May and June 2000.

Note: The questions in the above sample introduction were asked in an order that duplicates the order of the three points stated in the thesis statement that will come after the introduction, and the same order that they will be dealt with in the body.

8. What do I do next?

Write the **conclusion**.

If you used a quotation in the introduction, then come back to it. For example, if using the above headline about raves, you might say the following in the conclusion:

The media brought raves to our attention through its startling headlines and media coverage.

In other words, if you raised questions in the introduction, then answer them in the conclusion.

9. What do I do last?

- Fill in all the main **transition** words and phrases to link everything together.
- These go at the **beginning** of each paragraph.

STEP 14 IN THE RESEARCH ESSAY PROCESS: WRITING THE FIRST DRAFT

Here's what you need to do to write the first draft:

1. Type out the first draft of the essay using the outline.
2. For this first draft, just type without stopping.
3. Integrate the quotations/summaries/paraphrases into the essay.

Remember to include all the references for each one as you write.

Note: Refer to the research essays in Appendix E and Chapter 7 for examples of how to integrate quotations, paraphrases, and summaries.

4. Double- or triple-space this first draft because you are going to edit it after it is finished. It is much easier to do this when the essay is double-spaced or triple-spaced.
5. Save the essay on two separate disks or a disk and the hard drive.

STEP 15 IN THE RESEARCH ESSAY PROCESS: PROOFREADING THE FIRST DRAFT

Proofreading your first draft includes the following:

1. Put the essay through the spell checker and grammar checker after you have saved it.

Pay attention to every point highlighted.

The spell checker and grammar checker are only as good as the people using them. You must choose the correct spelling, the proper grammatical correction, or the right punctuation mark. These programs only give you the alternatives. One of these is to ignore the comment. Be sure to use your dictionary and grammar guide if you aren't sure which option to use. Remember, the spell checker does not pick out every error. e.g., If you type "fro" for "for", the spell checker will not highlight the word "fro" because "fro" itself is a word.

2. Be sure to save the changes on the word processor.

3. Print out the essay.

Why?

Very few people can proofread well from the screen of a computer. Also, remember that the spell checker and grammar checker don't point out all errors, so you must carefully proofread all words and punctuation on a printout.

4. Wait an hour.

Remember, when you are writing something like this, you become too "close" to the content, and you tend to read what you think should be written instead of what is really written down. Giving yourself a space of time allows you to take a break and let your mind rest for a bit. You are able to look at the written work with a fresh mind.

If you waited longer, like overnight, you would find more errors than you would if you waited only one hour.

5. Proofread the essay from the printout. It is not possible to see all the errors on the screen. You will find more when you print the essay.

6. What should I look for when I am proofreading?

Ask yourself these questions:

a) Is each grouping of words a **sentence?**
b) Does the writing **flow** from one thought to another?
c) Do I need to include more **transitions** to make it flow?
d) Did I use the **correct words**?
   Look carefully at words that are easily mistaken for each other:
   e.g., It's, its; their, there; for, fro, etc.
e) Is the **punctuation** correct?
f) Are all the sentences that include a series of things written in **parallel** form?

STEP 16 IN THE RESEARCH ESSAY PROCESS: WRITING THE SECOND DRAFT

To write your second draft, do the following:

1. Note that this is **still a draft.**
2. Go back into the essay on the computer and correct all the errors that you noticed when you proofread the printout.
3. Put the essay through the spell checker and grammar checker again.
4. Pay close attention to any points that these tools highlight.
5. Print out this second draft.

STEP 17 IN THE RESEARCH ESSAY PROCESS: WRITING THE LIST OF WORKS CITED

The next step is compiling and writing the list of works cited.

1. Now it is time for a bit of a break.
2. Collect your Form 7.1 First Page: Resources pages from all your different resources that you used to do this essay.
3. Remember that file folder with the notes that you didn't use in the essay? Go back to it now and put all the Form 7.1 pages from the resources that you didn't use into this file folder. These **will not** go into the list of works cited.
4. Take the remaining pages for the resources that you actually mentioned in your essay either in a sentence or in parentheses.
5. Put these pages in **alphabetical order** according to the first author's surname or the first word in the title if no author is named. Exclude the word "the" at the beginning of the title if it is used.
6. Consult Appendix B: MLA Documentation Style for how to create an MLA style list of works cited.

   Also, refer to the lists of works cited done for all the research essays in Chapter 7 and Appendix E.

   You will write each one of your resources that you used into your list of works cited. There are specific orders and specific punctuation marks that need to go into each entry. To ensure that you have done these correctly, consult Appendix B.

   The format for the list of works cited is unique as well. The first line of each entry starts at the margin, but the second and following lines of each entry are indented.

   Study and follow the information in Appendix B and in the sample essays before you start to write your entries.
7. Start a new page.
8. Entitle it "Works Cited."
9. List each resource **that you used in the essay** in this list of works cited in the proper order and format, as outlined in the MLA guide in Appendix B.
10. Also put this list through the spell checker and grammar checker.
11. Proofread it for every period and other punctuation mark that must go in it. Make sure that there is a period at the end of each entry.
12. Check that all book, newspaper, and magazine titles are typed in normal font and underlined. The titles of the articles should have quotation marks, "   ", around them.
13. Print out the list of works cited and include it with the essay as the **last** page.

STEP 18 IN THE RESEARCH ESSAY PROCESS: ALLOWING TIME TO ELAPSE

If at all possible, you should take another step, which is allowing time to elapse.

Tick . . . tock . . . tick . . . tock . . . . Allow at least one hour to pass again. The more time that you allow to elapse between printing out and proofreading, the more errors you will find. If you have planned well in advance, you can allow 24 hours to go by.

STEP 19 IN THE RESEARCH ESSAY PROCESS: PROOFREADING THE SECOND DRAFT

Proofread the printout of the second draft of the essay and the list of works cited again, following these suggestions:

Take a pencil and point it at each word as you read it.

Read the essay **out loud,** word for word. Be sure to read right to the **end** of a sentence.

Point with a finger to each word and read it out loud.

Read the essay **backwards**, starting at the last word and work towards the first word. This requires great concentration, but it certainly pays off in the end.

Save the corrections.

STEP 20 IN THE RESEARCH ESSAY PROCESS: WRITING THE FINAL COPY

1. The time has finally come for you to write and print out your final copy. Take your last corrected printout and use it as a reference to correct all the errors in the essay (on screen).
2. Be sure to correct the list of works cited, too.
3. Print out the essay and the list of works cited. However, before you actually press "print," make sure you've read Step 21, below!

STEP 21 IN THE RESEARCH ESSAY PROCESS: PREPARING THE ESSAY TO MEET SUBMISSION REQUIREMENTS

The last step in the process of writing a research essay involves a final check to make sure that you've covered everything. Check your essay to see that it meets the requirements for submission that are outlined in your subject outline, your course syllabus, or the assignment instruction sheet. Below are some common requirements. Use this list as a checklist for your essay.

The essay must

- be on **white** paper: $8^1/_2$ inches x 11 inches.
- be double spaced.
- be typed in a font such as Times New Roman or the one required by your teacher in your assignment instructions or your subject outline.
- be typed in a **point size** that is very easy to read. Use the same size as the one used for your subject outline, your course syllabus, or assignment instructions: usually 12.
- be typed in black ink. (Colours are great for graphics, not essays. Essays typed in colours other than black are hard to read and will probably not be acceptable. Refer to your subject outline, course syllabus, or assignment instructions.)

- have a simple title page with the following on it in the middle if your teacher/professor asks for a title page as part of the submission package:
  Your Name
  The Title of the Essay
  Your Class Number
  The date
- include the marking scheme from your assignment's instruction package immediately after the Works Cited page if the teacher requests this.
- include the printouts of anything that you used in the essay from the Internet, arranged in the same order that they are listed in your list of works cited: alphabetical by author or title if the author is missing.
- be stapled together before you hand the essay in. Enclose the essay in a duotang folder if it is too thick to be stapled together.
- See the section in your subject outline, syllabus, or assignment instructions entitled "Submission Requirements" to make sure that your finished essay will be accepted.

Refer to the research essays in Chapter 7 and in Appendix E for good examples of research papers and their lists of works cited.

You've just finished a big project! If you have: followed the information in Chapters 7, 8, and 9, and Appendices B and E; adhered to the information given to you in class either through a lecture or assignment; started your research early and obtained the minimum number of appropriate references; had your thesis statement approved by the teacher early on in the process; and sought help from the librarian, teacher, or other resources during this process, you should be able to submit a good research essay.

CHECKLIST: STEPS IN WRITING A RESEARCH ESSAY

Use the following checklist as you go through the process of writing a research essay.

Check off each step as you complete it. Remember that this will take a fair amount of time, but your hard work will pay off in the end. You will have written a research essay. Congratulations!

1. Choose a topic.
2. Compose a preliminary bibliography.
3. a) Summarize.
   b) Take notes from written sources and use direct quotations to avoid plagiarism.
   c) Take notes from videos.
4. Examine your notes to find three points to discuss.
5. Write the preliminary thesis statement.
6. Make more notes from other research material.
7. Write the second thesis statement.
8. Finalize the thesis statement.
9. Get the thesis statement approved by the teacher.
10. Sort through and throw out some of the research.
11. Cut and paste the research.
12. Prioritize the supporting details.
13. Compose the outline.
14. Write the first draft.
15. Proofread the first draft.
16. Write the second draft.
17. Write the list of works cited.
18. Allow time to elapse.

19. Proofread the second draft.
20. Write the final copy.
21. Prepare the essay to meet the submission requirements.

Summary

After you have written a thesis statement for your topic that meets the criteria of a three-point thesis statement, you should do the following:

- Get the thesis statement approved by the teacher.
- Throw out any irrelevant material.
- Cut and paste the remaining information onto sheets of paper: one for each point.
- Write an outline of your essay based on the five-paragraph essay style.
- Write at least two drafts and proofread each one from printouts.
- Write a list of works cited that follows all the rules for MLA documentation.
- Submit a final copy of the essay that has been proofread and a list of works cited that meets all the submission requirements.

It's a long process to write a research essay. So start early, don't be afraid to seek help, and apply yourself to the task. Good luck!

The Comparison/ Contrast Essay

Learning Objectives

After students have learned the content of this chapter, they should be able to do the following:

- Define a comparison/contrast essay.
- Apply the five-paragraph essay model to the comparison/contrast essay.
- Organize their discussion points in a logical and coherent manner
- Supply supporting details to back up their points.

Learning Benefits

We are constantly comparing and contrasting things: movies, books, teachers, and so on. Being able to compare and contrast things logically and coherently will allow you to state your points clearly so that they will be accepted by your readers or listeners. Also, having support for your points will give you further credibility.

In law enforcement, comparing and contrasting things is very common. During investigations, officers are always looking for similarities and differences in crimes to discover if there are any links to other cases. For example, consider serial murder cases, copycat cases, store robberies, etc. The discovery of one tiny commonality between cases might end up solving more than one incident. Knowing how to look for commonalities and differences—i.e., how to compare and contrast—is an important skill.

DEFINITION OF THE COMPARISON/CONTRAST ESSAY

The comparison/contrast essay should follow the five-paragraph essay model, just like the process essay described in Chapter 6 and the research essay described in Chapters 7 to 9. It is an essay that explains the differences and/or the similarities between two subjects. For example, you could compare two movies, two guns, two books, two services, or two aptitude tests, just to name a few possibilities. (Note: the word "compare" can be used to describe the process of both comparing and contrasting. It will be used this way sometimes in this chapter.)

If you were comparing two books (the two subjects of your essay), you might discuss the differences between or the similarities of these three aspects of the books:

a) the introduction;
b) the voice (first person/third person narration); and
c) the theme.

In a comparison/contrast essay, you can discuss a combination of differences and similarities in the one essay.

Examples:

Here are some combinations for comparison/contrast essays for your two subjects:

a) three differences
b) three similarities
c) two differences and one similarity
d) two similarities and one difference

1. What would some thesis statements look like for the above combinations?

For three differences—example (a), above:

Subject A and Subject B have three distinct differences: (point 1); (point 2); and (point 3).

For three similarities—example (b) above:

Subject A and Subject B are similar in (point 1); (point 2); and(point 3).

For two differences and one similarity—example (c) above:

Subject A and Subject B are different in (point 1) and (point 2), but they are similar in (point 3).

For two similarities and one difference—example (d) above:

Subject A and Subject B are similar in (point 1) and (point 2), but they are different in (point 3).

2. What are the steps involved when writing a comparison/contrast essay?

a) Choose a topic carefully. The best idea is to choose one with which you are familiar.
b) Pick your two subjects. You will need to prove that they have similarities and/or differences.
c) Decide which subject you will refer to first in each example.
d) List all the similarities of these two topics on one side of a piece of paper.
e) List all the differences between these two subjects that you can think of on the other side of the paper. This is just like the free writing exercise discussed in previous chapters.
f) Examine your lists carefully to see which is stronger: your similarities or your differences. Remember that you can have a combination of the two as well.

g) Narrow your points down to three points because you will discuss only three major points, regardless of how long your essay is supposed to be.
h) List your three points across a piece of paper, as in Figure 10.1, and write in as many examples as you can to support each point.

Figure 10.1 Three Points of Comparison

Essay topic: Comparing ________ (subject #1)	and ________ (subject #2)	
Point 1	Point 2	Point 3
________	________	________
________	________	________
Similar / Different (Circle one.)	Similar / Different (Circle one.)	Similar / Different (Circle one.)
Supporting details	Supporting details	Supporting details
________	________	________
________	________	________

i) Write your outline. See Chapters 4, 5, and 6 for a refresher on how to do this, if you need to. The outline used for this essay is the same outline that you used for the five-paragraph essay, the process essay, and the research essay.
j) Write your essay from your outline. Remember to keep the subjects in the proper order. See the sample essays below. In the first sample essay, Law and Security Administration is discussed first, then Police Foundations Programs.
   In the second sample essay, which discusses Lucy Maud Montgomery and the fictitious character, Anne of Green Gables, the examples related to Montgomery always come before the ones referring to Anne for each supporting detail, in order to keep the material consistent and to help the reader remain oriented as he or she is reading. This allows the reader to follow your argument more easily, and means your essay will be more effective in making its point.
k) Be sure to remember to proofread your essay thoroughly (and more than once!) before submitting it.

Exercise 10.1 Group Work

1. Form a group of three or four people.
2. Choose one of the topics listed below.
3. Decide on two subjects that you could discuss about that one topic.
4. Decide which of the above four combinations of writing a comparison/contrast essay you want to use.

5. Write a thesis statement for your topic that clearly states the following:
   a) the two subjects;
   b) the three points that are going to be compared; and
   c) whether the points are similarities or differences.

Use the section below to write your group's answer.

Topics
Compare one of the following:
a) two TV sitcoms (or other similarly formatted TV shows)
b) two movies
c) two movie actors/actresses
d) two schools
e) two countries: e.g., Canada and the United States, which are very similar but also have some major differences; or Canada and a European or Asian country.
f) two geographical locations, such as the west coast and the east coast of Canada
g) two sports
h) Don Cherry and another sports commentator
i) two golf courses
j) any other topic approved by your teacher

*Topic:*____

Subject 1, ________________, which will be compared to Subject 2, ________________.

Which combination? (Check off the one that your group is going to use in the thesis statement.)	_______ three differences
	_______ three similarities
	_______ two differences and one similarity
	_______ two similarities and one difference

Points 1 ____

2 ____

3 ____

Write your thesis statement here for your comparison/contrast essay. Make sure the points in the statement have a parallel construction.

____

____

____

____

SAMPLE COMPARISON/CONTRAST ESSAY: INFORMAL

This first essay is an informal comparison/contrast essay. (The covering page has been removed for space considerations.) It is followed by an exercise.

Helen Pawlak

Pawlak 1

Professor Doughty

Comunications 1

30 September 2004

Law and Security Administration and Police Foundations Programs:

What's the Difference Between the Two?

You are finally in college! You made it! You're in the Law and Security Administration Program at Durham College. You're proudly wearing your program's jacket, with LASA, Durham College, and your year of graduation embroidered on it. While you are wearing your jacket, you may have people ask you, "What is LASA?" Your response will probably be something like, "It's Law and Security Administration." The next question may be, "Is that the same or different than Police Foundations?" You can tell them that both programs are good preparation for getting onto a police service as a police officer; into a correctional institution as a prison guard; or into a security company as a security officer; however, the programs have one similarity and two differences at Durham College: similar courses are offered in first semester; different courses are offered in following semesters; and a different emphasis is put on field placement.

To begin with, the first semester at Durham College is the same for both the LASA and the PFP students. The students themselves are separated into classes by their programs, but they all take the same subjects. These subjects are considered the generic, basic courses required in each program: Canadian Criminal Justice System, Communications 1, Community and Social Services, Criminal and Civil Law, Political Science, Principles of Ethical Reasoning, Psychology, and Sociology and Canadian Society. These courses act as the foundations for all the other courses to come in the next three semesters of a two-year program. Also, some students decide to switch programs during the first semester, and they are able to do this easily because of the common course content covered in first semester.

Once the first semester is over, though, some differences in the course offerings start to show up. In second semester, both groups take a Communications course again, as well as Contemporary Social Problems, Criminology, and Interpersonal and Group Dynamics. However, the LASA students take Enforcement Procedure and Security Practices while the PFP students take Police Powers and Public Administration. Similarly, in the third semester, the common courses are Criminal Code, Interviewing and Investigations, and Lifestyle Management (fitness), but the LASA students learn about Alcohol and Gambling, Computer Literacy, Corrections, and Customs and Immigration. Meanwhile, the PFP students are studying First Nations People, Issues in Diversity, and Youth in Conflict with the Law. This brings them all up to the fourth semester when both groups of students study Conflict Management and Provincial Offences. Now the LASA students take Computer Crime and Advanced Security, Forensic Psychology, and Investigation and Surveillance. The PFP students also do Investigation, but they add Evidence to that course, and add Traffic Management to round off their studies. Therefore, although there are some similar courses in the LASA and PFP programs at Durham, even in the second, third, and fourth semesters, there are some major differences in the emphases.

The biggest difference in the two programs is the inclusion of field placement in the LASA program during the fourth semester. There is no field placement in Police Foundations. The LASA students obtain a placement in a law enforcement agency, including police services, where they receive hands-on work experience in their chosen career. It is a supervised situation, with the student directly responsible to an on-the-job supervisor and to a Durham College faculty member who is in charge of field placement. This three-week field placement tends to be the highlight of the year for many students as they put into practice many of the skills learned during their four semesters at Durham. This field placement opportunity is the main difference between the LASA program and the Police Foundations program at Durham College.

Now, if you are asked to compare the LASA and PFP programs, you can tell the questioner about the common first semester, different following semesters, and the LASA field placement. Hopefully, an explanation of the courses offered and the additional field placement for LASA will answer their questions. Wear your college jacket with pride knowing that you are in a program that is similar to another in at least one aspect but distinctly different in two others.

Exercise 10.2 Writing Exercise

Write a comparison/contrast essay comparing your college's LASA or PFP program with the one described at Durham College in the above essay. For more discussion points, go to Durham College's Web site: www.durhamcollege.ca. Refer to the programs under the title of "School of Justice." A drop box will come up, and you can choose the program you want from it.

Check that your essay meets all the criteria for a comparison/contrast essay. Use the summary on pp. 187–188 as a checklist.

Sample Comparison/Contrast Essay: Research

This next sample essay is not only a five-paragraph essay and a comparison essay; it is also a research essay. (The covering page has been removed for space considerations.) Research essays are discussed in depth in Chapters 7, 8, and 9.

If you have not studied research essays before your teacher teaches the comparison/contrast essay, there are a few points to understand before you read this essay.

1. As you read this next essay, you will notice quotation marks, " ", around words. The quotation marks mean that the author of the essay has copied the words within these quotation marks from another author to use as supporting material.
2. After the quotation marks, you will see parentheses, ( ). The information in the parentheses tells you the source of the information: (1) the author and page number or (2) just the page number on which that information can be found in that author's work.
3. This form of documentation, called the MLA style of documentation, is discussed in detail in Chapters 7 to 9 and Appendix B.
4. At the end of this essay, there is also a list of works cited. This is the bibliography for this essay. This, too, is explained in Chapter 7 and Appendix B.

As you read the essay, notice how the student author has compared the two characters.

Suzanne Edwards Edwards 1

Professor Doughty

Comunications 1

30 September 2004

Will the Real Anne of Green Gables Please Stand Up?

Who became best friends with a girl and made a solemn oath to stay best friends forever? Who lived in Cavendish on Prince Edward Island? Who refused the first proposal from a school friend because she did not love him? For all these questions, both Lucy Maud Montgomery and Anne Shirley, the character created by Montgomery, are correct answers. Although "Maud always insisted that the Anne books were not autobiographical" (Collins and Eriksson 5), research reveals that Montgomery wrote an autobiography when she wrote Anne of Green Gables and the Anne series because of the similarities in the people, places, and events in Lucy Maud Montgomery's life and Anne's life.

Initially, it is important to emphasize the people in Lucy Maud Montgomery's life who played an important part in her life, to show the likenesses between the real person, Montgomery, and the fictitious character, Anne. In Montgomery's childhood, she was adopted by Grandmother and Grandfather Macneil after her mother died. Although Montgomery did not like her grandparents, she put Grandmother and Grandfather into Anne's life in the forms of Matthew and Marilla, the aging brother and sister who adopted Anne. Characteristics of Grandmother Macneil, such as being tall, proper, unimaginative, rarely smiling and disapproving of imaginative, emotional girls (Bruce 34) were also character traits of Marilla. This woman was considered a no-nonsense type of person; she spoke very plainly but clearly when she wanted something done. When Marilla wanted Anne to come downstairs and eat breakfast, Marilla told her exactly what she was to do (32).

Edwards 2

> 'You'd better get dressed and come downstairs and never mind your imaginings,' said Marilla as soon as she could get a word in edgewise. 'Breakfast is waiting. Wash your face and comb your hair. Leave the window up and turn your bedclothes back over the foot of the bed. Be as smart as you can.' (Montgomery Green Gables 32)

Marilla's abrupt manner of speaking in imperatives was also characteristic of Grandmother Macneil's speech patterns. Not all of the people in Montgomery's life were fashioned after specific individuals. Sometimes, Montgomery would make up a character who had the same personality as people she met in her life. One of these personalities was the type "who pride[d] themselves on speaking their mind without fear or favour" (64). In the Anne series, this personality was personified in the character Mrs. Rachel Lynde. It was Mrs. Lynde who referred to Anne's looks in a derogatory way. During their first meeting, Mrs. Lynde refers to Anne as " 'a skinny, . . . homely, . . . freckle[d] [child with] . . . hair as red as carrots!' "(64). Fortunately for Anne, people who were positive influences in Montgomery's life were also incorporated into Anne's life: Montgomery's friend Amanda Macneil (Bruce 88) became Anne's " 'kindred spirit' " (Montgomery Green Gables 88), Diana Barry; Montgomery's favourite school teacher, Miss Gordon, (Bruce 89) became Anne's, Miss Stacey (Montgomery Green Gables 190). Both the real and the fictitious teachers encouraged their students to write and express themselves naturally (191). All the people mentioned above, both the negative and the positive influences, were common to both Montgomery and Anne, supporting the point that Montgomery and Anne are the same person.

Edwards 3

Along with the people in Montgomery's life, there were also many secret and favourite places of Montgomery's that were also the treasured places for Anne. One of them was the house in which Montgomery was born. Montgomery's birthplace was "small, wooden, yellow-brown and in a small town" (Bruce 20). Anne, too, was born in such a place: "a weeny-teeny little yellow house in Bolingbroke" (Montgomery Green Gables 39). Another house in Montgomery's life became Green Gables in Anne's life. This house was fashioned after the gabled Park Corner, Montgomery's cousin's house in Prince Edward Island which was the one place in which Montgomery experienced and evidenced love in a family setting (Bruce 22). Green Gables became a solace and refuge for the young orphan, Anne. This orphan was also given other natural spots which were favourite locales for Montgomery while she was growing up: the pathway leading to Green Gables (Bruce 28) became Anne's "White Way to Light" (Montgomery Green Gables 18); Montgomery's neighbour's pond (Bruce 29) became Anne's "Lake of Shining Waters" (Montgomery Green Gables 19); the "spruce grove" (Bruce 29) became the "Haunted Wood" (Montgomery Green Gables 29); and "Lover's Lane" (44) was the same for both characters. Besides natural locations, actual towns, schools, and societies in which Montgomery participated became the towns, schools, and societies in Anne's life. Bright River was the town of Hunter River; White Sands was the town of Rustico; the Avonlea school was the Cavendish school, and the ladies of the Cavendish Literary Society gave Maud all that she needed to describe a concert in Avonlea Hall (Bruce 143). Thus, after examining the environment in which Montgomery lived, and then comparing it to Anne's environment, one can note the similarities. Montgomery and Anne lived in the same settings.

Moreover, the events in the two women's lives are very similar. Both Montgomery and Anne were "orphans" (Smith 4) while they were young. Montgomery became an orphan after "her mother's early death and her father's departure for Western Canada" (4). Anne's mother "died of a fever when [Anne] was three months old… [and her] Father died four days afterwards from fever too. That left [Anne] an orphan" (Montgomery Green Gables 42). They both eventually became adopted by elderly people as mentioned before. Later in life, Grandmother Macneil and Marilla adopted twins. For Montgomery's Grandmother, they were David and Wellington Nelson (Bruce 56); for Anne's Marilla, they were Davy and Dora (Montgomery Anne of Avonlea 78). Marilla's compassion for the children was shown in this conversation:

> 'It's about Mary and those children . . . Mary is worse . . . [S]he can't last much longer. And the long and short of it is, Anne, that I'm sure Mary wants me to take those children. . . . She didn't say so but she looked it.' 'Oh,' Anne clasped her hands, all a thrill with excitement. 'And of course you will Marilla, won't you?'
>
> 'I daresay I'll tell Mary I'll take them.' (55)

Both Montgomery and Anne experienced living with two matriarchs with this caring attitude.

As well as this similarity, there are others. First of all, Montgomery chose to take a "First Class" licence to become a teacher (Bruce 96) and so did Anne (Montgomery Green Gables 277). This meant that they did three years of college in one (96). Secondly, both Montgomery and Anne refused a marriage proposal from a friend (Rubio and Waterson 58) because neither woman loved the man when he first proposed (63). For

Montgomery, this man was Reverend MacDonald (95) and for Anne, this man was Gilbert Blythe (Montgomery <u>Anne of Green Gables</u> and <u>Windy Poplars</u>). Therefore, many of the events in Montgomery's life duplicate the ones in Anne's, which makes the Anne series seem like an autobiography of Montgomery's life.

From the examples given, it is clear that Anne's life contains many of the same people, situations, and episodes as that of her author, Lucy Maud Montgomery. It is evident that Lucy Maud Montgomery is the real Anne of Green Gables. Considering all the similarities, it is difficult to understand why Maud said that she did not write an autobiography (Collins and Eriksson 5). Will the real Anne of Green Gables please stand up?

Edwards 6

Works Cited

Bruce, Harry. Maud: The Life of Lucy Maud Montgomery. Toronto: Bantam Seal Books, 1992.

Collins, Carolyn Strom and Christina Wyss Eriksson. The Anne of Green Gables Treasury. Toronto: Penguin Books Canada Ltd., 1991.

Montgomery, L.M. Anne of Avonlea. Toronto: Seal Books, McClelland and Stewart-Bantam Ltd., 1909.

Montgomery, L.M. Anne of Green Gables. Toronto: Seal Books, McClelland and Stewart-Bantam Ltd., 1908.

Montgomery, L.M. Windy Poplars. Toronto: Seal Books, McClelland and Stewart-Bantam Ltd., 1936.

Smith, Edith Katherine. "Lucy Maud Montgomery: Passionate Puritan." The Lucy Maud Montgomery Album. Com. Kevin McCabe. Ed. Alexandra Heilbron. Toronto: Fitzhenry & Whiteside Ltd., 1999.

Summary

When you write your comparison/contrast essays, make sure that you have incorporated the following:

- the five-paragraph essay model;
- two distinct subjects to compare;
- a thesis statement that clearly states the three points that will be discussed;
- words to state whether there are similarities and/or differences;
- a discussion of the three points from the thesis statement in the same order as they are stated in the thesis statement;
- a reference to the first subject when giving the supporting details to support your point (e.g., refer to an example from the Police Foundations program first and then state an example from the Law and Security program when giving the examples for every supporting detail);
- transitions to link the ideas; and
- a convincing argument, with good examples, that outlines the similarities and/or differences stated in your thesis statement.

The Oral Presentation

Learning Objectives

After students have learned the information in this chapter, they should be able to do the following:

- Present information in the form of an extemporaneous oral presentation to their class.
- Choose a topic for an oral presentation that meets their audience's needs.
- Research and gather information on the topic.
- Write an outline of the presentation and then write the information.
- Use several good delivery techniques during their oral presentation.
- Effectively include audio-visual aids in their presentation.
- Have backup plans for technology.
- Include an audience-participation activity within the presentation's timeframe.
- Demonstrate organization before and during the presentation;
- Use an outline to their advantage.
- Apply stress-reduction skills before and during their presentation.

Learning Benefits

Speaking in front of a group is considered by many to be a highly stressful situation. But learning the correct process, and actually implementing the process in a practical way, could significantly reduce the stress that is related to giving oral presentations. Practice will definitely improve your skills. Each time you give a presentation, you will learn at least one thing that you should stop doing; at least one thing that you should continue doing; and at least one thing that you should start doing. By applying the skills discussed in this chapter to your oral presentations, you, too, will be able to be at ease while giving your presentations. With time and practice, the majority of the stress will disappear when you give oral presentations.

Law enforcement officers are constantly talking to others and having to speak to groups of people. For example, officers speak to school children about road safety; to parents about the Neighbourhood Watch program; to college and university students about driving responsibly; and to seniors about elder abuse, to name just a few topics. Officers must take command of many situations. Giving oral presentations allows officers to develop and fine-tune their presentation skills.

Not all audiences will be as calm and attentive as your classmates when you speak to them, but through this exercise of giving an oral presentation, you will gain more confidence in public speaking. Furthermore, many officers become instructors, trainers, or teachers at their division's Police Learning Centre, at their security company's headquarters, or in the Schools of Justice at colleges or universities. As well, the art of speaking in front of an audience will become very important for promotions.

PREPARING THE ORAL PRESENTATION

An oral presentation consists of you standing up in front of your class and telling, not reading, the information; making direct eye contact with the audience; including audio-visual aids to keep the audience's attention; and including an audience-participation activity to reinforce/test the audience's listening skills during your presentation.

When you present your information in an "extemporaneous" manner, it means that you can stand up in front of your audience and talk to them about your topic without referring continuously to your notes. You know the content of your topic. You do **not** stand up in front of the class and do the following:

a) read the information to the class from pieces of paper;
b) read the information from small cue cards held in your hands;
c) put the majority of the information on overheads or PowerPoint® slides and read the information to the class; or
d) use any other technique in which you are simply standing there and reading the information to the class.

Speeches versus Presentations

1. What is the difference between a speech and an extemporaneous presentation?

A **speech** consists of someone reading a written document to the audience.

Examples:

- *Queen Elizabeth reading her Christmas letter to the world*
- *The Chief of Police reading a statement on television or for a radio broadcast about the progress of a particular case*
- *The Prime Minister of Canada reading the Throne Speech at the opening session of Parliament*
- *A person reading a eulogy at a funeral*

These speeches are written beforehand, and the speakers simply read the information from pieces of paper in their hands or a teleprompter. In the cases where the speech is on pieces of paper, the readers look up at the audience on occasion.

An **extemporaneous presentation** consists of the speaker standing up in front of an audience, facing the audience, making eye contact with the audience, referring occasionally to a point-form outline, and sharing the information with the audience without reading it.

Choosing a Topic

2. How do I choose a topic for an oral presentation?

Choosing a topic for an oral presentation is identical to choosing a topic for an essay.

i) Find out the overall topic.

Example: overall topic assigned = anything related to law enforcement

ii) Brainstorm every topic that you can think of that is related to law enforcement.

Examples:

1. *How to Become a Corrections Officer*
2. *The R.I.D.E. Program*
3. *The Neighbourhood Watch Program*
4. *How to Obtain a Firearms Acquisition Certificate*
5. *The K-9 Unit*
6. *The SWAT Team*
7. *The PREP Test*
8. *Preparing for the WCT (Written Communications Test)*

iii) Consider all the topics that you have written down and pick out three that interest you. You will enjoy doing the topic if you are interested in it, and you will show enthusiasm for the topic when you present it to your audience.

Example of narrowing down to three topics:

1. *The R.I.D.E. Program*
2. *The PREP Test*
3. *Preparing for the WCT (Written Communications Test)*

iv) Consider which of the three topics you can get the most information about and which one interests you the most. Fill in a chart similar to Table 11.1, below.

v) Make your final choice of topic.

Table 11.1: Analysis of Top Three Topics

Topics	Availability of information	Interest level
R.I.D.E. program	Easy—Police Learning Centre, newspapers, brochures, videos, officers	Medium
PREP test	Easy—Police Learning Centre, faculty members, other students who have taken it, information package, video available, posters available, equipment available	Medium—I will be taking Fitness next semester, and I will be exposed to it then
WCT	Easy—Police Learning Centre, faculty members, other students who have taken the test, Continuous Learning course and its teacher, a practice copy of it on the Internet	High—I have the opportunity to write it in two months
Final choice of topic = The WCT		

Exercise 11.1 Choosing a Topic

Fill in the blanks as you go through the process of determining your topic for your oral presentation.

1. Overall topic: ______________________

2. Brainstorm all the topics related to this overall topic:

____

____

____

____

____

____

3. Choose three of the topics above that interest you the most:

A ______________________

B ______________________

C ______________________

4. Analyze your three choices:

Topics	Availability of information	Interest level
A		
B		
C		

5. What is your final choice? ______________________

Gathering Information

3. How do I gather all the information for the content of the presentation?

You research and gather all your information for the content of a presentation just like you did for your essay. You might want to consider any or all of the following:

- Books
- Newspaper articles
- Magazines specifically related to policing, such as Blue Line
- Internet sources (All of the above can be found on the Internet.)
- Videos from your community's library, school library, or local Police Learning Centre
- Faculty members in your college
- Officers from the Police Learning Centre or your local police service

4. How much information should I get on this topic?

Keep in mind that your presentation should include the following:

- Content (the main information being included in your presentation)
- Audio-visual aids: posters, overheads/slides, pictures, video clips, etc.
- Audience participation: having your audience take part in some activity

Also keep in mind your time limitations. If your presentation is supposed to be fifteen to twenty minutes long, you should aim for approximately seventeen minutes in your planning and practising. Check to see if there are penalties for going over or under the required time. To help you plan the length of the actual content, keep in mind that it generally takes about one minute to present one double-spaced typed piece of paper of information if the information is typed in Times New Roman, point size 12.

Therefore, if you are planning to show a five-minute video clip on your topic and to do a fifteen-question quiz as an audience-participation activity, your timing might look like Table 11.2.

Table 11.2: Outline of Timing

Minutes	Content
1	Intro to video—title, producer, what's gone on before the clip starts, guiding question for audience to answer after the video clip
2–6	Video clip
7	Take up the answer from the introduction
8–11	Body of presentation
11–14	Fifteen-question quiz
15–16	Take up answers
17	Conclude

5. What do I do with all the sources of information once I get them?

You should take notes just as you would for an essay. Refer back to the section in Chapter 8 on note taking, particularly the information on how to summarize and how to take notes from a video. You should even record the source of information (author and title) in your notes because during the presentation you will tell the audience where you got your information. Sometimes you will give a direct quotation and state the author and title; at other times, you will simply state that this information came from these resources and then list them. Write your notes in point form.

The Outline

6. Do I write an outline like I did for the essay?

Yes. The outline is essential. Use an outline for the presentation similar to the one you used for the essay. See Form 11.1 on the next page.

Form 11.1 Outline for an Oral Presentation

Presentation title: ______________________________

CONTENT	**USE/DO (audio-visual aids)**
Introduction: (include an attention-getter) Insert a transition: Introduce the topic:	
Body (First Point): Insert a transition: Develop the point (details): Conclusion:	
Body (Second Point): Insert a transition: Develop the point (details): Conclusion:	
Body (Third Point): Insert a transition: Develop the point (details): Conclusion:	
Conclusion:	

Questions about Form 11.1:

1. In this form, what goes in the column that says, "Content"?

You will put all your information in here in point form once you have it all and have analyzed the audience.

2. In this form, what goes in the column that says, "Use/Do"?

After you fill in the "Content" side, you will write in all the audio-visual aids here, as well as the points when you are going to do your audience-participation activity.

Let's go back to the "Content" column of Form 11.1.

3. What goes in the "Introduction" section?

You will write in here the key words that you will use to get the audience's attention.You want to capture your audience's attention right from the start and then link it with a transition to your topic.

Do not start off with the following expressions:

The topic I have chosen to speak about is . . .

I am here today to tell you about . . .

I am doing my presentation on . . .

These are just a few of the overused and inappropriate openers for a presentation. Instead of the ones above, try using one of the following suggestions:

- Ask a question: e.g., *Have you written the Written Communications Test yet? This is one of the tests that you will need to write if you apply to some police services.*
- State a startling fact: e.g., *Before you write the Written Communications Test, you have the opportunity to see a sample test. It is available on the Internet for you to use, and today, you are going to see that sample test and learn how to write the test.*
- Ask for a show of hands: e.g., *How many of you will be writing the WCT in the next few months?* (Students raise their hands. You count them.)
- Read a quotation about your topic.
- Give a definition. (For an example of this technique, see how the discussion on plagiarism in Chapter 8 (page 152) is begun with a brief definition of the term, which then leads into a discussion of the topic).
- Do an activity that relates to your topic. (There will be more information about audience-participation activities later in this chapter).
- Show an overhead/PowerPoint® slide with the title of your presentation and some graphics.
- Introduce a video clip that relates to your topic and show it.

There are many more attention-getting introductions! They are only as limited as your imagination.

4. What goes in the "Body" section of the form?

Now you are ready to insert the main information of your presentation into the outline. This goes in the lines that say "Body (First point)" through to "Body (Third Point)" in Form 11.1.

The body of the presentation is equivalent to the body of the essay. This section contains the content. This section contains the majority of the information you want to present. In an essay, you develop your three points from your three-point thesis statement in the body; similarly, in the presentation, you develop your topic in a logical, coherent fashion. You may choose to use a thesis statement as the basis of your content for your presentation too. On the other hand, you may choose to explain a process in a chronological order that someone might need to do.

For each of your main points, fill in the point on the appropriate lines: e.g., Put the first point on the line that says, "Body (First Point)"; your second point on the line that says, "Body (Second Point)", etc. Then, go back and fill in the transitions that will link each point together and the information, in point form, that you are going to use to develop each point in the spaces provided.

5. What goes in the "Conclusion" section of the form?

Include in here the key words that you are going to say in order to bring the topic to a close and restate the topic.

Do not end by just blurting out: "That's it" or "I'm finished."

Instead of these overused and unprofessional ways of ending a presentation, try using something like one of the following:

Now that you know where to find a sample WCT on the Internet, have seen a sample WCT, and know how to answer the questions, I hope that you will be better prepared to write it. Please let me know how you do on the test when you do write it. I would appreciate having that information. All the best to you.

The R.I.D.E. program will be in full swing this holiday season. Hopefully, you now have a deeper understanding of its origin, its goals, its implementation, and its successes. When you see a R.I.D.E. stop, hear the statistics of the R.I.D.E campaign, or get stopped for one, I trust that you will have a better understanding of how and why our police service is working hard to Reduce Impaired Driving Everywhere.

Resist every urge to end with "That's it" after you finish your great conclusion to your topic.

KNOWING YOUR AUDIENCE

7. What should I take into consideration before I write my outline?

Before you write an essay, you consider **your audience and its needs**.

Do the same thing for your presentation. You will need to consider the following aspects of your audience: age, sex, education, culture, interest level, wants and goals, and expectations. For example, consider the following situation: You have been asked to do a ten-minute presentation to a group of Grade 12 high school students who have indicated that they want to go into policing. You are representing your college at the high school during its College Orientation Week, and you have been asked to tell these high school students why you chose this college to take your Police Foundations course. These students are coming to your session because they want to be there. It is being held during their lunch hour, and they are not getting extra marks for attending your session. There will be two staff members from your college's Student Services and Registration with you when you do this presentation.

For this situation, you would make up an audience profile something like that shown in Table 11.3. The information in a table like this one will be valuable to you as you prepare your presentation because you will know that you must gear your language to co-ed high school students just a year or more younger than you. You will, therefore, use an informal tone, and informal language is also acceptable. Since the audience has a high interest in what you are going to say to them, what you say may be the determining factor that helps them decide which college they will attend. Because of this information, you also know that you will need to include specific information about

Table 11.3: Audience Profile

Age	16–17
Sex	Males and females
Education	In Grade 12
Culture	Various
Occupation	High school students–graduating class
Interest level	High
Wants and goals, i.e., what they need from my presentation	To figure out if the college I go to is the one they want to attend
Expectations	To learn a lot about my college To see if I like the college and the course To hear a logical, organized detailed personal account of my experiences at this college

your college, such as food services, computer access, social groups and clubs, sports, and student life, as well as the course load, the faculty, and subjects taken. You will need to prepare three or more specific reasons why you came to this college and why the students should attend this college. Humour will be a good addition if you are good at telling humorous stories. This does not mean telling jokes. It could mean relating some of the funny things that have happened to you, such as getting lost many times during the first week, walking into the wrong room one time, and so on. Since you are representing your college, you are like an ambassador for the college; therefore, your tone must be polite and respectful to this attentive audience.

Exercise 11.2 Profiling Your Audience

Fill in the following table for your presentation's audience.

Audience Profile

Age	
Sex	
Education	
Culture	
Occupation	
Interest level	
Wants and goals, i.e., what they need from my presentation	
Expectations	

Now that you have gathered your information, seen the structure of the outline, and profiled your audience, it is time to put these three things together.

Assembling Your Presentation

8. Do I write the presentation out on the outline form as I did for the essay?

Yes, it is best to write in point form on the outline form (Form 11.1) in a logical coherent order. There is one main advantage to writing only the point form notes on the outline: you won't be tempted to read the notes. You will be more inclined to look at the point and then look up at the class and relate the information.

Try to limit the point form notes to the one-page outline. On the following pages there are two outlines (Form 11.1) for you to use: one is a one-page outline; the other is a two-page outline. (Some people use two pages of point form notes because their handwriting is larger than average, so for those people, the two-page version is included.)

Form 11.1 Outline for an Oral Presentation (one-page outline)

Presentation title: ____________________

CONTENT	**USE/DO (audio-visual aids)**
Introduction: (include an attention-getter)	
Insert a transition:	
Introduce the topic:	
Body (First Point):	
Insert a transition:	
Develop the point (details):	
Conclusion:	
Body (Second Point):	
Insert a transition:	
Develop the point (details):	
Conclusion:	
Body (Third Point):	
Insert a transition:	
Develop the point (details):	
Conclusion:	
Conclusion:	

Form 11.1 Outline for an Oral Presentation (two-page outline)

Presentation title: ______________________________

CONTENT	**USE/DO (audio-visual aids)**
Introduction: (include an attention-getter)	
Insert a transition:	
Introduce the topic:	
Body (First Point):	
Insert a transition:	
Develop the point (details):	
Conclusion:	

Body (Second Point):

Insert a transition:

Develop the point (details):

Conclusion:

Body (Third Point):

Insert a transition:

Develop the point (details):

Conclusion:

Conclusion:

Delivery Techniques

9. What should I know about delivery techniques for my presentations?

"Delivery" refers to everything that you do in front of the audience while relating your information. It includes how you present the information and all of the following:

- posture
- use of notes
- use of effective language
- effective use of volume, pitch, and tone
- dress
- use of audience-participation activity
- personalization of the presentation
- nonverbal communications
- organization before and during
- movements
- use of audio-visual aids

Adding a Personal Touch

10. How do I personalize a presentation?

Every person is unique, and everyone has a particular way of passing on information to other people effectively.

For example, some people are best at telling stories while others are best at simply stating the facts or main points. When presenters tell stories, for example, they are using a technique that they like doing, and by doing this, they personalize their presentations. These people also become known as storytellers when they give presentations. This is called "personalizing your presentation."

There are many ways to personalize your presentation. Consider which of the following you do best or like doing, and then try to use these personalization techniques in your presentation:

- story telling
- jokes
- comic strips
- drawings of stick people
- movies
- graphics
- overheads—handwritten in various colours/typed on coloured acetates/ coloured typing, etc.
- on-the-job examples
- cartoons
- flip-chart paper
- music
- drama
- blackboard
- PowerPoint® slides—key points of content on slides with graphics or added features

Try using one or more techniques in your presentations until you find the ones that suit you and that you are comfortable using. These will be the techniques that become your "signature." Your audiences will be expecting these from you and will look forward to your use of them. This doesn't mean that you have to use the same ones all the time. You can change and add as you become more skilled. Eventually, there will be one technique that is characteristically yours.

For example, some people always start their presentations with true-life stories. Others end their presentations with a poem, and others use a quotation to conclude.

Using Notes Effectively

11. How do I use my notes effectively so that I don't read the information?

Some ways to present, rather than read, the information are as follows:

a) Spend time learning and memorizing the information. You don't have to memorize it word-for-word as you would if you were learning lines for a play; however, you do have to know the information without looking repeatedly at the notes.
b) Do not take the completed copy of the information to the presentation. If you don't have the copy of all the written information with you, you won't be tempted to pick it up and read it.
c) Instead of using the copy of all the written information, use the outline you wrote prior to writing out all the information. There will be more details about this later in the chapter.
d) Practise! Practise! Practise your presentation in front of the following:
   - a mirror
   - your friends. Ask them to give you some feedback: three things you need to improve and three things to keep doing.
   - your family. Ask for the same type of feedback.

Nonverbal Communication Skills

12. What nonverbal skills should I be concerned about when presenting?

"Nonverbal" refers to all the things that you do with your body, from your head down to your toes, while you are presenting. The verbal aspect is the words you say. The non-verbal aspect is the language your body "speaks" to people while you are talking. You want to convey to your audience that you are a confident, knowledgeable person. You can give them that impression by controlling and/or breaking some bad habits that you may have when presenting.

The audience is watching you and listening to you; however, a great majority of the message that the audience receives is not from what you say but from how you say it and what you do with various parts of your body while presenting. These aspects are called "nonverbals."

Let's start at the top of your body and work our way down. Table 11.4 outlines some major nonverbals, with suggestions of how to use them.

Table 11.4: How to Use Nonverbal Communication to Your Advantage

Nonverbal	How to use it to your advantage
Hair	Your appearance, including your hair, should be neat; people should be able to see your face clearly. Avoid putting scarves and glittery hairpieces in your hair. Avoid flipping your hair, remaking your ponytail, running your fingers through your hair, or pushing your hair back while presenting.
Eyebrows	Try not to lift them up every time you make an important point.

(continued)

Table 11.4: How to Use Nonverbal Communication to Your Advantage (continued)

Eyes	Look at your audience while you are talking to them. Avoid reading from pieces of paper. Scan your audience as you talk. Be sure to look at the people in the far corners and to your front right and left. Try to look at everyone in the room. If you are reading a quote or a particularly relevant short passage, do look up from time to time. Moderate amounts of eye makeup are suitable. Avoid looking at your watch on your arm during the presentation. Many presenters put their watch on the podium so that they can see it at a glance.
Facial expressions	Try to keep a pleasant look on your face. Avoid frowning.
Mouth	Open your mouth when you speak, to avoid mumbling. Smile when appropriate.
Overall posture	Stand. Don't sit while presenting. This allows everyone to see you. Stand tall with your shoulders back. Stand with your legs slightly apart to give you balance and ease of movement. Avoid leaning on the podium, the desk, the TV stand, or any other piece of furniture. Stand on both feet at the same time. Face the audience when showing overheads or PowerPoint® slides. Avoid turning your back to the audience while you explain something on the screen. Use your finger on the overhead or the cursor on the computer to stress your point. Use the remote control to operate your PowerPoint® slide show and stand to the side of the screen rather than off to the side of the room where few people can see you. If you show a video, sit down while it is on.
Arms	Let them hang at your sides or hold them loosely at the wrists. Avoid swinging them unless you are doing it for a particular reason.
Hands	Keep them as still as is natural for you. People of different cultures use their hands differently. Some people just naturally use their hands expressively while others don't. Avoid holding onto the podium while talking. Keep all pencils and pens out of your hands to avoid playing with them or tapping them while you are talking. If you are using a pointer, pick it up only when you need it and then return it to its place. Avoid clicking your fingers, rubbing your fingers, cracking your knuckles, taking your ring off and on, playing with your ring, etc. Avoid tapping the desk, podium, or other furniture with your fingers. Clean your hands and fingernails before the presentation. Avoid shuffling your papers with your hands. If you are nervous, and you can't hold a piece of paper without moving it, put the paper on the podium and refer to it as needed.

(continued)

Table 11.4: How to Use Nonverbal Communication to Your Advantage (continued)

Legs	Stand with your feet slightly apart. Stand on both feet, not just one. Avoid crossing your legs while you stand.
Feet	Plant your feet firmly on the floor. Avoid tapping your foot, lifting your heel up and down, swinging your foot, taking your shoes off and on, and rubbing the back of one leg with the other foot.
Dress	Dress appropriately for your audience and your topic. Avoid wearing dangling earrings, especially ones that shine or glitter. Wear clothes that complement each other and you. Wear clean clothes. Last night's spaghetti stained shirt should be in the laundry. Wear simple jewellery that complements your clothes. Avoid any jewellery that makes a noise when you move, such as charm bracelets or loose bracelets that hit the podium or desk every time your hand comes in contact with the desk. Shoes should be clean and polished if applicable.
Perfume	Use caution when wearing perfume/scent. Some people have allergies to these. If possible, check with your audience first. If you do use scent, use it in moderation on the day of your presentation.

13. How do I use effective language in my presentation?

Use your words to your advantage by choosing words that are suitable to your audience. For example, if you were an officer talking to a Grade 5 class of boys and girls about bicycle safety, you could use the word "bikes" and "kids." However, if you were addressing a parents' group about the same topic, you might choose to use those words sparingly, but also use words like "your children," "your sons and daughters." That is how easy it is.

Also, using simple words is generally better than using long words. For example, if you said, "This act has a propinquity to disaster," your audience might not know what you were talking about unless they looked up the word "propinquity" in the dictionary. It would be better to say, "This act has a kinship or approximation to disaster." Better still, why not say, "This act could lead to disaster."

Furthermore, placing stress on certain words can also make your language effective.

If you were explaining the process of filling in the fingerprints of children on the Child Find folder, you might want to stress the words, "First . . . , secondly . . . , next" in order to establish the sequence of events. Just say those words a little louder, with a pause, and the audience will notice them.

Note: A word of caution about swearing should be mentioned here. Swearing is not acceptable or appropriate when giving a presentation. As the presenter, you are considered a professional and an expert in that field. Your audience expects to be treated with respect. You, as the presenter, need to take control of the situation during the presentation. Even if all your papers fall to the floor in the middle of the presentation, remain in control, and do not swear. If you are in the habit of swearing, practise your presentation in front of a few people, asking them to check your language in particular.

14. Can I also use volume, pitch, and tone to make my language effective?

Yes, volume, pitch, and tone can make your speech more effective.

Volume: Speak loudly enough so that everyone in the room can hear you. You most likely will have to speak more loudly than you do in a conversation with your friends. This is called "projection." To project, stand tall with your shoulders back, breathe in, open your mouth, and then speak. To you, it may sound like you are yelling when you first do it, but the audience will appreciate being able to hear you. Practise projecting by having someone go into another room of your house and carry on a conversation with you. The volume you have to use for that person to hear you is how loudly you will need to speak when presenting in front of a class.

Pitch: When people state that someone has a high voice or a low voice, they are referring to the pitch of the voice. Men's voices tend to have a lower pitch than women's. Men's voices are sometimes easier to listen to because of the lower pitch. Some women speak with a high-pitched voice. These women should try to drop their voices if possible and to speak slightly lower. Sometimes this high pitch occurs because of nervousness, so deep breathing exercises and good posture will often relieve the high pitch.

A common error is raising your pitch at the ends of sentences. The result is that the statements sound like questions and the audience isn't sure what you are saying. If you think you raise the ends of sentences in this manner, or have been told that you do so, try the following:

- Tape record your voice saying your presentation and listen to see if you are raising your voice at the ends of sentences. Ask others to listen to the tape for you and to evaluate your pitch.
- Present your information to a few friends and ask for their opinions.
- If a teacher or someone else mentions that you raise your voice at the ends of sentences, pay attention to that and work hard to correct it. You can do it with practice.

Tone: You will want to vary your tone when you speak. You do not want to use the same tone throughout the presentation; this is called a "monotone." A monotone tends to put people to sleep, and to cause them to yawn and get bored very quickly with what you have to say.

Also, your tone should not be condescending. This means that you do not want to "talk down" to your audience or speak in a lecturing or disrespectful manner to them. Vary your tone by doing the following:

- Speak in an enthusiastic manner. This shows your passion for the topic and what you are doing.
- Vary your types of sentences when you speak. Use questions and statements to add variety.
- Lower your volume slightly when telling a story.
- Raise your volume slightly when you say things like, "Let me give you an example."
- Plan pauses in your speech. For example, say, "Here is the first thing you have to do. . . . (pause) . . . First . . . "
- Let the audience read the content of a quotation from an overhead/PowerPoint® slide. Introduce the quotation, put up the overhead/slide and then ask the audience members to read it to themselves.
- You could arrange for volunteers to read certain things before you start your presentation. Be sure to arrange this before you start and to give them a copy of what they will be required to read. This allows the volunteers to practise the reading beforehand.

15. How can I use movement to my advantage when I deliver a presentation?

The use of appropriate movement can add a lot to your presentation.

- Try not to stick to the podium or desk area completely.
- Consider yourself a free agent who can move around in the room.

- Walking down the aisles while you speak, especially if you are asking questions, is very effective.
- Walk away from the podium or desk area where you have your point form outline while you are talking.
- Write things on the board. This will help you move away from the desk or podium to the board.
- If you have brought props of any kind, set them up in a location to either side of the middle of the room; this will force you to move there when it's time to show the props.
- Some people move to the back of the room while they show the PowerPoint® slides. You will need the remote control or an assistant to operate the computer.
- Sit down when you are showing a video.
- If you have put the audience into groups to discuss something as an audience-participation activity, then walk around and talk to each group during their work time.
- If you are referring to a poster taped to the board, or to something written on the board, go over to that area and point to it.

USING AUDIO-VISUAL AIDS

16. How can I use audio-visual aids to enhance my delivery of my topic?

People can get bored just listening to someone talk. Adding audio-visuals keeps the audience's attention. It has been said that the average attention span of an adult is somewhere between six and eight seconds. That's right: *seconds!* Since we live in a visual world in which many forms of entertainment are at our fingertips with a click on a remote control or the press of a key, you, the presenter, have to work hard to keep the audience's attention. You don't have to keep flashing things in front of your audience, but you do need to use some audio-visual aids to keep their attention.

Here is a partial list of audio-visual aids. There are as many as there are imaginations. Be creative!

Audio: CDs, tapes, playing of a musical instrument, singing, talking, etc.

Visuals: PowerPoint® slides, overheads, books, articles, pictures, photographs, charts, posters, bulletins, pamphlets, mimes, information on blackboards, etc.

Audio-visuals: Videos, DVDs, documentaries, movie clips, skits, puppets, etc.

17. What are some tips for using various audio-visual aids?

Listed below are five tips for using the most common audio-visual aids. Many of these tips can be applied to the majority of aids.

a) Visual aids such as PowerPoint® slides and/or overheads

i) Don't type/write all of your information or most of it onto the slide/overhead, and then read it to the audience.
ii) Use a minimum point size of 16 for the typing on the slide/overhead so that the people at the back of the room can read it.
iii) Have a maximum of fifteen lines of typing on one slide/overhead. Include only the key points in point form, not sentences or paragraphs
iv) Use colour, **bold,** *italics*, underlining, and all the different features of PowerPoint® to make your slides attractive. Do the same for all overheads.
v) Don't reveal the entire slide/overhead at once. Show only the point you are discussing. You control this on PowerPoint® by pressing "ENTER" only when you are going on to a new point. On overheads, use another piece of paper as a liner, and cover up what you don't want the audience to see.

See Figure 11.1 for an example of a PowerPoint® slide/overhead that could be used for the research essay based on Chris Morris's essay on the Supreme Court. (The essay is in Chapter 7.)

b) Visual props, such as books, objects, etc.

i) Hold them up high enough for everyone to see.
ii) Do not pass things around. The prop may be stolen or the audience members will be more interested in the prop than what you are saying.
iii) If an object is too small to be seen from the back of the room, walk around the classroom with it in your hand and make sure everyone has ample time to see it. This is a bit tricky. You should also be talking while doing this.
iv) Display the object on a table at the front, on top of the podium, on the blackboard ledge, or somewhere for all to see after you have shown it initially. You went to the trouble to bring it; make sure everyone gets to see it.
v) Make sure that the prop directly relates to the topic.

Example:
For a presentation on his essay about the Supreme Court, Chris could have used the following props:

- newspaper articles about the 1991 incident and the subsequent court case;
- an enlarged copy of the Canadian Charter of Rights and Freedoms;
- large pictures of the two men (Frank Boyle and Michael Feeney). Remember, the pictures have to be large enough to be seen from the back of the room.
- a poster with the title of his presentation on it. Tape the poster on the blackboard up high for everyone to see. Be sure the printing is very large so that the students at the back can see the words.
- a brochure from a victim's rights organization; and/or
- a Canadian flag either taped to the blackboard or hung from the blackboard.

c) Audio aids

i) Come prepared with all the equipment.
ii) Bring the correct CD, tape, etc.
iii) Preset the tape if needed.
iv) Do a test run before you start to make sure the volume is correct.
v) Do not play an entire song unless there is a specific reason for the entire song to be played. Most songs are three minutes long. Play the beginning of it and then let it fade into the background while you carry on speaking.

Some rap songs are very hard to understand. Print out a copy of the words onto an overhead/slide and let the students follow along with the words. Be careful with some music. The content may be offensive to some members of your audience. Make sure the music is specific to the topic and that it supports the topic.
Example:

For Shawna's presentation, based on her essay "How Paul (Bernardo) Teale Has Had an Effect on Canadian Society" (see Appendix E), she could start off by having the class stand up and sing "O Canada" since she started her essay off with a reference to it. Then she could start off with the attention-getting words of her essay. This would not only be an audio aid, but also an audience-participation activity because the entire class would be singing and/or standing during the singing of our national anthem.

If she didn't want to involve the class this way, she could ask the class to stand, and then play a CD or tape of "O Canada" until she got to the words "strong and free," which she states in the introduction of her essay. At this point in the song, she could lower the volume and talk over the remaining song as she introduced her topic.

Figure 11.1 Example of a Good Overhead or PowerPoint® Slide

The Supreme Court of Canada's final interpretation of Section 8 of the Criminal Code was not right because it showed disregard for

1. **The victim**
2. **Societal values**
3. **Public safety**

d) Audio-visual aids (videos, dramatic skits, etc.)

i) Bring all the necessary equipment to class.
ii) Be prepared. The video must be set at the exact starting place before you start your presentation. The drama must be rehearsed and ready for production during the presentation.
iii) Introduce the video or aid.
iv) Give a follow-up statement or two after using the aid to further support and explain how this aid supported your points.
v) Use these to complement your topic. These aids should be no more than one-third of your allotted time for your presentation.

Example of a topic, and audio, visual, and audio-visual aids suitable for its presentation:

Topic: The Child Find Program

Audio aids

- *a tape recording of a parent who tells the audience what she thought of this programme*
- *a tape recording of a child who tells the audience what she thought of this programme*

Visual aids

- *a copy of the Child Find pamphlet that is four to five times larger than the original one*
- *copies of the pamphlet—four times as many as the number of participants so that the parents can take enough home for all their children*
- *PowerPoint® slides outlining the content of the presentation*
- *text, graphics, charts, pictures, etc.*
- *an ink pad to use for the fingerprinting done in the Child Find pamphlet*
- *a finished Child Find pamphlet*
- *pictures of missing children who have been found through the use of this pamphlet*
- *wipes to wash the hands of the volunteers who take part in the demonstration of the fingerprinting part of the presentation*

Audio-visuals

- *a documentary on Child Find*
- *a video of a parent who benefited from this program*
- *a demonstration, such as how to take the fingerprints*

18. What are the pros and cons of the most typical audio-visual aids?

For your reference, Table 11.5 shows the pros and cons of using audio-visual aids (excluding computer-based aids, which are discussed below).

19. What are the pros and cons of using computer-based technology when doing presentations?

The following statement is commonly heard: "Technology is great . . . when it works!"

This is certainly true. Many students spend hours preparing fabulous PowerPoint® slides to use during their presentations, and for a variety of reasons, they can't use the slides.

Here are some of the most common problems encountered when using computer-based technology, as well as their solutions:

a) The disk/CD that the student did the slides on is not compatible with the computer in the classroom. In this case, the student should have gone to Media Services in the college and checked with the staff to see if that student's home computer was compatible with the one in the college.

Table 11.5: Pros and Cons of the Most Common Audio-Visual Aids (Excluding Computer-Based Aids)

Audio-visual aid	Pros	Cons
CD/tape	Adds variety Excellent background support if you can find the right one	Gets boring if played too long Need to remember to bring a CD player
Playing a musical instrument and/or singing	Adds variety Excellent background support if you can find the right song/tune	Make sure you can sing or play before you do this Be sure to provide the words if you want people to sing
Tape recording of someone discussing or telling a story about the topic	Adds variety Personal stories are always appreciated Good if short	Can have static background noises that detract from the content Requires a lot of time practising and recording
Overheads	Good visual aid Cheap and easy to use Can use a variety of colours Can be reused if you buy the write-on kind	Can be overused—too many overheads Can have too much information on them, which makes them hard to read If hand-written, the writing can be crooked, messy, etc.
Books/articles	Can show the exact source of information	Usually too small to be seen from the back of the room Need to be held up high and then placed for all to see
Pictures, photographs, charts, bulletins, and pamphlets	Complement the topic Show actual sources of information Good proof of points	Often too small to be seen from the back of the room Need to be enlarged on an overhead for all to see
Posters	Act as good title pages for presentations Usually add colour to the presentation	Printing and pictures need to be large enough so that the audience at the back of the room can see them clearly
Videos, video clips, DVDs, documentaries	Excellent audio-visual if on topic and set at the exact starting point	Setting the tape to start at the exact point is difficult at times Setting the DVD to start at an exact spot is very difficult, especially if the point required is not at the start of a scene
Skits, puppets, mime	A well-rehearsed drama is an excellent audio-visual aid	Need to rehearse beforehand Need to get volunteers Need to make the skit complement the topic

b) All of the PowerPoint® machines in the college have been booked by other students/teachers and the student can't get one for his/her presentation's due date. In this case, the student should have booked the machine long before the presentation date.
c) The most common problem is that the system is down in the college when the student is scheduled to do his or her presentation. Students need to have backup plans to allow for this. Often, the teacher can not reschedule your presentation if the system is down. Also, if you are an officer giving a presentation to a group and the PowerPoint® machine does not work for some reason, the audience is still expecting you to present. Many presenters print out their PowerPoint® slides and photocopy them onto overheads that they use as a backup plan. The use of the overheads might not be as interesting or entertaining as your PowerPoint® slides (with the added music and special techniques of entering each line separately, etc.), but if you have these overheads handy you can still do the presentation at the specified time.

20. How do I cope with these technological breakdowns?

You need to be flexible and be prepared with **backup plans**. Many students print out their slides and make overheads, as suggested above. Then if there is a problem with the system or the equipment, the student can still do the presentation as scheduled. Other students have made handouts of all their slides and given them out to the audience. Although these methods are not equal to the colours and movement that the student might have incorporated into the slide show, the presentation can still be given as scheduled.

Many speakers have backup overheads, flipcharts, posters, etc. in case the technology does not work. For example, if you, as an officer, have been scheduled to speak about Road Watch to the parents at an elementary school, they are expecting to see a presentation. If your computer and presentation machine do not work, you still need to fill that one-hour slot and give them the information they need. Just standing in front of them talking is not going to keep their attention. You need a backup plan.

The same applies for videos, DVDs, songs, etc. If the equipment does not work, then you need a backup plan. For example, if the DVD or video machine does not work or the tape is garbled for some reason, then the presenter could do the following:

a) State the title of the movie or documentary.
b) Tell the audience why this movie or documentary was chosen.
c) Relate the contents of the section that he or she was going to show. (Adding some acting into the telling of the content might add some entertainment.)
d) Conclude the information by restating how it applies to the topic.

Therefore, if the technology fails you at your time of need, you must still be prepared to make the presentation using different methods to keep the audience's attention.

INVOLVING YOUR AUDIENCE

21. How can audience-participation activities help my delivery?

Audience-participation activities help to keep the audience involved in your presentation by including them in the learning process. These are activities related to the topic, which the speaker instructs the audience to do during the presentation. The key thing about these activities is that **every member of the audience** takes part in the activity. Asking a few questions is **not** an audience-participation activity because only a few people get an opportunity to answer. These activities can be as simple as the following:

- Singing a song that relates to the topic—as discussed above;
- Taking a poll by a show of hands to see how many people agree or disagree with some point in your presentation;

- Asking each person to share their viewpoint on your topic;
- Asking the audience to get into groups and discuss a topic and then report back to the class; or
- Having the audience write the answers to a ten- to fifteen-question quiz based on the information you've just told them. Be sure to take up the answers. Prizes such as candy act as a major motivator for this activity.

More elaborate audience-participation activities can be used, such as the following:

- Divide the audience up into groups and ask each group to make up a poster related to your topic. You provide the paper, pens, and tape.
- Make up a game similar to popular board games (e.g., Trivial Pursuit) or TV game shows (e.g., Jeopardy), and change the rules so that everyone in the class has a turn. Search the Internet for game templates. All you have to do is enter the questions and the answers. Then you just run the program like the TV game-show host.
- Divide the audience into groups and ask them to create and perform a one-minute skit based on a topic related to your topic. Be sure you have enough time for each group to perform.

22. Why should I include audience-participation activities in my presentation?

These types of activities keep your audience's attention, as well as helping the audience to understand the point you are trying to make and to remember what you presented. Besides that, they are fun!

FINAL PREPARATIONS

23. What is the key to making a good presentation?

Organization is the key ingredient to a good presentation.

24. How do I get organized to do this oral presentation?

Now that you have your outline, your audio-visual aids, and your audience-participation activity figured out, you can organize your presentation. You should now go back to your outline and fill in the right column, "Use/Do", with the audio-visual aids and the activities that you are going to use during the presentation. (See Figure 11.2 for an example.)

Figure 11.2 Example of a Completed Outline for a Presentation—Form 11.1 (based on Chris Morris's Essay on the Supreme Court)

Presentation Title: Whose Rights are Paramount?

CONTENT	USE/DO (audio-visual aids)
Introduction: (include an attention-getter) Question: What are our basic rights?	Flag taped to board Large copy of Canadian Charter of Rights and Freedoms presented to class Audience-participation activity: Ask students to answer question, adding one short example to support answer.

(continued)

Figure 11.2 Example of a Completed Outline for a Presentation—Form 11.1 (based on Chris Morris's Essay on the Supreme Court) (continued)

Story of incident: 85-year-old man found beaten to death • 3 BC courts convicted Feeney for second-degree murder • Appeal—Supreme Court asking for protection under Charter • Defence claimed improper search and violation of rights of Section 8 • Feeney—free	
Topic:	Write thesis on overhead
State thesis: The court's ruling was not right—showed disregard for the victim, societal values, and public safety.	Let students read it to themselves
Point #1: Disregard for the victim	Volunteer reads the quote I gave him before class
Transition—to begin with Court's ruling showed disregard for the victim.	Show video clip of court case
Supporting points: Add relevant quotation from Canadian Charter of Rights and Freedoms. —introduce video	
Conclusion of Point #1	
Sum up—jury's decision to free Feeney not reasonable in the interest of the victim	
Point #2: Societal values	
Transition—*Secondly*	Audience-participation activity:
Ten Commandments	Lead a discussion on the Ten Commandments; show Bible.
Supporting points: • 1986 case of R v. Landry • Explain the mistakes the officers made • Stress that they were not "lawless vigilantes" (L'Heureux-Dubé 51)	Quote from 1986 ruling
Conclusion of Point #2	
Murderer's rights were upheld.	Read the synopsis from this case

(continued)

Figure 11.2 Example of a Completed Outline for a Presentation—Form 11.1 (based on Chris Morris's Essay on the Supreme Court) (continued)

Point 3: Public Safety Transition: *Lastly* Supporting points: • Ruling allowed "a savage killer on the loose in the community" (Leishman 2) • Precedent set—may result in overturning of other convictions • Ruling resulted in concern about public safety—because of delay in getting warrants • State process of getting warrants	Show pictures of the two men—Boyle and Feeney Ask class: What convictions have been overturned? Why? Results? (e.g., Guy Paul Morin, "Hurricane" Carter) Audience-participation activity: three minutes to prepare; one minute group presentation Group activity three to five students per group Pretend that they are members of a Victim's Rights Group. Their group's mandate is to provide one-minute presentations on situations they can think of where victim's rights might be or have been compromised.
Conclusion of Point #3 One man free but another dead and society at risk	
Conclusion: Revisit thesis Feeney freed under Section 24(2) Madam Justice Claire L'Heureux-Dubé's point of view Was justice served for the crime against Mr. Boyle? No. Police should be commended for acting quickly.	 Write revisited thesis on overhead Students read it to themselves Have a student read this from Criminal Code. Show overhead with her view written on it. Let class read it.
Conclude The appeal should have been quashed in the interest of Mr. Boyle, society, public safety, and, ultimately, justice. Explain pamphlet.	 Distribute pamphlet from an actual victim's rights group.

Points to note about the outline in Figure 11.2:

1. Most of the notes are in point form. Resist the urge to write out your notes in sentences. The point form notes will serve as cues to the topics. Remember: Don't read the information; tell it to the audience as if you were an expert on this topic.
2. There are many audio-visual aids listed. That is great. There could be even more! For example, you could include an overhead/slide as the introduction to each new point from the thesis. These could act as transitions to the next point.
3. There are three audience-participation activities: the discussion about basic rights, the debate about the Ten Commandments, and the role-playing activity, as members of a Victim's Rights Group. Audiences like to be involved and to participate actively because this makes your presentation more enjoyable for them. Also, more learning and remembering of your presentation takes place because people learn by doing.

Exercise 11.3 Props and Aids

Now, make a list of all your props and audio-visual aids that you are going to need. See the example below before you do yours.

Example:

Chris would have the following list for his presentation:

List of Audio-Visual Aids Needed for Presentation

- Canadian flag (and masking tape)
- Overhead 1: thesis; overhead 2: revisited thesis
- Enlarged copy of Canadian Charter of Rights and Freedoms
- Pictures—large ones/ photocopied onto overhead:
  Frank Boyle; Michael Feeney
- Quotations from essay written on pieces of paper
- Video clip of crime report; court case
- Bible (to present Ten Commandments)
- Newspaper clippings about the case
- Copy of the Criminal Code with bookmarks in it at the exact reference
- Pamphlets on Victim's Rights—one for each student

Exercise 11.4 Completing the Outline

Look back at your outline and use the list you just completed to fill in the audio-visual aids you are going to use in the right-hand column ("Use/Do").

25. What do I do now?

Now, put all of this information together and practise, practise, practise!

How to Relieve Stress Prior to Your Presentation

26. How can I relieve the stress of doing an oral presentation?

Even though you may have all your content ready and be prepared with audio-visuals and audience-participation activities, you might still be feeling some stress. Here are the top ten ways to relieve stress before doing an oral presentation

1. Realize that you are not alone. Others feel stressed too.
2. Realize that other people are cheering you on. Your audience wants you to succeed. They are hoping for a great presentation.

3. Practise, practise, practise!
4. Do some deep breathing exercises every time you get anxious about the presentation and just before you do it.
5. Do some stretching exercises before the presentation. You can do many neck exercises just sitting in your seat. Most of the tension will be in your neck, so neck stretches will help you relieve some of that tension. Make the stretch and hold it to a count of fifteen rather than doing repetitive jerky stretches.
6. Be yourself! Have fun!
7. Visualize yourself doing well. See yourself up at the front of the room being the best presenter there is.
8. If you are going to use PowerPoint®, check that your home computer is compatible with the college computer.
9. Book all your audio-visual equipment a month in advance.
10. Have a backup plan in case the technology does not work. Be prepared.

QUICK CHECKLIST FOR ORAL PRESENTATIONS

Oral presentations should keep your audience's attention, and the content should be told, not read, to the audience. In order to accomplish these goals, be sure that your presentation includes the following:

- an attention-getter, a statement of the thesis statement, a discussion of the three points, and a conclusion, all linked together with transitions;
- a variety of audio-visual aids throughout the presentation to complement the content; and
- at least one audience-participation activity that involves every person in the class actively doing a task

When delivering the content, remember to do the following:

- Use techniques that you do best.
- Use the notes on the outline as memory joggers.
- Pay attention to your nonverbal communication.
- Use effective language, varying your volume, pitch, and tone.
- Move around naturally.
- Dress appropriately.
- Use stress-reduction techniques.
- Be organized before and during the presentation.
- Have fun.
- Be yourself! (And good luck!)

Exercise 11.5 Class Exercise

The teacher should write the following on two blackboards:

- "Audio-Visuals" on one blackboard; and
- "Audience-Participation" on another blackboard

1. Form groups of three people.
2. Each person should have paper and pen and be ready to write.
3. One person in the group acts as the recorder.

4. In the groups, each person, in turn, states the topic of the essay that he or she is going to present to the class. Each student shares what he or she is going to use as audio-visual aids and as the audience-participation activity at this point in the process.

5. The other two members of the group contribute more ideas about both the audio-visual and the audience-participation activities that the member could use.

6. Once everyone has completed these steps, each group should have a list of all the audio-visual aids and audience-participation activities that they have created.

7. Now, two members from the group that finishes first go up to the board and list their group's ideas under the appropriate headings: "Audio-Visuals" and "Audience-Participation." Then the next group comes up to write its ideas down. If a group gets up to the board, and its idea has already been written under the heading, this group doesn't write the same idea down. Write only the ideas that are not on the board. This continues until every group has recorded every idea.

8. Together, the teacher and students examine the lists for some creative ideas from the class. Students write down the ideas they like.

Summary

All the steps discussed in this chapter may seem like a lot of work, but remember—you want to keep your audience's attention, and you want to relieve a lot of the stress of doing the presentation.

Being prepared with various audio-visual aids and at least one audience participation activity will keep your audience's attention and help relieve some of your stress. The audience will be looking at the overheads, watching the video clip, taking part in the activities, reading quotations, etc. Before you know it, your time will be used up, and you will have presented a presentation from memory that deserves a high mark.

Resource and Note Taking Pages

Form 7.1 First Page: Resources

Title of article/chapter/video clip (in quotation marks): ______________________

Name(s) of author(s): ____

Title of book/magazine/journal/newspaper/video (underlined):

____

Editor: ________________________ Edition: ________________________

City of publication: _______________ Publisher's name: _________________

Volume number: _________________

Year/date of publication: _________ / _______ _______ _______
year only date month year

Page number(s): __________

For Internet/CD ROM resources only:

Starting page number of article: _____

Number of words/paragraphs/pages in article: _____
short/long? _____

Site/path/file address: ____________________________________

Date you visited the site: ______ _______ _______
date month year

For interviews only:

Name of person interviewed: ______________________________

Person's job title: _______________________________________

Date of interview: ______ ______ ______
date month year

For videos only:

Name of producer: _________________

Production date: __________________

Date you viewed the video: ______ ______ ______
date month year

Form 7.1 First Page: Resources

Title of article/chapter/video clip (in quotation marks): ______________________

Name(s) of author(s): ______________________________________

Title of book/magazine/journal/newspaper/video (underlined):

____

Editor: ______________________ Edition: ______________________

City of publication: ______________ Publisher's name: ________________

Volume number: ________________

Year/date of publication: ________ / ______ ______ ______

year only date month year

Page number(s): __________

For Internet/CD ROM resources only:

Starting page number of article: _____

Number of words/paragraphs/pages in article: _____
short/long? _____

Site/path/file address: ______________________________

Date you visited the site: _____ ______ ______

date month year

For interviews only:

Name of person interviewed: __________________________

Person's job title: ________________________________

Date of interview: _____ _____ _____

date month year

For videos only:

Name of producer: ________________

Production date: ________________

Date you viewed the video: _____ _____ _____

date month year

Form 7.1 First Page: Resources

Title of article/chapter/video clip (in quotation marks): ____________________

Name(s) of author(s): ____________________

Title of book/magazine/journal/newspaper/video (underlined):

____

Editor: ____________________ Edition: ____________________

City of publication: ____________________ Publisher's name: ____________________

Volume number: ____________________

Year/date of publication: ________ / ________ ________ ________
year only date month year

Page number(s): __________

For Internet/CD ROM resources only:

Starting page number of article: _____

Number of words/paragraphs/pages in article: _____
short/long? _____

Site/path/file address: ____________________

Date you visited the site: ______ ______ ______
date month year

For interviews only:

Name of person interviewed: ____________________

Person's job title: ____________________

Date of interview: ______ ______ ______
date month year

For videos only:

Name of producer: ____________________

Production date: ____________________

Date you viewed the video: ______ ______ ______
date month year

Form 7.1 First Page: Resources

Title of article/chapter/video clip (in quotation marks): ______________________

Name(s) of author(s): ______________________________________

Title of book/magazine/journal/newspaper/video (underlined):

____

Editor: ______________________ Edition: ______________________

City of publication: ______________ Publisher's name: ______________

Volume number: ________________

Year/date of publication: ________ / _______ _______ _______
year only date month year

Page number(s): __________

For Internet/CD ROM resources only:

Starting page number of article: _____

Number of words/paragraphs/pages in article: _____
short/long? _____

Site/path/file address: ______________________________

Date you visited the site: ______ _______ _______
date month year

For interviews only:

Name of person interviewed: ______________________________

Person's job title: ______________________________________

Date of interview: ______ ______ ______
date month year

For videos only:

Name of producer: ________________

Production date: ________________

Date you viewed the video: ______ ______ ______
date month year

Form 8.1 Second and Following Pages: My Notes

Notes taken from:

Title: ____________________

Author(s): ____________________

Page number(s): __________

Question	My Notes: Direct Quotations	My Words

Form 8.1 Second and Following Pages: My Notes

Notes taken from:

Title: ______________________________

Author(s): ______________________________

Page number(s): __________

Question	My Notes: Direct Quotations	My Words

Form 8.1 Second and Following Pages: My Notes

Notes taken from:

Title: ____

Author(s): ____

Page number(s): __________

Question	My Notes: Direct Quotations	My Words

Form 8.1 Second and Following Pages: My Notes

Notes taken from:

Title: ______________________________

Author(s): ______________________________

Page number(s): __________

Question	My Notes: Direct Quotations	My Words

Form 8.1 Second and Following Pages: My Notes—Additional Pages

Question	My Notes: Direct Quotations	My Words

Form 8.1 Second and Following Pages: My Notes—Additional Pages

Question	My Notes: Direct Quotations	My Words

Form 11.1 Outline for an Oral Presentation

Presentation title: ______________________________

CONTENT	**USE/DO (audio-visual aids)**
Introduction: (include an attention-getter) Insert a transition: Introduce the topic:	
Body (First Point): Insert a transition: Develop the point (details): Conclusion:	
Body (Second Point): Insert a transition: Develop the point (details): Conclusion:	
Body (Third Point): Insert a transition: Develop the point (details): Conclusion:	
Conclusion:	

Form 11.1 Outline for an Oral Presentation

Presentation title: ______________________________

CONTENT	**USE/DO (audio-visual aids)**
Introduction: (include an attention-getter) Insert a transition: Introduce the topic:	
Body (First Point): Insert a transition: Develop the point (details): Conclusion:	
Body (Second Point): Insert a transition: Develop the point (details): Conclusion:	
Body (Third Point): Insert a transition: Develop the point (details): Conclusion:	
Conclusion:	

APPENDIX B MLA Documentation Style

When you are composing a research paper, you must give credit to your sources. Using the ideas, information, or expressions of others without properly documenting the source of the information is considered **plagiarism**. Plagiarism is a serious academic offence and is sometimes referred to as "intellectual theft."

If you (a) quote material verbatim, (b) paraphrase materials, (c) present statistics or findings from a survey or study or (d) use ideas, information, or expressions that are not common knowledge, you must cite or acknowledge the source.

Different academic disciplines use different systems of documentation, but students of Justice Studies should use the Modern Language Association (MLA) style, presented in the MLA Handbook for Writers of Research Papers.

A. Parenthetical References

In MLA style, a parenthetical reference identifies a source and refers readers to the full citation of the source in the list of works cited. Following are some sample MLA-style parenthetical references.

Author and page (short quotation)

Prose quotations that run no more than four lines in your essay are integrated into the text and enclosed in double quotation marks. The author's name need not appear in the parenthetical reference if it is included in the signal or introductory phrase, as in the first example:

Mark Kingwell defines happiness as "the possession of virtuous character and the performance of virtuous action" (327).

The search for J.D. Salinger, the New Hampshire recluse whom one reviewer called "the Greta Garbo of American letters" (Swados 119), became something of a minor national obsession in the early 1960s.

Author and page (long quotation)

Prose quotations that run more than four lines are set off from the text by indenting one inch (2.5 cm) from the left margin. Block quotations are not enclosed in quotation marks.

Swift's ironic "A Modest Proposal" paints a devastating portrait of Ireland's poor:

Some persons of a desponding spirit are in great concern about that vast number of poor people, who are aged, diseased, or maimed, and I have been desired to employ my thoughts what course may be taken to ease the nation of so grievous an encumbrance. But I am not in the least pain upon that matter, because it is very well known that they are every day dying, and rotting, by cold, and famine, and filth, and vermin, as fast as can be reasonably expected. (58)

Author of more than one source

If the list of works cited contains more than one work by the same author, name the title in the parenthetical reference or in the text.

In Larry's Party, the central metaphor for human existence is the maze, "a circling, exquisite puzzle of pain, and pain's consolation" (Shields 160).

The central metaphor for human existence is the maze, "a circling, exquisite puzzle of pain, and pain's consolation" (Shields, Larry's Party 160).

If the title of the work is long, use a shortened version in the parenthetical reference.

In "Canadian Monsters: Some Aspects of the Supernatural in Canadian Fiction," Atwood describes the wendigo and Coyote as "supernatural forces in the environment [. . .] against which the human characters measure themselves" (235).

The wendigo and Coyote are "supernatural forces in the environment [. . .] against which the human characters measure themselves" (Atwood, "Canadian Monsters" 235).

Authors—two or three

If the source has two or three authors, include them in the parenthetical reference or name them in the text.

A good English essay comes from asking good questions since, as Rosenwasser and Stephen note, "if you don't take the time to look for questions, you might end up writing a tidy but relatively pointless paper" (11).

Some writers stress that good essays come from asking good questions: "If you don't take the time to look for questions, you might end up writing a tidy but relatively pointless paper" (Rosenwasser and Stephen 11).

Authors—more than three

If the source has more than three authors, include in the text or parenthetical reference only the name of the first author followed by *et al.* ("and others").

According to Simpson et al., depression among stroke victims tends to deepen with time (45).

A recent study found that depression among stroke victims tends to deepen with time (Simpson et al. 45).

Author—corporate (group of people or organization)

Place the names of corporate bodies in the parenthetical reference or in the text. (The preferred placement for long names is in the text.) In the parenthetical reference, shorten words that are commonly abbreviated.

In the mid-1980s, the Women's Legal Education and Action Fund sought to force positive changes in family benefits law in Ontario (174).

A diatom was identified as the cause of the mysterious outbreak of food poisoning (Natl. Research Council 36).

The same source two or more times in succession

If you document a source and include the author's name in the first reference, you need not repeat it again in successive references. As long as the subsequent references follow the first reference directly, it is acceptable to include the page number only.

In 1998, Canada's crime rate edged up. According to a 1999 report, Canada's crime rate increased in the wake of a sharp jump in car thefts and increases in minor crimes such as bail violations and mischief (Kornell and Zelland 124). Police reported "65,000 more criminal incidents in 1998 than in 1997, resulting in a 1% increase in the rate of total Criminal Code offences" (125–126).

Example from Crystal Vasiloff's essay on DNA (Appendix E):

With a powerful tool, such as DNA, Madam Justice Louise Arbour, stated that "'Effective law enforcement benefits society as a whole . . . [and] . . . [f]orensic DNA analysis is capable of both identifying and eliminating suspects—a feature that seriously reduces the risk of wrongful convictions'"(Makin 1). Before the involvement of DNA, there was also a chance of being an innocent suspect who must go through a lengthy and humiliating trial to be proven not guilty. However, the issuance of DNA warrants "'have the capacity to exonerate an accused early in the investigation'" (1). This will save officers a lot of time and money, and most importantly, will save the reputation of an innocent person. DNA is vital in merely proving that someone has had no part in a crime. The easiest thing to do would be voluntarily giving DNA, like Vaughan did in the Alberta case where "Mounties wanted to analyze his DNA to prove he was not the serial rapist who has attacked three women" (Plischke A.6). If someone is not guilty, DNA is the best tool to prove such innocence, and therefore, is considered effective in law enforcement.

Author—unidentified

If the name of the author is unknown, either use the source's full title in the text or use the first two or three words of the title in the parenthetical reference.

According to a recent article entitled "The Poverty Trap in Ontario," there is a direct link between welfare reform and increased levels of homelessness (28).

There is a direct link between welfare reform and increased levels of homelessness ("Poverty Trap" 28).

Authors with the same last name

If the list of works cited contains works by two or more authors with the same last name, include the first initial in the parenthetical reference.

(J. Smith 13)

(D. Smith 45–49)

If the initial is shared, write the first name in full.

(Alan Greenfeld 167)

(Abe Greenfeld 22)

Documentary film

If you use a documentary film as part of your essay, do the following:

1. Include the name(s) of the director(s) in the same sentence as the name of the documentary.

   Ben Addelman and Samir Mallal's documentary, Discordia, explores the September 2002 riots at Concordia University in Montreal, Quebec.

2. Start the entry for the list of works cited with the name(s) of the director(s).

   Addelman, Ben and Samir Mallal. Concordia. Pr. Adam Symansky. Ed. Hannele Halm. Ex. Pr. Sally Backner. The National Film Board of Canada, 2004.

Electronic sources

Electronic sources include Web sites, online publications, e-mail correspondence, and postings, as well as films, television programs, videos and CD-ROMs. When citing text from an electronic database, it will often be necessary to refer to a paragraph or line number, as electronic sources rarely include page numbers. Keep in mind that "par." is the short form of "paragraph", and "l." is the short form of "line." (See Section B in this appendix, "List of Works Cited," to learn how to properly document electronic sources at the end of your paper.)

In 1997, adult males accounted for "64.6% of all Canadians charged for criminal incidents" (Halliwell par. 6).

In 1885, juvenile convictions accounted for "96 percent of all crimes in Ontario"(Statistics Canada l. 1-2).

Indirect quotation

Use the abbreviation *qtd. in* to indicate that you are using someone else's report of a writer's or speaker's words.

Voltaire once said, "As for the obvious, leave it to the philosophers" (qtd. in Kingwell 14).

(Note: The MLA prefers that material be taken from an original source rather than quoted indirectly).

Legal Act

When referencing a section of an Act, such as the Youth Criminal Justice Act, sources may be cited in parentheses in the text. Use the following order of information: name of Act, statute volume, jurisdiction, year, chapter, section.

The Lieutenant Governor in Council may make regulations prescribing forms for the purposes of this Part (Children's Law Reform Act, R.S.O. 1990, c. C-12, s.17).

Literary works (e.g., poems, plays, novels)

When citing literary works that are available in several editions, you should help readers locate the passage by providing more than just the page number.

Multivolume work

If your essay cites more than one volume of a multivolume work, include the volume number in the parenthetical reference. Note that a space separates the colon and the page number.

In her diary, Virginia Woolf expressed her reservations about Ulysses (2: 199–200).

For a classic prose work, follow the page number with the chapter or part number.

In Women in Love, Gerald's death in the Tyrolese mountains is observed by "a small bright moon" (Lawrence 532; ch. 30).

For a classic verse play, include the act, scene, and line numbers in the parenthetical reference. Use arabic numerals unless roman numerals are preferred by your instructor.

In King Lear, the dying Edmund reveals a touch of humanity when he asserts, "Some good I mean to do / Despite of mine own nature" (Shakespeare 5.3.244–45).

Note: If you are using an edition of a play that numbers the lines by page, ask your instructor if he or she wants you to include page numbers in the citations.

For a poem, cite the part (if the poem is divided into parts) and the line numbers. Reflecting on mortality, the speaker in Anne Bradstreet's "Contemplations" concludes,

"Nor wit nor gold, nor buildings scape time's rust; / But he whose name is grav'd in the white stone / Shall last and shine when all of these are gone" (33.230-32).

Quotation within a quotation

If the words that you are going to quote in your essay already have double quotation marks around them in the original, then use double quotation marks and single quotations marks around these quoted words.

The punctuation would look like this: "' . . . '".

After three Durham Regional officers were allowed to return to work after being suspended, Doug Cavanaugh, President of Durham's Regional Police Association said, "'They never refused to cooperate with the investigation; they just wanted to make assurances'" (Bovie A1).

Section of the Criminal Code

When referencing a section of the Criminal Code, sources may be cited in the body of the paragraph. Use the following order of information: abbreviation for Section, Section number, and abbreviation for Criminal Code.

According to the Criminal Code S. 745, "a person who commits first degree murder will be sentenced to imprisonment for life without eligibility for parole until the person has served twenty-five years of the sentence."

Verbal sources

If you quote from a lecture, conversation, or personal interview (that you have conducted yourself), cite the speaker's surname.

"We believe that it's going to help us get tougher sentences for gun crimes" (Bryant).

For sample research essays using the MLA style, see Chapter 7 and Appendix E.

B. LIST OF WORKS CITED

The list of works cited, which starts on a separate page at the end of the essay, contains complete bibliographical information for all the sources cited in the text. When constructing a list of works cited, follow these guidelines:

- Start the list on a separate page and title the list *Works Cited.*
- Centre the title an inch (2.5 cm) from the top of the page.

- Arrange the list *alphabetically* by the surnames of the authors or editors.
- If a work has no author or editor, alphabetize it according to the first word of its title. If the title's first word is *a*, *an*, or *the*, use the second word to determine placement.
- Do not indent the first line of each entry in the list of works cited. Indent the second and following lines five spaces (or 1.25 cm). This format, called a *hanging indent*, makes the authors' surnames stand out for easy reference. (If your word processor has the hanging-indent feature, use it to format entries.)
- Double-space between the title and the first entry, and between and within entries throughout the list. To make this easier for you, before you start your list of works cited, set up the double-spacing function on your computer, and this criterion will be met. See the sample lists of works cited for the spacing required.

For sample lists of works cited, refer to Chapter 7 and Appendix E.

Italics/Underlining

Most word processors allow you to use italics for titles of complete works and special categories of words. However, the MLA recommends the use of underlining rather than italics on the ground that italicized text is not always as readable as underlined text. If you wish to use italics, the MLA suggests that you obtain your instructor's approval before doing so.

Refer to the sample lists of works cited in the essays in Chapter 7 and Appendix E. Note how the titles of complete works, such as books and newspapers, are underlined.

Books and Other Nonperiodical Works

Anthology or compilation Follow the name of the editor or compiler with a comma and the abbreviation *ed.* or *comp.*

Douglas Glover, ed. Best Canadian Stories 99. Ottawa: Oberon, 1999.

Downie, Mary Alice, and Barbara Robertson, comps. The New Wind Has Wings: Poems from Canada. Toronto: Oxford UP, 1984.

Article in an encyclopedia or entry in a dictionary Name the author of the article (if there is one), the article's title, the title of the encyclopedia, any edition number, and the year of publication. (Full publication information is not necessary if the encyclopedia is well known.) Omit volume and page numbers if the articles are arranged alphabetically. Follow the same guidelines when citing an entry in a dictionary.

Doucette, Leonard E. "Drama in French." The Canadian Encyclopedia. 2000 ed.

Author—corporate (group of people or organization) Begin the entry with the corporate author's name, even if it is the name of the publisher as well.

Canadian Authors Association. Canadian Writer's Guide. Markham, ON: Fitzhenry, 1997.

Canadian Museum of Civilization. In the Shadow of the Sun: Perspectives on Contemporary Native Art. Hull, QC: Canadian Museum of Civilization, 1993.

Author—one You will find on a book's title page and copyright page the three basic units of a book entry: (1) author; (2) title; and (3) place of publication, publisher, year of publication. Use a shortened form of the publisher's name (for example, *Scribner's* for Charles Scribner's Sons, *Norton* for W.W. Norton and Co., Inc., *Oxford UP* for Oxford University Press, or *Simon* for Simon and Schuster, Inc.).

Choy, Wayson. The Jade Peony. Vancouver: Douglas & McIntyre, 1995.

Author of more than one source If your list of works cited contains two or more works by the same author, name the author only in the first entry. Begin subsequent entries with three hyphens followed by a period. List the entries alphabetically by title.

Mistry, Rohinton. A Fine Balance. Toronto: McClelland, 1995.

---. Such a Long Journey. Toronto: McClelland, 1993.

Authors—more than three Name only the first author listed on the title page, and follow the name with a comma and *et al.* ("and others").

Betcherman, G., et al. The Canadian Workplace in Transition. Kingston, ON: IRC, 1994.

Authors—two or three Name the authors according to the order in which they appear on the title page. Invert the name of the first author so that the surname comes first. Separate the authors' names with commas.

McNaught, Kenneth, and David Bercuson. The Winnipeg General Strike. Don Mills, ON: Longman, 1974.

Smith, David, John Adams, and Chris Cook. Writing Online. New York: Macmillan, 2000.

Author with an editor After the author and the title, write the abbreviation *Ed.* ("Edited by") followed by the name of the editor.

McClelland, Jack. Imagining Canadian Literature: The Selected Letters of Jack McClelland. Ed. Sam Solecki. Toronto: Key Porter, 1998.

Author—unidentified Begin the entry with the title. Recall that titles are alphabetized by the first word other than *a*, *an*, or *the*.

The International Guide to English Language Programs, 1998. Victoria: EI Educ. Intl., 1997.

(Note: In this example, "Educ." stands for "Education".)

Book in a series If the book is part of a series, name the series (and any series number) after the title.

Davison, Michael. The San Francisco Renaissance: Poetics and Community at Mid-Century. Cambridge Studies in American Literature and Culture. Cambridge: Cambridge UP, 1989.

Book published before 1900 If the book you are citing was published before 1900, omit the name of the publisher. Use a comma, rather than a colon, between the place of publication and the date.

James, William. The Principles of Psychology. New York, 1890.

Conference proceedings List conference proceedings (published collections of papers presented at a conference) as you would books. After the title, add relevant information about the conference that is not included in the title (such as the name of the conference).

King, Karyn, and Rita M. Bean, eds. Literary Instruction: Practices, Problems, Promises.

Proc. of the Annual Conf. and Course on Literacy, June 1990, U of Pittsburgh.

Pittsburgh: U of Pittsburgh P, 1990.

(Note: In this example, "Proc." stands for "Proceedings.")

Cross-references If you are citing two or more selections from the same collection, create an entry for the collection and cross-reference individual selections to the entry. For each selection, write the name of the author and the title, the last name of the collection's editor, and the inclusive page numbers.

Blaise, Clark. "The Bridge." Lecker and David 43-48.

Di Michele, Mary. "Poem for My Daughter." Lecker and David 270-71.

Lecker, Robert, and Jack David, eds. The New Canadian Anthology: Poetry and Short

Fiction in English. Scarborough, ON: Nelson, 1988.

Ondaatje, Michael. "King Kong Meets Wallace Stevens." Lecker and David 250-51.

Thomas, Audrey. "Déjeuner sur l'Herbe." Lecker and David 411-22.

Edition other than the first If a book's title page indicates a later edition of the book, name the edition, in abbreviated form, after the title in your entry. An edition may be identified by number (*2nd ed.*, *3rd ed.*, etc.), by year (e.g., *2000 ed.*), or by name (*Rev. ed.* for "Revised Edition").

Siegel, Arthur. Politics and the Media in Canada. 2nd ed. Whitby, ON: McGraw, 1996.

Editor Follow the name or names with the abbreviations *ed.* ("editor") or *eds.* ("editors").

Benson, Nancy, ed. Ten Great American Plays. New York: Columbia UP, 1998.

Government publication If the name of the document's author is not identified, begin with the name of the government that issued the document, followed by the name of the government agency.

Canada. Federal Cultural Policy Review Committee. Report of the Federal Cultural Policy Review Committee. Ottawa: Dept. of Communications, Information Services, 1982.

Introduction, preface, foreword, or afterword Name the author of the element, identify the element, and then give the title of the book, the author (after the word *By*), and the editor (if there is one). Capitalize the name of the element but do not underline it or enclose it in quotation marks. After the publication information, give the inclusive page numbers of the element.

Vernon, Lorraine. Afterword. Time Capsule: New and Selected Poems. By Pat Lowther. Victoria: Polestar, 1996. 247-51.

Multivolume work If a work has more than one volume, indicate (using the abbreviation *vols.*) the total number of volumes before the publication information.

Bell, Quentin. Virginia Woolf: A Biography. 2 vols. London: Hogarth, 1972.

If your essay cites only one volume, write the volume number before the publication information and the total number of volumes at the end of the entry.

Bloom, Harold, ed. The Art of the Critic: Literary Theory and Criticism from the Greeks to the Present. Vol. 9. New York: Chelsea, 1989. 11 vols.

Pamphlet Treat a pamphlet entry as you would a book entry.

Leduc, Paul. A Walking Tour of Old Montreal. Montreal: City of Montreal, 1973.

Publisher's imprint Imprints are special names under which publishers group their books. If the title page of a book you are citing includes the name of an imprint along with the name of the publisher, cite the imprint name followed by a hyphen and the publisher's name. (In the example below, "Vintage" is an imprint of Random Publishing.)

Shields, Carol. Small Ceremonies. Toronto: Vintage-Random, 1976.

Republished book Add the original publication date after the title of the book. Then give the publication information for the edition you are citing.

Mitchell, W.O. The Vanishing Point. 1973. Toronto: Macmillan, 1992.

New material contained in the republication, such as an introduction or afterword, should be added after the original publication date.

Austen, Jane. Mansfield Park. 1814. Introd. Tony Tanner. Harmondsworth, Eng. : Penguin, 1966.

Selection in an anthology or compilation Name the author of the selection, the selection title, and the title of the book. If the book has an editor and/or compiler, write the abbreviation *Ed.* ("Edited by") and/or *Comp.* ("Compiled by") after the title, followed by the person's name. Give the inclusive page numbers of the selection after the publication information.

Klein, A.M. "Haunted House." The Collected Poems of A.M. Klein. Comp. Miriam Waddington. Toronto: McGraw, 1974: 22–25.

Richler, Mordecai. "The Summer My Grandmother Was Supposed to Die." The New Canadian Anthology: Poetry and Short Fiction in English. Ed. Robert Lecker and Jack David. Scarborough, ON: Nelson, 1988: 374–83.

Smith, Edith Katherine. "Lucy Maud Montgomery: Passionate Puritan." The Lucy Maud Montgomery Album. Comp. Kevin McCabe. Ed. Alexandra Heilbron. Markham, ON: Fitzhenry and Whiteside, 1999: 4–7.

Translation Begin the entry with the author's name. After the title, write the abbreviation *Trans.* ("Translated by") and follow the abbreviation with the name of the translator.

Gravel, François. Miss September. Trans. Sheila Fischman. Dunvegan, ON: Cormorant, 1998.

Articles and Other Publications in Periodicals

A periodical is a publication, such as a scholarly journal, a magazine, or a newspaper, that appears at regular intervals. When citing a publication in a periodical, follow these general guidelines:

- If an article in a periodical is not printed on consecutive pages, write the first number and a plus sign; for example, to cite the page numbers of an article that appears on pages 34–41 and 78–79, write *34+* (not *34–79*).
- Treat titles of works that appear in titles in quotation marks as you would stand-alone titles: "The Role of Fate in Macbeth" (an article about a play).
- Abbreviate the names of months except for May, June, and July.

Article in a daily newspaper List the author (if there is one), the article's title, the title of the newspaper, the complete date in this order: date month year, and the page number (including the section letter). Omit any initial article in the newspaper's name (Vancouver Sun, not The Vancouver Sun). If an edition is identified on the masthead, add a comma after the date and name the edition (e.g., *metro ed.*).

O'Reilly, Finbarr. "Books in Canada Brought Back to Life by Amazon." National Post 17 Jan. 2001: B2.

Article in a journal paginated by issue For a periodical that numbers pages separately within each issue, follow the volume number with a period and the issue number.

Olson, Gary A. "The Death of Composition as an Intellectual Discipline." Composition Studies 28.2 (2000): 33–41.

Article in a journal paginated by volume For a periodical that numbers pages continuously within each annual volume, write the volume number (in arabic numerals) after the journal's title. The issue number and the month or season may be omitted.

Woodcock, George. "Managing Hatred in Two Centuries." Queen's Quarterly 100 (1993): 827–31.

Article in a monthly or bimonthly periodical For a periodical that appears every month or every two months, give the month(s), year, and page numbers.

Kareda, Urjo. "Behind the Scene." Toronto Life Feb. 2001: 61–66.

Article in a weekly or biweekly periodical For a periodical that appears every week or every two weeks, list the day, month, and year with no comma between the information.

Parks, Tim. "Hell and Back: A New Translation of Dante's Inferno." New Yorker 15 Jan. 2001: 84–89.

Editorial or letter in a periodical Add the word *Editorial* or *Letter* after the title (if any) or author's name.

Bly, Robert. Letter. Harper's Sept. 1999: 8.

"Where's the Humanity?" Editorial. Toronto Star 10 Jan. 2001, metro ed.: A22.

Review To cite a review, give the reviewer's name and (if there is one) the title of the review. Then write *Rev. of* followed by the title of the reviewed work, the name of the author (or editor, director, etc.), the name of the periodical, and the rest of the publication information. For a film or theatre review, add relevant information about the production.

Silverberg, Mark. Rev. of Mean, by Ken Babstock. Dalhousie Review 78.2 (1998): 327–29.

Taylor, Kate. "The Air's a Bit Thin on Lepage's Moon." Rev. of The Far Side of the Moon, by Robert Lepage. Dir. and Perf. Robert Lepage. Premiere Dance Theatre, Toronto. Globe and Mail 21 Apr. 2000: R12.

Unidentified author in a periodical Begin with the title if no author's name is given.

"Freezing the Taxman." Maclean's 21 Mar. 1994: 19.

Other Sources

Cartoon Begin with the cartoonist's name and (if there is one) the title of the cartoon. Then write the word *Cartoon* and conclude the entry with the rest of the publication information.

Chast, Roz. "The N.R.A.'s Written Test for a Gun License." Cartoon. New Yorker 2 Aug. 1999: 90.

Johnston, Lynn. "For Better Or For Worse." Cartoon. Toronto Star, 26 April 2004: E8.

Film or videocassette List the title, the director, the distributor, and the year of release. Other relevant information, such as the writer, producers, or performers, may be added.

Just Watch Me: Trudeau and the '70s Generation. Dir. Catherine Annau. Prod. Yves Basaillon and Gerry Flahive. National Film Board, 1999.

If you wish to focus on a particular individual's work on the production, begin the entry with that person's name,

Annau, Catherine, dir. Just Watch Me: Trudeau and the '70s Generation. Prod. Yves Basaillon and Gerry Flahive. National Film Board, 1999.

To cite a videocassette, write the word *Videocassette* before the distributor's name. Include the original release date if relevant.

Henry V. Dir. Kenneth Branagh. Perf. Kenneth Branagh, Paul Scofield, Derek Jacobi, Ian Holm, and Emma Thompson. 1989. Videocassette. CBS/Fox Video, 1990.

Interview To cite a published interview or an interview broadcast on television or radio, begin with the name of the person interviewed and the title of the interview. Conclude with the appropriate bibliographical information.

Ricci, Nino. "The Ascension of Nino: An Interview with Nino Ricci." Books in Canada Dec. 1992: 10-12.

If the interview is untitled or has a title that does not indicate the nature of the source, use the descriptive identifier *Interview.* Add the interviewer's name if known and relevant.

Richards, David Adams. Interview with Antanas Sileika. Imprint. TVOntario, Toronto. Oct. 18 2000.

Shields, Carol. Interview. "More Spice than Nice." Globe and Mail 26 Feb. 2000: D2-3.

If you conducted the interview, state the type of interview (*Personal Interview, Telephone Interview, E-mail Interview*).

Marchand, Benoit. Personal Interview. 9 May 2000.

Legal Act When referencing an Act, use the following order of information: title , statute volume, jurisdiction, year, chapter, section.

Children's Law Reform Act, R.S.O. 1990, c. C-12, s.17.

Lecture, speech, address, or reading State the speaker's name, the title of the oral presentation, the sponsoring body (if any), and the location and date of the presentation.

Atwood, Margaret. "In Search of Alias Grace: On Writing Canadian Historical Fiction." Charles R. Bronfman Lecture in Canadian Studies. U of Ottawa, Ottawa. 21 Nov. 1996.

Ignatieff, Michael. "The Rights Revolution." The 2000 Massey Lectures. U of Toronto,

Convocation Hall, Toronto. 7 Nov. 2000.

If the presentation has no title, write an appropriate description (*Lecture, Address, Reading*, etc.) after the speaker's name.

Carey, Peter. Reading. Harbourfront Reading Series. Brigantine Room, York Quay Centre,

Toronto. 28 Feb. 2001.

Live performance Begin with the title of the play, concert, ballet, or opera. Add relevant information, such as director, conductor, or performers, and conclude the entry with the location and date of the performance.

Billy Bishop Goes to War. By John Gray. Dir. and Perf. Eric Peterson and John Gray.

Bluma Appel Theatre, Toronto. 24 Sept. 1998.

Don Giovanni. By W.A. Mozart. Libretto by Lorenzo Da Ponte. Dir. James Conway. Cond.

Nicholas Cleobury. Perf. Davide Damiani, Gilles Cachemaille, and Isabel

Bayrakdarian. Hummingbird Centre, Toronto. 30 Jan. 2000.

Map or chart Treat a map or chart as you would a book with an unidentified author, but add the word *Map* or *Chart* after the title.

Newfoundland and Labrador. Map. St. John's: Newfoundland and Labrador Department

of Tourism and Culture, 1992.

Personal communication To cite a letter you have received, begin with the sender's name. Then write the phrase *Letter to the author* followed by the date.

Page, P.K. Letter to the author. 16 Apr. 1994.

Section of the Criminal Code When referencing a section of the Criminal Code, use the following order of information: abbreviation for section, section number, abbreviation for Criminal Code, name of publication (underlined), year of publication, edition, annotations by names of annotators, city of publication, province, name of publishing company, copyright year.

S. 238 C.C. Martin's Annual Criminal Code 2004. Student Edition. Annotated by Edward

L. Greenspan and Marc Rosenberg. Aurora, ON: 2004.

Sound recording Arrange the information in an entry (for example, composer, performer, conductor) according to your research emphasis. Include relevant information such as manufacturer and year of issue. If the recording is not a compact disc, indicate the medium by writing *Audiocassette* or *LP* before the manufacturer's name.

Corigliano, John. The Red Violin. Perf. Joshua Bell. Philharmonic Orchestra. Cond. Esa-

Pekka Salonen. Sony Classical, 1998.

Fleming, Renée. Strauss Heroines. Weiner Philharmoniker. Cond. Christoph Eschenbach. Decca, 1999.

Enclose the title of a specific **song** in quotation marks.

Krall, Diana. "Devil May Care." By Bob Dorough. When I Look in Your Eyes. Verve,1999.

Treat a **spoken-word recording** as you would a musical recording.

Thomas, Dylan. "A Child's Christmas in Wales." Read by the author. Dylan Thomas: Volume 1. LP. Caedmon, 1952.

Television or radio program List the episode's title (if any), the title of the program, the title of the series (if any), the network, the local station and city (if any), and the broadcast date. Add other relevant information such as narrator, performers, or director.

"Episode 5: A Question of Loyalties, 1775-1815." Canada: A People's History. CBC-TV. 12 Nov. 2000.

"Marcel Proust: In Search of Lost Time." Ideas. Narr. Barbara Nichol. 3 episodes. CBC Radio One. 1-15 June 1998.

Work of art State the artist's name, the title of the work, the name of the organization in which the work is housed, and the city. If the work is part of a private collection, follow the title with the name of the individual who owns it.

Colville, Alex. Hound in Field. National Gallery of Canada, Ottawa.

Electronic Sources

Electronic sources include CD-ROMs, e-mail, software programs, Web sites, on-line databases, and information available using telnet, gopher, file transfer protocol (FTP), and other access modes. This section deals specifically with e-mail, CD-ROMs, and Web sources.

CAUTION: Be aware that sources on the World Wide Web lack the stability of their print counterparts; an on-line document may be revised or it may even disappear altogether. In addition, there is no guarantee that the information contained in a Web document is of good quality and error-free. For these reasons, you should evaluate Web sources carefully and obtain your instructor's approval before using them in an essay.

CD-ROM Treat a publication on CD-ROM as you would a book, but indicate the medium (CD-ROM) before the publication information.

The 1999 Canadian Encyclopedia World Edition. CD-ROM. Toronto: McClelland, 1998.

If you are citing only part of the CD-ROM, state the author of the part and/or the title of the part before the CD-ROM's title.

Vastokas, Joan M. "Native Art." The 1999 Canadian Encyclopedia World Edition.

CD-ROM. Toronto: McClelland, 1998.

Electronic communication To cite electronic mail you have received, begin with the sender's name and, if there is one, the title (taken from the subject line). Then write the phrase *E-mail to the author* followed by the date.

Chiang, Valerie. "Re: Archetypes." E-mail to the author. 7 Mar. 2001.

Web Sources

A citation of an electronic source contains information similar to that found in citations of print sources. When citing a Web source, you must provide information that identifies the source and allows readers to locate it. In MLA style, the electronic address (or URL) of a Web source is enclosed in angle brackets.

<http://www.nelson.com>

NOTE: In MLA style, an URL that must be divided between two lines should be broken only after a slash.

A Web source citation consists of applicable items from the list below. Following the list are sample MLA-style entries for various types of Web sources.

1. Name of the author or site owner, or name of the editor, translator, or compiler followed by the abbreviation *ed.*, *trans.*, or *comp.*
2. Title of a short work within a scholarly project, book, database, or periodical
3. Title of the scholarly project, book, database, or periodical; or, for a professional or personal site with no title, a descriptive identifier such as *Home page*
4. Name of the editor, translator, or compiler of the on-line book, preceded by the abbreviation *Ed.*, *Trans.*, or *Comp*; or name of the editor of the academic project or database
5. Publication information for any print version of the source (relevant publication facts not given in the source may be added in brackets)
6. Version number of the source or, for a journal, identifying information such as the volume and issue numbers
7. Date of the electronic publication or of the latest update
8. Name of any sponsoring body associated with the Web site or, for a journal, the number range or total number of pages or paragraphs (if they are numbered)
9. Access date (the date that you visited the site)
10. Electronic address, or URL
11. Period at the end after the > symbol.

Academic project

Anthology of Middle English Literature. *Ed. Anniina Jokinen. 5 Sept. 2000. 13 Nov. 2000*

<http://www.luminarium.org/medlit/>.

Nineteenth-Century German Stories. Ed. Robert Godwin-Jones. 1994. Foreign Lang. Dept., Virginia Commonwealth U. 12 Jan. 2001 <http://www.vcu.edu/hasweb/for/menu.html>.

Article in an information database

"Canadian Literature: 1960 and Beyond." Encyclopedia Britannica Online. 18 Jan. 2001<http://search.eb.com/bol/topic?eu=108739&sctn=3>.

Article in a journal

Ward, Ian. "Shakespeare and the Politics of Community." Early Modern Literary Studies 4.3 (1999): 45 pars. 3 Jan. 2001 http://www.shu.ac.uk/schools/cs/emls/ 04-3/ward-shak.html>.

Article in a magazine

Bemrose, John. "Finding Reality in Fiction." Maclean's Online. 17 July 2000. 8 Aug. 2000 <http://www.macleans.ca/xta-asp/storynav.asp?/2000/07/17/ Cover/37130.shtml>.

Article in a newspaper

Richler, Mordecai. "Fighting Words." New York Times on the Web. 1 June 1997. 31 Aug. 1999 <http://www.nytimes.com/books/97/06/01/reviews/970601.01richlet.html>.

Book

Montgomery, Lucy Maud. Anne of Green Gables. [1908.] Project Gutenberg. 14 Nov. 2000 <http://www.literature.org/authors/montgomery-lucy-maud/anne-of-green-gables>.

Document within an academic project

Schiller, Friedrich. "The Sport of Destiny." Trans. Marian Klopfer. Nineteenth-Century German Stories. Ed. Robert Godwin-Jones. 1994. Foreign Lang. Dept., Virginia Commonwealth U. 12 Jan. 2001 <http://www.vcu.edu/hasweb/for/schiller/sport_e.html>.

Personal site

Atwood, Margaret. Margaret Atwood Information Site. 6 Sept. 2000 <http://www.web.net/owtoad/index.html>.

Lancashire, Ian. Home page. 1 Mar. 2001 <http://www.chass.utoronto.ca/~ian/>.

Professional site

Periodical Writers Association of Canada. Home page. 30 Oct. 2000 <http://www.web.net/~pwac/welcome.html>.

Sample Memo, Police Narrative Report, and Business Letter

1. **Sample Memo**
2. **Sample Police Narrative Report**
3. **Sample Business Letter**

The following sample documents are included for instructors who wish to incorporate into their courses a discussion of the skills involved in writing within these types of communication formats.

SAMPLE MEMO
MEMORANDUM: SMITHVILLE POLICE SERVICE

TO:	Chief Ronald SCHUHARDT
FROM:	Constable Suzanne LO
DATE:	Friday, March 12, 2004
SUBJECT:	REQUEST TO ATTEND AN UPCOMING TRAINING SEMINAR — INVESTIGATIVE INTERVIEWING

I request permission to attend a 02-day workshop entitled "Investigative Interviewing"; this is a seminar organized by Blue Line magazine.

Here are the particulars:

When:	Tuesday, April 27 and Wednesday, April 28, 2004 09:00–16:00 each day Held during the Blue Line Trade Show & Exhibition
What:	02-day multi-media seminar with certificate accreditation
Cost:	$250.00 + GST
Where:	LeParc Conference Centre Leslie Street, Markham, Ontario
Some of the Topics:	Witnesses and Witness Psychology The "Non-Accusatory Interview Technique" Tactics for Overcoming Deception Analysis of Statements by both Witnesses and Accused

I feel that it is beneficial for me to go because it would enhance my performance during interviews. The new "Non-Accusatory Interview Technique" is of particular interest to me. Upon my return from this seminar, I would be pleased to run in-house workshops so that I can share what I have learned with the officers of Smithville Police Service.

For complete details of the seminar, please refer to its Web site: www.blueline.ca/tradeshow.

I look forward to your reply. Please contact me at extension 4556.

Source: "Blue Line Training Seminars." Blue Line March 2004: 43-44

SAMPLE BUSINESS LETTER

Constable Rion Singh
Smithville Police Service
642 Queen Street
Smithville, ON
U1P 4X5

Monday, March 15, 2004

Mr. William Starchuk
St. John's Ambulance
98 River Street
Smithville, ON
U1P 3Y4

Dear Mr. William Starchuk,

SUBJECT: REQUEST FOR YOU TO CONDUCT FIRST AID AND CPR RECERTIFICATION WORKSHOPS

Please consider conducting First Aid and CPR Recertification Workshops for twelve officers at Smithville Police Service's Headquarters during the month of June 2004.

All twelve of the officers need to recertify the following by Wednesday, June 30, 2004:

First Aid and Infant, Child, and Adult CPR

We would appreciate receiving a written proposal outlining the following:
- dates and times that you are available in June
- accreditation
- costs
- course descriptions
- an agenda of the session(s)
- your résumé

Please phone me at 905-443-5847 extension 4311 before Thursday, April 01, 2004 to let me know if you are or are not going to submit a proposal.

If you choose to submit a proposal, please mail it to me before Thursday, April 15, 2004.

I can be reached at the above phone number or by e-mail: rion.singh@srp.ca.

Yours truly

Rion Singh

Rion Singh

SAMPLE NARRATIVE POLICE REPORT

Incident # 04-132

Reported by Officer Lucas STRONG

Date: Wednesday, December 01, 2004 Report started at 18:00; completed at 18:25.

On Wednesday, December 01, 2004, I, Officer Lucas STRONG, received a call from the dispatcher at 16:25 to go to Smithville College's Parking Lot B. A female, Alice LEIGH, had called into 9-1-1 at 16: 22 to report a possible Break and Enter and Theft from her 2000 Toyota RAV 4. I was to meet her in the south end of Parking Lot B. I was to look for a brunette female, approximately 5 feet 7 inches tall, twenty years old, wearing a red "Roots" jacket and blue jeans, standing beside her red RAV 4.

I arrived on the scene at 16:45, got out of the cruiser, and asked the brunette female approaching me if she was Alice LEIGH. She confirmed that she was.

She led me over to a red RAV 4, which was backed into a parking spot in the second row of parking spots at the south end of Parking Lot B.

She said that the red RAV 4, licence plate TRGB* 987, was her car. The passenger front window was broken; shards of glass were on the front passenger's seat and on the floor of the front passenger's side; the lock to the glove compartment was on the floor of the RAV 4; chisel-like instrument marks were around the hole which had formerly held the lock; and the car owner's manual was on the floor. There was nothing in the glove compartment.

Alice LEIGH told me that she had locked five hundred dollars ($500.00) in cash into the glove compartment prior to leaving her car in this parking lot at 09:05 when she arrived at school that morning. LEIGH said that she didn't want to take all that cash into the college. LEIGH said that she was planning on depositing that money in the bank on her way home from school.

LEIGH said that she got the last parking spot in Parking Lot B when she arrived at school this morning. She could not remember what any of the other cars looked like. There were no other cars parked in the first row or second row in the south end of Parking Lot B when I arrived. There were two other cars in this lot at this time, 16:58: a 1986 gold Cutlass Cierra, licence plate ABDF* 123, and a 1999 red Toyota Corolla, licence plate ADRE* 643. These cars were parked near the doors at the north-east side of the lot.

LEIGH did not remember seeing anyone in the parking lot when she arrived at school this morning.

At 17:05, LEIGH showed me her ownership and insurance for the red RAV 4 upon request.

Insurance Policy # 5473 Insurer: PROTEC Insurance Company
V.I.N. for red RAV 4 TYDKV88763X135752

At 17:10, I went to my cruiser to verify the ownership and licence plates on the RAV 4.

At 17:20, I received a positive confirmation of ownership.

At 17:22, I went back to Alice LEIGH who was sitting inside her RAV 4. I suggested that she get the window fixed quickly and the lock replaced for the glove compartment. I gave her my business card and suggested that she call me if she remembered the descriptions of anyone she saw in the parking lot or the descriptions of any of the cars that were in the parking lot.

At 17:25, I went back to my cruiser. Alice LEIGH drove out of the lot at this time.

At 17:26, I left Smithville College and returned to Headquarters. I arrived at Headquarters at 17:50 and went to my desk.

I started this report at 18:00 and finished it at 18:25.

I filed it in the Filing Cabinet #34 bottom drawer marked "Nov.–Dec. 04".

Student's Personal Spelling List

Note to the Student

This appendix has blank sheets of paper, broken down alphabetically—similar to an empty telephone book where you would keep the phone numbers of your friends and family.

To help improve your spelling, write into this directory **all** the words that you misspell during this course (and you should also keep it as future reference, so that you can keep adding to it and continue to work on correcting your errors). Then, when you use a particular word, look it up and make sure that you are spelling it correctly.

Here is an easy way to take advantage of this directory:

1. When you get an assignment back or when the teacher corrects in-class assignments, take the time to write every word you misspell into this directory. You will discover that you are repeatedly spelling some very simple words incorrectly.
2. To help you further, underline or circle the letters in the words that you are writing incorrectly.

   Example:

   If your teacher indicates that the word "recieve" is spelled incorrectly on your paper, then check a dictionary or find out from the teacher the correct spelling and write the correct spelling of that word in the "R" section of the directory. You would write in "rec<u>ei</u>ve." Be sure to add the underline, so you can be reminded of where your original error was.
3. Another good thing to do is use different coloured pens to highlight the corrections.

   Example:

   For "receive," you would write the "rec" in blue pen; the next "e" in red pen, and the "i" following the "e" in green pen. The rest of the letters, "ve", would be in blue pen. This will make the "ei" after the "c" stand out.
4. Every time you want to use the word, you look it up in your directory to make sure that you are spelling it correctly. After a while, you won't have to look the word up; you will know the correct spelling every time.

   Good luck with working on improving your spelling!

A

B

C

D

E

F

G

H

I

J

K

L

M

N

O

P

Q

R

S

T

U

V

W

X/Y/Z

Sample Research Essays

DNA: A Criminal's Nightmare
by
Crystal Vasiloff

Crystal Vasiloff

Professor Doughty

Comunications 1

30 September 2004

DNA: A Criminal's Nightmare

What is DNA? DNA is the short form of "deoxyribonucleic acid," which carries the genetic code within cells. These tiny cells, which can often be found at crime scenes, carry very relevant information that often gives police investigators the extra verification they needed when considering evidence. The use of DNA to determine the innocence or guilt of an individual has had positive impacts on law enforcement because it has solved previous cases; has provided strong evidence; and helped reduce wrongful convictions.

DNA has provided solid evidence that has given police investigators the chance to take another look at unsolved crimes. DNA information in the DNA Data Bank contributed to charges laid on 36-year-old Gerald Benard for his sexual assault on an 18-year-old woman in 1998 (Shaw 1). This "conviction is the first in Durham Region attributed to the DNA bank since it was created two years ago. Police are confident it won't be the last" (1). Along with valuable police investigation, a large amount of credit for this conviction must go to the incorporation of DNA in the investigation since "[i]t [was] the only piece of evidence that link[ed] Mr. Benard to the attack" (8). Although good police investigations are valuable in making these convictions, DNA gives them extra creditable evidence to work with. Detective James Stewart-Haas, who was the head of this investigation (8), said, "'[DNA] [was] very significant. It show[ed] that money spent on the...[DNA]...data base is leading to police finding and convicting sexual predators, where [police] had very little evidence'"(8). Therefore, science has played a substantial role in creating a safer environment for Canadians because "'[w]ithout the DNA bank this predator would still be out there in our midst'"(8). Police investigators have had an overwhelmingly difficult job in trying to solve some cases, but with DNA, it is now possible to go back in time to find the missing pieces of the puzzles.

Furthermore, DNA acts as reliable evidence that can be extremely significant when making a conviction. "The DNA Data Bank helps investigators identify suspects, eliminate suspects, and determine if a serial offender may be involved in a crime" (Munroe 1). These tiny cells, which are naked to the human eye, can give valuable information about a crime scene or a person that no police officer would be able to tell. For instance, in the case against Benard from 1998, the DNA match of Benard to the one in the Data Bank was credible because "[t]he scientific odds that a person other than Benard could match the DNA left behind by the rapist are one in 82 billion, more than 13 times the world population"(8). This amount of certainty leaves behind little doubt that Benard was, in fact, the rapist. There are also times when investigators are not able to speculate on who a suspect might be. When this occurs, DNA can help narrow down some possibilities. For example, when the Alberta police were searching for a serial rapist in Alberta, "[s]amples taken from the 240 men [were] analyzed in an RCMP lab in Edmonton for DNA 'fingerprints,' which [were] then matched against the DNA pattern of the rapist" (Plischke A.6). This saved the police a lot of time trying to track down a suspect while ruling out so many possibilities. The advancement of using DNA findings in investigations will, ultimately, "'help ensure that those guilty of serious crimes will be apprehended more quickly while excluding the innocent from suspicion'"(1). The involvement of DNA and the DNA Data Bank are now crucial parts of investigations and have shown credibility in law enforcement and convictions.

Lastly, DNA has had a positive impact on Canadians by ruling out the chance of an innocent person being convicted. Even though police investigations are effective in many ways, doubt of guilt is decreased dramatically when DNA in used as evidence. With a powerful tool, such as DNA, Madam Justice Louise Arbour, stated that "'[e]ffective law enforcement benefits society as a whole . . . [and] . . . [f]orensic DNA analysis is capable of both identifying and eliminating suspects—a feature that seriously reduces the risk of wrongful convictions"(qtd. in Makin 1). Before the involvement of DNA, there was also a chance of an innocent suspect going through a lengthy and humiliating trial, only to be proven not guilty. However, the issuance of DNA warrants "'have the capacity to exonerate an accused early in the investigation'" (1). Therefore, the use of DNA will save officers a lot of time and money, and most importantly, will save the reputation of innocent people. DNA is vital in proving that someone has had no part in a crime. The easiest thing for a suspect to do is volunteer for DNA testing like Vaughan did in the Alberta case where "Mounties wanted to analyze his DNA to prove he was not the serial rapist who ha[d] attacked three women" (Plischke A6). If someone is not guilty, DNA is the best tool to prove such innocence; therefore, it is considered effective in law enforcement.

To sum up, Canada's justice system is based on the belief that rights will be protected and wrongs will be punished. This basic idea is becoming more and more accurate now that law enforcement can use DNA to reopen cold cases, have valuable credibility in court, and free the innocent of convictions. DNA is an exceptionally reliable source in the justice system. The issuance of the National DNA Data Bank, according to the Solicitor General of Canada, is "'a major step forward for law enforcement in Canada'" (RCMP 1), and it and DNA will continue making law enforcement in Canada more effective.

Vasiloff 4

Works Cited

"DNA." Webster's Pocket Dictionary. Trident Press International. 2002.

Makin, Kirk. "Police Get Their DNA." The Globe and Mail. 31 October 2003: 1, Short. 01 March 2004 <http://www.globeandmail.com/servlet/story/RTGAM.20031031>.

Munroe, Susan. "DNA Data Bank in Canada." Canada Online. 2004: 6 par., Short. 01 March 2004 <http://canadaonline.about.com/cs/crime/a/dnadatabank.htm>.

Plischke, Helen. "Widespread DNA tests used for tracking rapist: An investigation in Alberta." Vancouver Sun. 15 June 1996: A6, Short. 01 March 2004 <http://www.durhamc.on.ca/mycampus>.

RCMP. "Canada opens National DNA Bank." Royal Canadian Mounted Police. 05 July 2000: 1-2, Short. 01 March 2004 <http://www.rcmp-grc.gc.ca/news/2000/n_0010_e.htm>.

Shaw, Stephen. "DNA bank check leads to rape conviction." This Week. 12 April 2002: 1, 8.

Source: Crystal Vasiloff, "DNA: A Criminal's Nightmare." Reprinted with permission.

How Paul (Bernardo) Teale Has Had an Effect on Canadian Society
by
Shawna Hayes

Shawna Hayes

Professor Doughty

Comunications 1

30 September 2004

How Paul (Bernardo) Teale Has Had an Effect on Canadian Society

The national anthem suggests that Canada is a country that is "strong and free" (Lavallee 1). Are Canadians actually as "free" as they believe themselves to be? The reality is that no one is truly free when contained in a society corrupt with brutality and murder. Who confines the human race to this violent society? The answer lies within the psychotic minds of killers and rapists, such as Paul Bernardo, who destroy the lives of innocent, harmless people. Bernardo (who later assumed the name Paul Teale) made an impact on Canadian society by taking the lives of innocent girls, having an influence on many Canadians, and alerting some Canadians to potential murderers.

Bernardo began to impact Canadian society when he brutally murdered innocent girls. His victims were 14-year-old Leslie Mahaffy and 15-year-old Kristen French ("The Homolka–Bernardo Murders" 1). It was not simply that Bernardo had murdered these young women, but it was the way he had savagely tortured the girls which caused him to be "accused of the most heinous murders in Canadian history" (1). Canadians had never been more disgusted by a member of their nation, and this is what caused "this particular murder case . . . to become notorious throughout Canada" (Davey 1). It was not only the citizens' disgust of the murders that changed Canada; the citizens were also changed by their anger toward Bernardo for having killed the girls. One author, Frank Davey, illustrated the anger of Canadians when he stated that "the abduction and sex-slaving of two young women, each of whom had barely emerged from childhood, not only provoked the outrages such crimes deserved, but . . . it touched raw nerves across an already unsettled Canadian nation" (309). Canada was also changed by the sadness brought about by the murders. The families and friends of the victims were extremely upset, especially Kristen French's mother, Donna

French. She expressed her remorse to an interviewer when she asked, "'How could anyone hurt someone so beautiful? I don't just mean physically beautiful, she was a beautiful person. She was kind and she was just very sensitive. And I think, how can anyone destroy that?'" ("The story the Canadian government doesn't want you to see" 1). Canadians were also saddened because "the victims were not only daughters of southern Ontario communities but were also everyone's imaginary daughter" (Davey 309). Thus, the merciless murders committed by Bernardo wiped out the lives of two innocent, beloved girls.

Furthermore, Bernardo affected Canada because many Canadians were negatively influenced by his disgusting acts of violence. Although there was a public ban in Canada of any information regarding the trial, details about the case were easily accessible from American sources and the Internet. The high rate of publicity that the case received allowed Canadians to see and hear all of the vivid details about the murders. Some of the outcomes of people receiving this information were quite surprising. Apparently, some women began to view Bernardo's acts as being appealing (109). Bernardo "now has a circle of groupies" (109). These women claim that what he did was not wrong (109), and "one woman claimed she may be in love with Bernardo" (109). If his violence could influence Canadian women, chances are he influenced Canadian men as well. Another event which illustrated that Canadians were negatively influenced by Bernardo's violence occurred when "a computer buff, reportedly named Justin Wells, set up the Internet computer news group "alt.fan.karla-homolka" (109). The establishment of this "fan club" (109) of Bernardo and his wife shows just how easily other people can begin to admire and possibly begin to "copy-cat" when they are exposed to violence. Therefore, Paul Bernardo had a negative impact on this country by influencing Canadians' behaviour with his violence.

Hayes 3

Finally, Bernardo forced the nation to have a stronger awareness of potential murderers. This is one of the very few positive outcomes of the Bernardo murders. Canadians have now seen someone who looked so sweet and innocent turn out to be a monster underneath that exterior. They have been forced to realize that they must take further precautions in order to protect themselves from murderers and rapists. Bernardo and his wife were known by their friends as "the 'Ken and Barbie' couple" ("The story the Canadian government doesn't want you to see" 1) because "they had beautiful smiles, clean cut good looks, and lived in a sweet little pink house" (1). Canadians now realize that trusting people who appear this way could be a fatal mistake. More and more women are now carrying a rape whistle or can of pepper spray in their purse, and Bernardo can be considered the cause of this. Bernardo may have "always looked like he was coming out of church" (Davey 121), but his actions taught Canadians that looks can definitely be deceiving. Consequently, Bernardo made a positive impact to Canadians by making the nation more aware of potential murderers.

Bernardo stole the lives of young women, influenced some Canadians' behaviour with his violence, and forced a nation to better recognize potential killers; Canada was altered by these factors. Bernardo took away some of society's freedom: the freedom to live free from fear. This created "a sense that a country had changed . . . and that in some small, extremely unpleasant but important ways the accused—Paul Bernardo—had forced Canadians to confront those changes" (5). How can Canada ever be truly "free" when violence and murder exist today? The answer means little now for Leslie Mahaffy and Kristen French, but it means a great deal for people still trying to shape their lives in our often corrupt civilization.

Works Cited

Citizens Coalition for Responsible Government. "The Homolka–Bernardo Murders." 5 April 1994. 17 Oct. 1999 <http://grouchy.cs.indiana.edu/canada/citizens.coalition>.

Davey, Frank. Karla's Web. Toronto: Penguin Books Canada, 1994.

Lavallee, Calixa. "O Canada." The national anthem of Canada, 1880. 25 October 1999 <http://canada.gc.ca/canadian/anthem_e.html#h2>.

"The story the Canadian government doesn't want you to see." A Current Affair. 26 October 1993. 17 October 1999 <http://grouchy.cs.indiana.edu/canada/CurrentAffair>.

Source: Shawna Hayes, "How Paul (Bernardo) Teale Has Had an Effect on Canadian Society." Reprinted with permission.

The Blue Jays Win the 1992 World Series
by
Sarah Mathieson

Sarah Mathieson

Professor Doughty

Comunications 1

30 September 2004

The Blue Jays Win the 1992 World Series

On October 24, 1992, history was made at Atlanta's Fulton County Stadium. The crowd watching the Blue Jays play against the Atlanta Braves in game six of the 1992 World Series went wild when the Blue Jays won the game, four to three, and brought the Championship home to Toronto. Because the Blue Jays won the 1992 World Series, they had a huge impact on Canada, especially Toronto, because the World Series financially benefited Toronto; the World Series brought Torontonians closer together; and the winning Blue Jays brought pride to Canada. They did all this because they were the first team in Canada to win the World Series.

First of all, when the Blue Jays won the 1992 World Series, they had an impact on Toronto because the series financially benefited Toronto. "Some financial experts estimated that Toronto's presence in the World Series would generate revenues in excess of $25 million" (Barnes et al. 59). One of Toronto's biggest profits was made in the sale of souvenirs. These were sold in the SkyDome, from street vendors, or in malls during and after the series had finished. The souvenirs ranged from T-shirts, flags, hats, balls, and jackets to posters, all with the Blue Jay logo on them. Not only did the souvenirs bring money to Toronto, money came from other sources too. The hotels were full and restaurants were booked with fans coming to see the games. Toronto also profited from ticket sales during the World Series because the SkyDome was almost filled to capacity for every game. The following year, in 1993, a study indicated that because the Blue Jays had won the World Series, "the SkyDome generated an annual $264.8 million in goods and services in Metro Toronto, and $351.9 million to the province of Ontario. SkyDome also generated about $60 million in tax revenues for Metro Toronto, $70 million to the province" (O'Malley 8). Because of the large number of fans buying souvenirs and tickets, fans staying in hotels and eating in our restaurants, the City of Toronto financially benefited from the World Series.

Second, the Blue Jays winning the World Series had an impact on Toronto because it brought Torontonians closer together as a city. Spectators united together in bars, restaurants, and in their homes to watch the World Series' games in anticipation of a win. Furthermore, when the game was held in Atlanta and many of the Jays' fans could not see the game in person, "50 000 Toronto fans filled SkyDome to view game six on the giant screen [the Jumbotron at SkyDome]" (Kinsella 24). "Frantic fans at SkyDome cheered on the Jays from afar" (Gamester and Hall 95). Because the fans could not attend the games in Atlanta, the Jumbotron was the best place to watch them. Even when the Canadian flag was flown upside down in Atlanta, at the beginning of game two, the Jays' fans never lost hope that their team would come out as winners. "On a night when the Canadian flag was accidentally flown upside down by the colour guard, in the end, Ed Sprague turned the Blue Jays' world right side up" (Morrison 24). The final proof of Torontonians drawing closer together occurred when the Blue Jays won the coveted trophy, for "400 000 fans swarmed the streets of Downtown Toronto" (Kinsella 24). "Blue Jays' fans [felt] as tall as the CN Tower. The celebration culminated with a parade to SkyDome" (137) on the next Monday when

> [t]ens of thousands of fans [lined] the way as the Jays and their families [drove] to the SkyDome on the Monday following the final game for the biggest love-in in Toronto's history. We're all number one, Joe Carter [told] fans who [jammed] the Dome for a final tribute to the World Series' winners. (Gamester and Hall 5)

Therefore, because of the win and the unity of the fans, Torontonians became closer as a city during the World Series of 1992.

The third and final way that the Blue Jays winning the World Series had an impact on Toronto was that it brought pride to Canada because the Jays were the first team in Canada to win the World Series

> [w]ith a convincing 9–2 victory over the Oakland A's before 51 335 witnesses at SkyDome. [T]he Blue Jays finally had turned the page and begun a new chapter in their history. And the only word beginning with "c" that applied to them was not choke, but champions, winners of the ALCS in six games, the first Canadian team to advance to the World Series. (Morrison 18)

To see the Blue Jays play at this level, fans from across Canada travelled to Toronto to witness history in the making. According to Gamester and Hall, "wall to wall people jammed Yonge Street after the game to celebrate Canada's first World Series' victory" (Morrison 95). The people of Toronto cheered for joy that their team had won and were even more proud of every player who wore the blue and white, from the pitcher, Mike Timlin, to first baseman, Joe Carter because "America's pastime officially became Canada's property" (38). After the end of game six, "on the streets of Toronto, . . . thousands upon thousands of fans celebrated into the early morning hours" (39). These fans and the thousands of fans watching the game at home, restaurants, clubs, and bars mark the 1992 World Series as "the greatest moment in Toronto sports' history" (Gamester and Hall 2), for the Jays were the first team in Canada to win the World Series.

In conclusion, the 1992 World Series being won by the Toronto Blue Jays had a great effect on Toronto because it brought wealth to Toronto, united the Blue Jays' fans, and brought patriotism to Canadians because the World Series was finally won outside of the United States of America. The 1992 World Series was a moment in history that will be remembered in the hearts and minds of Canadians forever.

Works Cited

Barnes, Doug et al. "The Blue Jays Win the World Series: Financial Returns." News in Review. Canadian Broadcasting Corporation, Toronto, 1992.

Gamester, John and L. Hall. "The Taste of Victory . . . At Last." On Top of the World. Ed. Brad Henderson and Gerry Hall. Toronto: Doubleday Canada, 1992. 95.

Kinsella, W.P. "Crossing the Border." A Series For the World. Ed. Jon Rochmis. San Francisco: Woodford, 1992. 24.

Morrison, Scott. "World Series Game Six." Toronto Blue Jays: 1992 World Champions. Toronto: Toronto Sun Publishing Corporation, 1992. 36–38.

O'Malley, Martin and Sean O'Malley. "Travels at SkyDome." Game Day: The Blue Jays at SkyDome. Toronto: Viking, 1994. 24.

Source: Sarah Mathieson, "The Blue Jays Win the 1992 World Series." Reprinted with permission.

The Holocaust and its Impacts
by
Jennifer Kelloway

Jennifer Kelloway

Professor Doughty

Comunications 1

30 September 2004

The Holocaust and its Impacts

"'I saw with my own eyes Germans tossing babies in the air and shooting them'" (qtd. in Witness 67). This is how one Jew remembered the Holocaust, and as disturbing as it may sound, every witness to the Holocaust has memories equally as horrifying as this one. The Nazis, under Hitler's rule, brutally murdered millions of Jews during what has become known as The Holocaust. As defined by the New Lexicon Webster's Encyclopedic Dictionary, the Holocaust is the "destruction of European Jewry by the Nazis" (462). The Holocaust has had a tremendous effect on Jews, Germans, and the world.

First of all, the Holocaust has had an impact on the lives of millions of Jews. Jews who were victims of the Holocaust have to live with the horrific memories and "'the scars . . . [they] seem to be carrying'" (qtd. in Witness 226) for the rest of their lives. In the years following the Holocaust most Jews had "'more nightmares than [they] ever had in the immediate events'" (228). The memories of this unspeakable event can never be erased no matter how hard the Jews try. The Nazis killed entire families of Jews. After the war, one survivor stated that "'[i]n 1939, there were 117 people of [his] family. In 1945, 11 survived'" (248). Some Jews, like Simon Wiesenthal, sought justice and "became world famous Nazi hunter[s]" ("About Simon Wiesenthal" 1) who dedicated their lives to "gathering information on the whereabouts of fugitive Nazis" (1). They wanted people to know that "the Nazis weren't able to kill millions of people and get away with it" (1). Jews have taken it upon themselves to make sure that the Holocaust is never forgotten. Simon Wiesenthal went on to open the "Simon Wiesenthal Centre" ("Simon Wiesenthal: Nazi-hunter" 5), where the focus is on "keeping at least the memory of the Holocaust alive" (5). They believe that "[i]t's got to be recorded" (qtd. in Witness 249) as it is one of the most horrific events in history. The Jews will never forget the Holocaust because of the impact that it has had on their lives.

Furthermore, the Holocaust affected the lives of many Germans, and many had to face the consequences of their involvement. Although Hitler committed suicide on April 30, 1945 ("Nuremberg Trials: A Chronology" 1) and could not be prosecuted, many of his followers were brought to justice during the Nuremberg Trials. In addition to the sentencing of war criminals, the Nuremberg trials established the "principle of individual responsibility" ("Nuremberg Trials" 786); this means that following orders is not an excuse for committing these crimes. Many of the more than 200 Germans who were tried were sentenced to death (786). Also, many of the German Nazis who were not sentenced immediately after the war were later hunted by Nazi-hunters. Nazis such as Konrad Kalejs, who is "86-year[s]-old" ("Nazi Suspect Set to Leave" 1), are still being hunted to this day. Nazis are even deported from countries, making them the "most unwanted, wanted [men] in the world" (4). Some governments have "stopped World War Two veterans from receiving government pensions more than five decades after their involvement in 'crimes against humanity'" ("Germany Halts War Criminals' Pensions" 1). Many Germans' lives were forever ruined when they became involved with the Nazi party, and later, the Holocaust.

Finally, the Holocaust has had a profound impact on the entire world. When World War II was finally over, and the world had learned of the atrocities committed in the concentration camps, many countries took action, collectively and individually, to ensure that something like the Holocaust can never happen again. In 1945, the Allies formed the United Nations, a group of 51 countries ("United Nations" 1120), which joined together

Kelloway 3

with the goal of "promoting peace and international cooperation" (1120). In addition, after the Second World War the Geneva Conventions, which are "4 international agreements signed by a large majority of sovereign nations for the protection of . . . civilians from the effects of war" ("Geneva Conventions" 427), adopted the fourth international agreement, which "established rules in international law for the protection of prisoners of war" (427). In Canada specifically there is the Crimes Against Humanity and War Crimes Act, which makes genocide, crimes against humanity, and war crimes indictable offences punishable by life imprisonment (Department of Justice Canada 1). Are these deterrents working? Yes, because when the Ethnic Cleansing was taking place in Yugoslavia, it was stopped before it could become as large an atrocity as the Holocaust. Lessons have been learned. An event like the Holocaust will never happen again because of the impact it has had on the world.

The Holocaust has ruined millions of Jewish people's lives, many German lives, and changed the world's standards towards crimes against humanity. The Holocaust must never be forgotten and never be repeated. With new international laws, rules, and regulations, and the Jewish survivors' determination to ensure that the memory of what happened lives on, the Holocaust will never be forgotten or repeated. It was learned that it

> may start from a little prejudice or name-calling or whatever it is, and can blow up into the most horrifying experience, either for a whole community, for a whole nation, for a whole people, or for an individual. And this must not be permitted to go on if we—if we are humans. And I hope we are human. (qtd. in Witness 250)

Kelloway 4

Works Cited

"About Simon Wiesenthal." Simon Wiesenthal Center. 27 October 2002 <http://www.wiesenthal.com/about.wiesenthal.cfm>.

Department of Justice Canada. "Crimes Against Humanity and War Crimes Act." 20 Oct. 2002 <http://laws.justice.gc.ca/en/C-45.9/3806.html>.

"Geneva Conventions." The New Webster's Encyclopedia. Ed. Michael D. Harkavy. Naples, Florida: Trident Press International, 1996.

"Holocaust." The New Lexicon Webster's Encyclopedic Dictionary of the English Language. Canadian Edition. New York: Lexicon Publications, Inc., 1998.

"Nazi Hunters Say Germany Halts War Criminals Pensions"." HateWatch.org. 27 October 2002 <http://www.hatewatch.org/article.php?sid=1077>.

"Nazi Suspect Set to Leave." BBC News. 27 October 2002 <http://news.bbc.co.uk/I/hi/uk/589237.stm>.

"The Nuremberg Trials: Chronology." The Nuremberg Trials: A Chronology. 28 October 2002 <http://www.law.umke.edu/faculty/projects/ftrials/nuremberg/NurembergChronology.html>.

"Nuremberg Trials." The New Webster's International Encyclopedia. Ed. Michael D. Harkavy. Naples, Florida: Trident Press International, 1996.

"Simon Wiesenthal: Nazi-hunter." BBC News. 27 October 2002. 27 October 2002 <http://news.bbc.co.uk/i/hi/uk/58119.stm>.

"United Nations." The New Webster's International Encyclopedia. Ed. Michael D. Harkavy. Naples, Florida: Trident Press International, 1996. 462, 1120.

Witness. New York, NY: Joshua M. Greene Productions, Inc., 2000.

Source: Jennifer Kelloway, "The Holocaust and its Impacts." Reprinted with permission.

Answer Key

Chapter 1 Answers

(excluding Writing Exercises 1.2, 1.4, 1.6, and 1.10)

Exercise 1.1

1. admissible
2. Chief, February
3. lieutenant, I, sergeant, tomorrow
4. I , was, Wednesday
5. received

Exercise 1.3

1. choose, affect
2. complement, quite
3. used to, their
4. You're, used to, It's
5. Desert

Exercise 1.5

1. well, well, well
2. went
3. saw
4. drove, the, test

Exercise 1.7 (Answers may vary.)

1. Officer Kim removed his gun, his holster, and his badge.
2. The menu for the recruits' banquet consisted of tossed salad, roasted potatoes, Yorkshire pudding, roast beef, and *chocolate* cake.
3. The instructor told the officers to bend down and shoot low.
4. Black pants, white shirt, black socks, and black shoes was the dress code for those Police Foundations students.
5. For about an hour, the residents heard the sirens and the ambulances.

Exercise 1.8 (Answers may vary.)

1. I like eating peas, carrots, and corn.
2. I should be physically fit so that I can run after suspects, reduce heart attack risks, and relieve my stress level.
3. A police officer should be honest, approachable, and controlled.
4. I am studying communications, psychology, sociology, and politics.
5. I enjoy swimming and playing basketball.

Exercise 1.9 (Answers inserted and underlined. Answers may vary.)

1. The police sirens were going from 12:09 until 12:28 (delete the comma,) while the officer chased the speeding car along the 401 on Friday, August 19, 2005.
2. During the chase, all the cars going eastbound pulled over to the shoulder and stopped to give the officer free access to the road.
3. When the officer got up to the speeding car and pulled it over, the officer found the following people in the car: a teenaged boy; a middle-aged father; a middle-aged mother; and a ten-year-old girl.
4. The father was not driving the car; the son was.
5. The father's licence had been suspended, and the sixteen-year-old who had his G1 was driving the car; the mother had a valid licence.

Chapter 2 Answers

(excluding Writing Exercises 2.5, 2.6, 2.7, and 2.10)

Exercise 2.1 and Exercise 2.2

Write an F in the column if the group of words is a Fragment. Write IC if the group of words is an Independent Clause (Sentence).

__F__ 1. Police arrested that man after the police found 650 pot plants in his house.
__F__ 2. The street value of the pot plants was $330,000.
__IC__ 3. The police also confiscated $32,000 worth of hydroponics equipment.
__F__ 4. The police investigators also found a bypass (delete the "a") hydro line that was being used to illegally connect electricity to the man's house.
__F__ 5. This man is facing charges of (delete "the") growing and producing marijuana, possession for the purpose of trafficking, and stealing hydro.

Exercise 2.3 (Answers will vary.)

Change these fragments to complete thoughts/sentences.

1. Officer James gave chase to a speeding car.
2. Because the suspect was speeding, an officer on radar traffic duty noticed him.
3. The officer asked the suspect for his gun, which he gave to him.
4. Rather than wait until they got to the station, the officers filled in their reports on the computer in their cruiser.
5. The inmates are given three one-hour breaks per day in the yard during the summer in that prison.

Exercise 2.8

a) The officer in patrol car #24 noticed a vehicle with an expired licence plate. He pulled the driver over to investigate.
b) The officer in patrol car #24 noticed a vehicle with an expired licence plate; he pulled the driver over to investigate.
c) The officer in patrol car #24 noticed a vehicle with an expired licence plate, so he pulled the driver over to investigate.
d) The officer in patrol car #24 noticed a vehicle with an expired licence plate; subsequently, he pulled the driver over to investigate.
e) The officer in patrol car #24 pulled a driver over because the officer noticed the expired licence plate on the car.
f) Because the officer in patrol car #24 noticed a vehicle with an expired licence plate, he pulled the driver over to investigate.

Exercise 2.9

a) The officer wrote his notes in his notebook. Then, the officer wrote his reports.
b) The officer wrote his notes in his notebook; the officer then wrote his reports.
c) The officer wrote his notes in his notebook, and then the officer wrote his reports.
d) The officer wrote his notes in his notebook; then, the officer wrote his reports.
e) The officer wrote his reports after he wrote his notes in his notebook.
f) After the officer wrote his notes in his notebook, he wrote his reports.

CHAPTER 3 EXERCISES

(excluding Writing Exercise 3.2)

Exercise 3.1

1. Police, con-artist, made-in-Canada
2. the positive identification of a con-artist
3. – officers checked for tattoo on file- buttocks- “Made in Canada”
   – 55-year-old- male- Quebec- wanted for breaking parole and fraud-related charges in Quebec, Ontario and Alberta-Canada-wide warrant
   – arrested in West Van- used fake cheques to buy pizzas
   – police reported- man = 22 different names and birthdates
4. “Officers” in {2} links to “Police” in {1}
   “the man” in {2} links to “con-artist” in {1}
   “ ‘Made in Canada’” in {2} links to “made-in-Canada” in {1}
5. “Quebec man” in {3} links to “the man” in {2}
6. “He” in {4} links to “Quebec man” in {3}
   “fake cheques” in {4} links to “fraud-related charges” in {3}
7. Concluding sentence words: “police, positive identification, and con-artist” link to Introductory sentence words: “police, positive identification, and suspect”

CHAPTER 4 EXERCISES

(excluding Writing Exercise 4.3)

Exercise 4.1

Example	Topic	Opinion	3 reasons/points
a)	Law & Order TV show	It's my favourite program.	• characters • situations • outcomes
b)	In order to succeed	students need to	• attend their classes • do their homework • study for tests
c)	Ecstasy	can cause	• physical changes • mental changes • emotional changes

Exercise 4.2

√ 2. In order to be effective communicators, officers need to write reports that are free of spelling, grammar, and punctuation errors.

3. Before officers become profilers, they need years of experience on the force, special psychology courses, and certification. {**The points are not parallel.**}

4. Officers are well-educated individuals. {**opinion or fact**}

√ 5. Courses in defensive driving, report writing, and court preparation are all necessary courses for police officers.

6. All police services need helicopters to protect the public and the officers. {**only two points stated, not three**}

√ 7. This crime could have been solved more quickly if the officer had written detailed notes at the crime scene, submitted his reports at the designated time, and prepared the Crown Brief by the deadline.

8. This college offers the best Police Foundations program. {**opinion only**}

9. In order to be successful in the Police Foundations program, students must be prepared to work hard, do all assignments, and attend all classes. {**The first point is not parallel to the second and third points.**}

10. The LASA program is offered at many colleges. {**fact only**}

CHAPTER 5 ANSWERS

(excluding Writing Exercises 5.3 and 5.4)

Exercise 5.1

1. a question
2. " you" and "leader"
3. "you need to be a motivator, a participant, and an initiator."
4. "If this is your desire…"

Exercise 5.2

1. It was the first point in the thesis statement. Therefore, it goes in the first paragraph of the body. The body starts in the second paragraph.
2. The third point of the thesis statement goes in the fourth paragraph of the essay, which is the third paragraph of the body.
3. The transition goes at the start of the new paragraph.
4. No
5. They are replaced with different words.
6. "definition" and " friend"
7. three, or one for each point
8. three, or one for each detail.
9. a) to make it easier to write the essay
   b) to help the writer get organized
   c) to help the writer meet the criteria of a developed essay
   d) to keep the thesis statement up front
   e) to make sure the paper is an essay
   f) to make sure all three points are discussed in a logical order and equally.

CHAPTER 8 ANSWERS

Exercise 8.2

1. a) article/magazine
   b) article/magazine (whichever one wasn't used in 1a)
   c) magazine
2. first
3. details, information
4. a) names
   b) cities
   c) organizations
5. parentheses, page numbers
6. a) MLA
   b) page number
7. yes, would not
8. have not, after, within, before
9. do not

Exercise 8.4

First quote	Second quote
a) yes	j) yes
b) five	k) more than
c) yes	l) no
d) yes	m) yes
e) reference information, MLA	n) after

(continued)

First quote	Second quote
f) plagiarism	o) plagiarism
g) surname	p) sentence, second, succession
h) reference, first	q) double-
i) page, after	r) a new
	s) page

Exercise 8.5

1. left side
2. right
3. no
4. main
5. point
6. were
7. video clip, put quotation marks around, underline

Chapter 9 Answers

Exercise 9.3

1. one
2. the death of Jamie Brittain
3. a) an awareness of the dangers of Ecstasy
   b) a desire to get raves back to their original time of love and peace
4. has resulted in

Index

E

F

G

H

I

J

L

M

Q

R

S

V

W

Y